Instrumental Music for Today's Schools

ROBERT W. HOUSE, *1920-*

Head, Department of Music
University of Minnesota, Duluth

PRENTICE-HALL, INC., ENGLEWOOD CLIFFS, NEW JERSEY

PRENTICE-HALL INTERNATIONAL, INC., *London*
PRENTICE-HALL OF AUSTRALIA, PTY., LTD., *Sydney*
PRENTICE-HALL OF CANADA, LTD., *Toronto*
PRENTICE-HALL OF INDIA (PRIVATE) LTD., *New Delhi*
PRENTICE-HALL OF JAPAN, INC., *Tokyo*

© 1965 by Prentice-Hall, Inc.
ENGLEWOOD CLIFFS, NEW JERSEY

Library of Congress Catalog Card Number 65-10331
C-46800

Preface

                 This book is primarily addressed to public school band and orchestra directors and to those preparing for such a vocation. The intent is to cause a re-evaluation of the purpose and pattern of instrumental music instruction and to produce more enlightened teaching. The work is not heavily documented with quotations and statistics; neither is it designed to cover every item of information and method of operation in the field. This mass of material is partially known to the reader or can be further described by his teacher and found in the Selected References at the end of each chapter. On the other hand, the book does go into sufficient detail to assure a comprehensive grasp of the instrumental music program.

    The author is an experienced performer, and he has taught band, orchestra, individual and class lessons on every instrument, and music methods classes for future teachers. He has supervised student teachers and has served as an adjudicator and clinician on many occasions. Growing out of this background, this book should be useful as either a text or as a basic reference in any undergraduate or graduate course where the teaching of instrumental music is a topic.

    Editorial assistance was provided by: John Shepard of Mankato State College; Clayton Hathaway, music supervisor of the Duluth schools; and James Murphy, Robert Beverley, Shirley Munger, and Addison Alspach of the University of Minnesota, Duluth.

R. W. H.

iii

Contents

CHAPTER 1

The Role of Instrumental Music in the Schools

This book is written in the belief that music is, and should be, a vital part of the school curriculum, and that this purpose cannot be accomplished without a strong program of instrumental instruction. Such instruction should include not only the usual areas of band and orchestra (and the training of players for the necessary instruments), but also those activities which are sometimes considered subsidiary—instrumental forms in music listening, pre-band instruments, keyboard, solo, and small ensemble experience.

Strangely, the instrumental music program is seldom considered an integrated whole but is treated in terms of either the band or marching band, or string instruction, or piano class. These topics are then compartmentalized with all other phases of music instruction appropriate to the elementary and secondary levels since this is the way that schools are organized and responsibilities defined. Consequently, we seldom see a unified and balanced approach to instrumental music instruction from kindergarten through twelfth grade.

Yet in the process of their professional preparation, most music teachers acquire an orientation toward either vocal or instrumental work. Entering college as a violinist, for example, one might develop some skill as a percussionist in order to play in the band, and might also acquire some useful piano facility. He will possibly study the clarinet and trumpet and no doubt will include some choral experience. His work in music theory and history will cover a very broad field. Since some understanding and appreciation of all the varied forms of music literature should result, we will have produced a fairly balanced musician. His preparation for teaching will be similarly broad. It cannot be forgotten, however, that this educative process was undertaken

1

by one who considered himself a violinist and who probably saw it as a means of playing and teaching the violin and the orchestra. He will teach band, and chorus, and even mathematics if need be but, unless his self-image changes, he will eventually find himself a position where his chief work is in strings. It seems that the field of work—either playing or teaching at any age level in any part of the country—is relatively less important to the individual than this sense of mission and familiarity within a particular phase of music.

Vocational drive is found everywhere but it seems peculiarly strong among instrumental music teachers. It is a source of amazement to laymen and fellow teachers to observe the great energy expended by a band or orchestra teacher. Upon assuming his duties, he typically revamps the music library; purchases all the new instruments he can; recruits as many beginners as possible; and then manages to arrange schedule time for instruction of these people. Concert and contest appearances are planned and money is raised for transportation, more instruments, and new uniforms. Teaching before and after school hours, planning at night, repairing instruments, transporting the major jobs to the nearest repair shop, as well as enlisting his wife to alter uniforms, and arranging the chairs and racks himself for each rehearsal, this creature manages to weld his ill-assorted human material into musical units and to present them as planned.

Such aggressiveness is responsible for the great strides made in instrumental music. It is also the cause of much ill feeling and resistance on the part of professional colleagues, misunderstanding by the public, disillusionment on the part of the instrumental teachers themselves, and some negative educational results.

How can this energy and musicianship be applied more effectively in the true cause of music education? The answer, to which this book is dedicated, is to develop a reasoned philosophy, and a program of instruction in instrumental music which will mesh with the school curriculum and will result in sustained efforts toward better musicianship of the students. Before proceeding to that task, however, it seems wise to review some primary errors which need correction.

Possibly the fundamental weakness in approach has been the tacit admission that music is either extracurricular or co-curricular. Some educational authorities have regarded music in the schools as an activity or an *enrichment* of the curriculum, and we have almost begun to believe it.

Those who accept music in this secondary role are easy marks for the theory that school music is justified because of its supposed useful effect on character and health. They forget that our hospitals and prisons have their fair share of musicians.

Still others seem to regard music chiefly as an agency for public relations. They teach children to play in order to create greater spectacles on the gridiron, to amaze and entertain concert audiences, and to bring honor and glory to the school, community, and the director.

Another long-standing idea is that playing musical instruments, involving some mechanical problems, is too difficult for the many, and the director's time is better reserved for the talented few. We want to *choose* our students but feel thwarted when some of these show a preference for science, mathematics, or a foreign language.

It is just one more step to the belief that true success is measured by the number of future music teachers and symphony players that can be produced. Thus, the welfare of the majority becomes secondary to those few who show the spark. This view is bound to make any teaching career frustrating.

We draw attention finally to the prevailing misconception that the inherent purpose of instruction is to create superb performing groups. According to that view, whatever contributes to that result is justified regardless of any side effects. What if the music is too difficult and requires many extra rehearsals? What if there is no time for sight reading or development of appreciation? Some of the music may be more entertaining than educational; perhaps more students should be learning to play, but these deficiencies are supposedly overlooked so long as the group maintains full instrumentation and sounds better than competing groups.

As an alternative to these points of view, a balanced, integrated program of music education will be the concern of this book. This chapter will develop a background to deal with the more specific problems. First, it will be necessary to outline past developments in instrumental music and discuss the present situation. A firm basis for an instrumental music program will be proposed and a general pattern of activity will be outlined.

THE GROWTH OF INSTRUMENTAL MUSIC IN THE SCHOOLS

There are many who deplore "the vanishing strings" and sense a drop in the number of good bands and fine players. This estimation would be difficult to prove. While conditions fluctuate in various sections and localities of the nation, it seems that the total number and quality of instrumental performers and groups have exhibited a rather remarkable rise. Historically, instrumental music in the schools is a recent phenomenon. It is well to review briefly how this came about.

European Tradition

General music is the principal form of music education in the common schools of Europe. This situation results from the fact that the specialized forms of music education arose first and were entrusted to special agencies.

In ancient Roman and early Christian practice, musical study for the intellectual class was included among the "seven liberal arts," as part of the Quadrivium. Later, the church schools, private tutors, and the medieval universities regarded music as a scientific and theoretical study of great importance in the development of intellectual powers. This influence is still strong in European universities.

Because of the liturgical importance of music, however, special *scholae cantorum* were established during and after the fourth century to develop singers and instrumentalists for the church.

There was also a strong secular tradition, as evidenced by the traveling troubadours and *Meistersinger*. Outside the sphere of the church and university there were the village dances and celebrations, from which so much of our folk music derives. Musicians also began to gather at the courts, where their services were in great demand. This secular phase of music, in contrast to the academic and religious, was largely concerned with the playing of instruments. The necessary skills were acquired by simple imitation, tutoring, and apprenticeship. From the latter, the music guilds, guild schools, and finally the modern European conservatories arose. Thus we see how instrumental music acquired the aspect of a trade, limited to those carefully chosen and specially trained.

The Reformation led Europe to the idea of popular education, because the early Protestant leaders felt that the common people should have the tools to read and interpret the Bible and become good citizens of the state. In answer to this need, schools were first established in sixteenth-century Germany and then throughout Western Europe. They emphasized the ability to sing and read music, which was important to hymn-singing congregations.

This is the background of today's system of state-controlled elementary schools. Academic examinations are used to select qualified students for the secondary schools and universities; others have a choice of vocational schools, including the music conservatory.

Establishment of Music Education in America

This was the heritage which the Puritans, Cavaliers, Germans, Swedes, and Dutch brought to our shores—a belief that singing and reading music was a basic part of education, and that developing special talents was a matter of professional training professional. However, for many years, there were very few professionals.

In 1700, the first pipe organ was installed, at Port Royal, Virginia; a century later the New York Philharmonic Society sponsored its first concert. There were sporadic attempts at instrumental performances in the interim, including the use of an orchestra for *The Beggar's Opera* at Upper Marlborough, Maryland in 1752. But vocal music was in the forefront well into the present century.

Music in the schools was the result of much effort and fortuitous circumstance. About 1720, singing societies and singing schools were established in New England. They were closely identified with local church choirmasters and their choir members in an effort to upgrade their contribution to church services. In 1829, the first music convention was held in Concord, New Hampshire. As the name implies, this took the form of a short course or institute for musicians and teachers, for demonstrations in vocal problems, harmony, conducting, and the latest in methods and materials. The plan of these music conventions had much in common with the normal institutes and Chautauquas of a later time, and the music clinics and workshops of today.

The great movement toward universal, free public education occurred prior to the Civil War. It is identified with Horace Mann and, in music, with his good friend Lowell Mason. Mason and his associates were able to establish music in the Boston schools in 1838 and to spread the word by means of the various music conventions of the time.

About this same time, pestalozzian philosophy began to take effect in the schools, and was largely responsible for the firm foothold of music in the curriculum. In brief, Pestalozzi reacted against the exclusive presentation of second-hand or "book knowledge." He contended that the purpose of education was to develop individual powers and talents, and that the key to this process was through direct sense impression. On this premise, music's place in the curriculum could hardly be challenged.

Widening Musical Horizons

At this point there was nothing to suggest the future development of instrumental music in the schools. It is time to examine those factors with which we are more directly concerned.

The prime factor in the establishment of instrumental music was the relative success of vocal music in the schools. The number of people who had been taught to sing and read music also learned to appreciate it and to like the sound of instruments. After all, a strict diet of music *a cappella* is somewhat severe.

The natural appetite for instrumental music led various organizations and communities to sponsor concerts by instrumentalists. There were no radios, recordings, television, or motion pictures, so live performances had to be arranged. Lacking enough local and American players of stature, European artists were engaged for the concert circuit. We can mention Ole Bull, Jenny Lind, and the Germania Orchestra, followed by the orchestras of Theodore Thomas and Walter Damrosch and the bands of D. W. Reeves, Patrick Gilmore, and John Philip Sousa. Permanent symphonies and opera companies were established in some of the larger cities, and town bands were organized in many smaller localities. For a time, however, the majority of players were imported from Europe. These people largely staffed the conservatories and university music departments which developed, and many became private teachers when they could not identify with such institutions.

One further development helped create the impetus for instrumental teaching in the schools. This was the philosophy of pragmatism as expressed in *progressive education*. It is an American creation, of little effect elsewhere, which gathered strength throughout the first half of this century. It is based upon the theory that knowledge is discovered by application. Education is thus not simple exposure to, and mastery of facts but a process of experimentation and application proceeding from "where the pupil is." It is easy to see why the formerly basic subjects lost ground and the interesting fringes gained at their expense. There followed the great proliferation in athletics, home economics and industrial arts, business courses, art and music; even driver education and such courses as "home and family relationships" are included. The activity curriculum (without subject lines) and the core curriculum (centering instruction upon certain cultural institutions) evolved during this period.

Regardless of the validity of progressive education, instrumental music was granted its chance to develop in the schools. The development of skills on musical instruments was in keeping with the progressive spirit. In music, experimentation is constant. There are few eternal truths; individual progress is clearly demonstrable.

Thus instrumental music acquired its foothold. "The kids wanted to play" and the parents wanted to hear them. The band and orchestra directors were given a rather free hand in promoting and developing their activities. Only now, in the reaction against progressivism, do we understand the dangers inherent in association with the fringe areas of the curriculum. Music can and must claim its place on a different basis.

Developing Pattern of Instrumental Music

School orchestras began in a rather haphazard fashion. In some localities, small ensembles (whose members had studied with private music teachers) were organized for special events such as Christmas programs, commencement exercises, etc. Qualified conductors were found among the academic teaching staff or within the local community. Permanent organizations are recorded at Richmond, Indiana, in 1889; at Wichita, Kansas, and New London, Connecticut, in 1896; and at Hartford in 1898. These and other early orchestras possessed a very limited instrumentation, and had not acquired full school status in terms of scheduling and finance. By 1910, however, over a hundred orchestras were found in the American schools.[1]

The school band movement began about this time and grew quite rapidly. One reason lay in the adaptation of class instruction to the teaching of instruments. The British schools gave us the idea and it was successful with American string pupils. When tried with wind and percussion players, the results were astonishing. By class instruction, a comparatively respectable concert band could be developed in three or four years.

[1] Edward Bailey Birge, "High School Orchestras," *School News*, November, 1910, pp. 12-14.

The first World War was another factor in stimulating the development of school bands. There were service bands to imitate and parades to see. Then veterans with band experience returned home, and some became teachers in the schools. Also, bands became identified with the surge of interest in interscholastic athletic events.

Finally, there were commercial interests which helped in the school band movement. The music publishers, uniform makers, and band instrument companies saw great possibilities and aided in the general process of promotion and organization.

During the Twenties and Thirties instrumental music spread to the schools of the entire nation. Most schools can trace their first bands and orchestras to this period. The first strength was in the Midwest, then in the larger schools in all sections, and finally, as more teachers were produced, the smaller schools established instrumental music in the curriculum.

Instrumental music also shared the exuberance of the "jazz age." There was a new emphasis on youth; people liked to support causes; and there was much "community boosting" sentiment. In such an environment, music contests grew rapidly. Some were sponsored by colleges, music companies, and business groups, until music teachers combined to set up district, state, and national contests on an official basis. In 1928 the first national contest was held.

At first, contests were quite rigidly organized. For each event and class, there usually was one required number, or a choice among two numbers. Contestants competed for first, second, and third place rather than being rated superior, excellent, or good. As a result of the fierce competition and the growing maturity of the profession, the contest system was modified and decentralized into its present form in the late Thirties.

As we have said, the music contests were closely identified with various organizations of music teachers. The National School Band and Orchestra Association was developed to control the contests. Later, it divided and these groups are associated with the Music Educators National Conference. The Conference itself originated in music section meetings of the National Education Association. First organized in 1907 at Keokuk, Iowa, it now functions on the national, regional, and state levels and numbers nearly fifty thousand members. Most of the special interest groups, such as the American String Teachers Association, the College Band Directors National Association, and the National Association of College Wind and Percussion Instructors, are also affiliated with the Conference.

A significant outgrowth of the professional meetings has been the organization of various select bands and orchestras. The National Orchestra at the 1926 Conference in Chicago led directly to the organization of the National Music Camp at Interlochen, Michigan. Now, there are hundreds of such summer camps in existence. Many more groups are organized yearly on a one or two day basis for various university clinics and professional gatherings. These festival or clinic groups have probably overtaken the contests in popularity and educational impact.

THE CURRENT SCENE

As the school instrumental program evolved, it was accompanied by some very natural developments:

(1) The number of certified teachers has greatly increased, and their preparation has been enriched. Previously, many instrumental music teachers secured their jobs on the basis of demonstrated or assumed abilities; some were spectacularly successful and some were not. Today, most teachers possess a four year degree with a more deliberate exposure to the various aspects of musicianship.

(2) Partly due to the above fact, there is evidence of a broader form of activity in the instrumental program, including some attention to keyboard instruction, non-orchestral instruments, and music appreciation. This process is only in the opening stage.

(3) At the same time there has been a tremendous development of marching bands. This phenomenon was especially marked in the Thirties and Forties.

(4) Music enrollments have kept pace with rising school enrollments. String instruction suffered considerably during and just after the second World War, but the trend is now reversed.

(5) The first generation of graduates of the instrumental music program are now mature citizens. The effect is seen in the increasing number of American composers, conductors, and symphony players. Both positive and negative results are evident in the attitudes of parents toward music in the schools and in their participation in local musical endeavors.

(6) Scientific discovery and technological development have created the motion picture, recording, radio, and television industries. These media have become part of the curriculum in the schools as audio-visual aids. A more important aspect is that they provide a great variety of out-of-school musical experience. Their effect is difficult to measure but is undoubtedly great. They do create a familiarity with music and musical device, an acquaintance with many musical idioms, and certain expectations with regard to the music used in the schools.

(7) A large repertoire of published music has been adapted and created for the school instrumental program. Formerly, orchestras were often forced to use theatre arrangements of standard classics, and bands used the available marches and orchestral transcriptions. There was little usable material for the small ensemble and individual soloist. Composers

and publishers worked strenuously to provide music but the main criterion seemed to be salability, and many of the works were complete trash. In the process, however, the better things have survived and the demand has become more discriminating, so that a reasonable repertoire is now available in most fields of the school instrumental program.

(8) Finally, instructional facilities have gradually improved. It has been proverbial that music departments operate in the oldest, least desirable setting. Previously, it was necessary to use any practical means to put instruments in the hands of the players. The heterogeneous collection of silver cornets, helicons, mellophones and upright altos, tenor horns, C melody saxophones, and Albert system clarinets that used to be found in school bands can be remembered. Such conditions are now the exception rather than the rule. New music buildings or wings have been constructed in many of the new schools that have been built to meet the increased enrollments. The number and quality of instruments provided by the schools has improved.

Here, some observations may be drawn from a careful and objective survey undertaken by the National Education Association. In early 1962, questionnaires were sent to a systematic sample of school principals. Usable replies were tabulated for 657 elementary and 696 secondary schools. It was found that the music program is more than holding its own. In the elementary schools, "music was being given as much or more time in the school program in 1961-62 as it was five years before."[2] During this same period, in the secondary schools, "enrollments increased 28.6 percent. . . . Naturally, enrollments in music would be expected to rise during this period. But the schools reported that enrollments in music tended to increase not only in *number* but in *percent* of the student body."[3]

The situation is not all positive. The survey shows that 70 to 80 percent of the classroom teachers were expected to teach music, with or without the help of a specialist, yet "training in music was *not* a requirement for elementary school teachers in 63.3 percent of the schools in the survey."[4] And "30.6 percent of the schools reporting said they offered no instruction on instruments at all."[5]

Comparative size of schools has a striking influence on the music program. According to the survey, it is the smaller schools which most often fail to provide the needed staff, offerings, and equipment. Orchestra, for example, is offered in 9.8 percent of the high schools classified as "small" and in 69.5 percent of the "large" ones.[6] Yet the smaller secondary schools possess the greatest *proportion* of full time staff in music. They

[2] NEA Research Division, *Music and Art in the Public Schools*, Research Monograph 1963-M3 (Washington, D. C.: National Education Association, 1963), p. 12.

[3] *Ibid.*, p. 34.

[4] *Ibid.*, p. 12.

[5] *Ibid.*, p. 16.

[6] *Ibid.*, p. 45.

consequently enroll an average of 45.2 percent of the student body in music while the large schools do about half as well.[7]

The bright and dark aspects of the scene are summed up in these words:[8]

> . . . nearly 95 percent of the secondary schools in the country offered music. Student enrollments . . . were on the increase. However, well over half of all high school graduates had less than a year of music in high school . . . The music program as it stood in most secondary schools appeared to be geared to the interests and abilities of students who could perform, rather than to efforts to insure that *every* student learn something about music before he graduated from high school.

Organizational Patterns

Another way to look at a school program is in terms of the number of teachers and their responsibilities. Having given some of the statistical facts on a national basis it is safe to portray the typical local scene. It is clear that school size is a major factor in determining the local pattern for instrumental music. However, arbitrarily selected enrollment figures can not be the sole gauge, since other variables include total enrollment within the local school system, the number of faculty, tax support, etc. The most direct means of classifying school instrumental programs is in terms of the relative degree of specialization expected of the teachers.

VERY SMALL SCHOOLS. Very small schools are ones in which instrumental music instruction is a part-time job. In addition, such a teacher teaches vocal music or some other subject, or is assigned to handle instrumental instruction in two or more nearby localities. Schools of this type usually enroll less than one hundred students in grades 10 through 12 and are often grouped in county systems.

In such schools the chief responsibilities are to assist the classroom teachers in music instruction, and to develop some high school choral groups and as large a band as possible. Teachers working in more than one school often combine their players into one group for concerts and festivals. Music facilities and equipment are often at a bare minimum.

SMALL SCHOOLS. The typical small school has one full time teacher for instrumental music. He usually has a limited budget and severe scheduling problems. By a combination of individual and class teaching, he starts his beginners and welds them into a band. Sometimes, he is able to produce a few small wind and string ensembles. Class piano is offered in only a few instances.

MEDIUM-SIZED SCHOOLS. In medium-sized schools, the instrumental teacher is part of a two or three man team. Work is divided according to

[7] *Ibid.*, p. 35.
[8] *Ibid.*, pp. 53-54.

need and individual qualifications. Often, one teacher handles the high school band and related ensembles, while another works similarly in the intermediate grades and junior high school. Another typical plan is to have one teacher for band and beginning woodwind or brass (whichever is his specialty) while the other teaches strings and the remaining band instruments. A larger staff of three or four divides its work on the same principle.

Schools in this category typically have a high school enrollment of some three to eight hundred. Facilities and equipment are often excellent in this size school.

LARGE SCHOOLS. In large schools, the task of the instrumental teacher is quite highly specialized. Each is assigned to a specific phase of music in a particular building. There is a band director and an orchestra director working in each high school and in each junior high school. Others may be assigned to beginning instruction in the intermediate grades. In the metropolitan systems, with a multiple network of elementary and secondary schools there is an instrumental supervisor with coordinating and administrative responsibility, and a corps of special teachers for the various instruments. There is often more than one band and orchestra per school, and sometimes a city wide organization of the best players. There is usually a large system of beginning classes and small ensembles, as well as additional offerings such as music theory and history, class piano, and the like. Equipment and facilities are usually fair to good.

Nothing quite like this stair step effect is noted in subjects other than music. Small schools may not attempt shorthand classes nor will they be able to arrange fast and slow sections in the various subjects. However, the basic core of English, social science, natural science, and mathematics will be offered in every school. Even vocal music retains this position of stability. Since many of its components are not being taught on a universal basis, instrumental music is readily classified as a frill. Those who wonder why their school has neither string nor piano instruction are easily answered that it must be unnecessary since other schools do not have it.

Another factor that keeps the instrumental music program to an insecure, unstable plan is that, historically it has been developed on a free enterprise basis. When teaching personnel changes, parts of the program are often abandoned, reintroduced, or markedly revised. A large marching band may be found in a school that did little in this line a few years ago, but the orchestra program was discontinued. Another school, which was not adequately supporting its program, is now adding teachers and buying equipment; and still another is revising the pattern of beginning instruction. Thus instrumental music in a school depends more on individual motives, competence, and personality of its director than does the rest of the curriculum. It is still in a period of flux and experimentation.

The situation is further compounded by this uncertain status, so that the instrumental program is unusually affected by the philosophy (and whims) of the administrator and the expectations of the local community. There are constant pressures to pacify the service club (who sent the band to the big festival) and the parents' club (who purchased the new uniforms). The superintendent is torn between the desire to display the instrumental groups and the feelings of the other teachers who resent this apparent favoritism. As a result, the instrumental teachers are tempted to stress propaganda and promotion rather than stable educational enterprise.

The Public Viewpoint

The instrumental music teacher is not wrong in considering the public viewpoint. Social consensus is the rock upon which the schools are built. However, the public does not consist of a few outspoken critics, nor of the parents of the students. The local school board is not even the public, although they undertake to represent it fairly. The public is the entire nation and its will is not determined by a questionnaire addressed to fifty or a hundred individuals. Public demands are best discovered by examining individual actions. Nationwide, if we can see an increase in concert audiences, in the support of symphonies, in the purchase of musical merchandise, and sales of good musical recordings then there is no doubt that music does seem important in the life of America.

More specifically, however, the *kind* of school music desired by our society must be determined. Emphasis could be placed upon musical literacy, appreciation, performing skills, or even public entertainment, but looking at the public interest, instead of at a few pep club members, we sense a mandate for developing balanced musicianship. The truest support comes from those who acquired a taste for music and the desire to play while in school. They sense the value of good musical literature and stimulating instruction and encourage their children to register to play in school groups. We must not misinterpret their enthusiasm as a reaction for our pageantry-of-the-moment, but as an expression of general support of worthwhile musical activity.

Since the advent of Sputnik and ensuing debate on the school curriculum, there has been public concern with the programs in science and mathematics. Some interpret this as involving a retrenchment in the other subjects, including music. It may, indeed, have this effect wherever the music program has been unproductive. For the real enemy that is being uncovered in this clamor is *time-wasting*. We may always count on support for instrumental music if the results, in terms of pupil learning, match the time involved. The public viewpoint is that musical study is a good thing, if it results in concrete achievement. Wide opportunity to participate is endorsed, pedantry is decried. How the task is accomplished is left to us.

School Philosophy

Educators generally reflect the public's attitude. They accept music as a school subject and respect its public relations value. They like to see students developing their musical knowledge, skills, and appreciation. However, our teaching colleagues are very close to the scene of our operation and as fellow pedagogues they can readily analyze its faults.

To many teachers and administrators, the instrumental music program seems to be a source of irritation. There are unusual requirements for space, expensive items of equipment, trips to finance, too many emergencies, and schedules disrupted. Although these conditions are unavoidable in instrumental music, nevertheless, there is some suspicion among non-musicians that these demands are not always legitimate.

The objectives of instruction constitute a more fundamental point of difference with our colleagues. In their eyes we seem to concentrate upon the performing skills far beyond the needs of the layman, and at the expense of ordinary musical understanding. They fear we are building little conservatories, whereas the school subjects should be general and liberal in character. Many educators feel this situation could be remedied by presenting more intellectual content. These same people have been partially convinced, however, that music is a unique subject, being based on non-verbal forms, and educational principles and procedures must be applied somewhat differently in this field. Hence the typical reaction is to put the instrumental teacher in his field and keep him there. He is granted a certain license to proceed but is watched carefully for signs of fanaticism. Unfortunately, our position as music teachers is not invulnerable. It must be strengthened.

THE BASIS FOR INSTRUMENTAL MUSIC

We have thus portrayed the phenomenal growth of instrumental school music and some of the stresses and strains which have developed en route. The future of the movement depends upon more than a few corrective measures. The weaknesses are more fundamental than that. What is needed is a re-examination of the values and problems of instrumental instruction so that an inherently stronger and more vital program may be built.

Work of the School

Education in the broadest sense is the universal and continuing process by which individuals acquire an understanding and command of their environment. It is accomplished through experience—by means of constant exposure to environmental situations and the consequent reactions in favor of certain lines of behavior. Well integrated and meaningful reactions constitute learning. Schooling is that form of education which society has instituted in an attempt to transmit and improve those elements of knowledge and conduct which it considers important. The curriculum is the instrument by which this task is undertaken and comprises all the content and procedures used by a school in producing the goals it seeks. In order to evoke the necessary experiences purposefully and cumulatively, the curriculum is built on discrete levels (grades) and phases (subjects and topics). Thus we speak of the science program or the music program and the various activities these comprise.

The process of curriculum building is three-fold: (1) to determine objectives—to decide what the students should know, if the school is to fulfill its mission to society and to the individual; (2) to select the experiences—to decide what situations and reactions should be sought in developing the desired objectives; (3) to organize instruction—to plan the materials (books and music), subject matter (facts and beliefs), the mode of presentation, and all other factors which will create the necessary educative environment.

It must be understood that each curriculum is unique because it is created by and for individual teachers and their students.[9] This quality of variation leads to many educational debates: what areas of knowledge should be covered; what our students should be learning; what is effective teaching; how does music, especially instrumental music, qualify as a school subject; and what are the inherent values in it.

The public schools are primarily dedicated to what is called *general education*—promoting the fundamental tools of human existence and social usefulness. Any vocational values growing out of this process are encouraged but not specifically sought.

Knowledge is not the sole province of the school and much general education is acquired from parents, associates, and many other sources. We learn to speak, eat, and manipulate concrete objects; we learn social conduct and morality; we develop personality, varied values, and some aesthetic responses outside the schools.

Conversely, many of the practical skills of life require more thorough, technical study; unless it is provided, the complex phases of civilization established over the centuries would be lost. Our grandchildren would be unable to read, write, or figure; there would be few who could build and create, and certainly few who could either play music or compose it.

Therefore, the elementary and secondary schools must see that *all* secure the essential elements for a full life. This philosophy has been

---

[9] A full treatment of curriculum planning by this author is found in "Curriculum Construction in Music Education," *Basic Concepts in Music Education,* Fifty-Seventh Yearbook, Part I, of the National Society for the Study of Education (Chicago: University of Chicago Press, 1958), pp. 236-260, and in Charles Leonard and Robert W. House, *Foundations and Principles of Music Education* (New York: McGraw-Hill Book Company, 1959), pp. 142-226.

stated more precisely by the author: "The bases upon which any subject claims a place in the school curriculum are (1) that it is a field of knowledge or a practice which exists as an integral part of ordinary existence, and (2) that the essential competence is not likely to be acquired through ordinary existence."[10]

These criteria are implicit in construction of the curriculum. To the extent that a subject can demonstrate these qualifications it will be maintained. However, it is useless to deny the existence of a rank of importance among school subjects. Wherever schooling is poor and limited, the available time and money will be spent on those subjects considered most vital; where conditions allow, greater breadth is sought.

The weight of opinion has shifted on this matter from time to time. From the classical emphasis upon languages and mathematics, the modern trend has been to give prominence to the natural and social sciences. The fine arts, however, have always retained a place in the curriculum. Any balanced philosophy of education recognizes the inherent need to provide (1) skills necessary to the maintenance of thoughts and ideas among people, (2) a sense of civic responsibility and social relationships, (3) the tools to aesthetic satisfaction, and (4) knowledge of facts and methods required to cope successfully with the physical environment. Music educators can thus rest assured that music will always be taught in their school. Their mission is to see that the essential elements of that subject are taught and taught effectively.

·*Values of Music*

It is generally agreed that the ends of education involve the needs of both the individual and of society. The evidence that music contributes to those needs must be clarified. There is a common persuasion that music is so abstract, so ephemeral, that it could be totally abandoned. Yet this very quality of abstractness is the basis for music's peculiar contribution to man's existence. If music is so impractical, it is strange that man made music even before he could speak or write.

SOCIAL FUNCTION. All evidence points to rhythm and song as being ingredients of culture since man's beginning. Music developed as an accompaniment to tribal ceremonies and religious rites, and became wedded to song and dance. As civilization progressed, music retained this role, and became an indispensable part of church services, court functions, dances, and folk activities. It has always been a universal art, shared by the elite and masses. Music is subject to cultural diffusion, radiating from the point of origin to other peoples and classes, and adjusting to new situations and institutions. For example, those Americans who could

[10] Robert W. House, "The Role of the Fine Arts in the Preparation of Teachers," *Music Educators Journal*, November-December, 1960, p. 39.

neither read music nor obtain established artists to perform, created spirituals, hill tunes, and jazz—without formal tuition.

It would be interesting to estimate the amount of time, in a week, that some form of music strikes the ear—through recordings, radio, television, movies, at church services, athletic events, meeting and luncheon programs, concerts, social gatherings, and work. Total exposure time will vary among individuals, but it will be substantial in any case. Any element of life so prevalent is certain to have great meaning.

The amount of active participation in music is significant. It is claimed that there are thirty-four million people in America today who can and do play instruments. Of these, about 21.5 million play some piano, 3.3 million play the standard string instruments, 5.3 million the guitar, 1.3 million the accordion, and about six million altogether on the woodwinds and brasses.[11] "In the fall of 1962 it was estimated that elementary, junior high, and high schools had 15,000 orchestras and 48,000 bands"; besides this, there were "approximately 1,200 symphony orchestras."[12]

Statistics show that music in America is big business. Retail sales of new instruments, accessories, and sheet music in 1962 amounted to $630 million; this compares with $380 million spent on operas, concerts, and the theatre, and $90 million on "classical" records. This figure also surpasses the total spent on all spectactor sports, cameras, comic books, and playing cards.[13] Such figures are not conclusive, but indicate that music is not a minor factor in American life, although much of the music surrounding us is strictly incidental—almost background noise to our growing income and leisure. Only a small proportion of it really affects us significantly, but there is something which apparently appeals to the deep springs of human nature.

INDIVIDUAL VALUE. The common belief is that music is a sort of captured emotion and that by listening to it we should reflect the indicated mood. To an extent this is probably true, for music may indeed arouse vague sentiments of happiness, nostalgia, exhilaration, and apprehension, but these feelings are only pale versions of the elemental emotions—joy, passion, anger, and fear.

Music may be descriptive but it never creates more than an illusion of the authentic sensations, When music descriptive of fires is heard, the listener neither sees fires, lights them, nor does he feel warmer, and when the music rages, he does not rage. He only imagines those sensations or feelings.

Musical tones in themselves are very weak stimuli (except when produced with strong intensity). They may pass unnoticed unless the mind

[11] "Report of Amateur Music in the U. S. A.," *Music Journal,* October, 1963, pp. 60-62.

[12] *Loc. cit.*

[13] *Loc. cit.*

perceives the patterns of tonal relationships. We can take it or leave it. Due to this fact, music is all about us and strongly tied to a recreational role. It has also been shown, experimentally, that music can affect the pulse rate and digestion, and is sometimes effective therapeutically since it produces calmness by occupying the mind.

Delving further for an explanation of music's value, some have claimed that music can improve individual character and promote understanding among nations. If so, these effects have never been clearly evident in history. Musicians have behaved much like other people and nations have waged foreign policy with little regard for their neighbors' music.

However, music is admittedly valuable as a means of self expression. This is a legitimate reason for its inclusion in the curriculum, although it is evident that millions of citizens sing and play with great difficulty and remain well adjusted. They apparently secure self-expression by other means.

The fact is that music has a mild influence in all these ways—as an emotional stimulant, therapeutic and moral agent, cultural representative, and vehicle for self-expression. However, these values are only side effects of music's basic function.

Music is a powerful factor in human experience because it is essential in giving meaning to its full range. Through the transformation of vibrations into tones, patterns may be created and perceived. Man can relate these patterns which involve an illusion of time, space, and movement to his own experience. Thus musical relationships are *symbolic* relationships.[14] The composer does not speak to us in actual terms, for music is not a language in the strict sense. Words represent specific things and ideas among individuals, while musical patterns have no concrete, referential meanings. This is why it is so difficult to express what music means; instead, we each commune with ourself. Pasternak calls this, the state of "transposed reality."[15]

Any explanation of music's power is necessarily obscure, but it cannot be said that we can do without music. Man would be starved without this unique method of access to his inner, inexpressible thoughts. Believing this is the case, it is necessary to unlock this kind of responsiveness in the students. It is the true role of music instruction and puts a new light on the musical activities sponsored by the school.

The Music Team

School music activity is classified in several ways. The field is divided into general music (including music in the elementary classroom), band,

---

[14] For a full explanation of this theory, see Susanne Langer, *Philosophy in a New Key* (New York: New American Library, 1948) and *Feeling and Form* (New York: Charles Scribner's Sons, 1953).

[15] Boris Pasternak, *Safe Conduct: Autobiography* (New York: The New American Library of World Literature, Inc., 1959), p. 59.

orchestra, chorus, music theory, and various other subjects. All of these have their listening, performing, rhythmic, and creative aspects. There is an even more basic property: all music is either sung or played.

Vocal music, as previously stated, holds the position of seniority in the schools. Everyone can be taught to sing and little equipment is required. Whereas the success of instrumental groups depends upon their school size, instrumentation, and level of individual proficiency, choral groups can be formed from almost any material. Singing is the most universal form of musical activity, and since teachers and supervisors have been oriented in that direction, it has been the traditional core of the general elementary and secondary music programs.

Instrumental music, on the other hand, often develops more dedication and team spirit. Bands *are* naturally spirited and compelling and lend themselves well to brilliance and pageantry, while orchestras can achieve the ultimate in musical subtlety and complexity.

School music cannot favor either vocal or instrumental music, and it cannot limit itself to one or the other without disastrous consequences. Each field has its special values to contribute to the child's musical responsiveness. Thus, schools hire instrumental and vocal teachers and expect them to cooperate and coordinate their programs to serve the ends of music education.

Unfortunately, there is usually very little real cooperation among the music personnel *at the point of instruction*. The teachers may be friends, and unite on matters of general policy and procedure, but each works at developing his own organization. In many instances the members of a music staff are unaware that they are working at cross-purposes. As a result, students come to associate vocal music with rote learning and free rhythm, and think instrumental music means technical drill and strict discipline. A situation has been allowed to arise whereby students cannot possibly acquire a rounded background in voice, strings, and band instruments even if they so desire.

One cause of this condition can be found in the pattern of instruction in the elementary school. The student, typically, sings all kinds of songs (first by rote and then by syllables) and strenuous efforts are made to teach him to read music. Occasionally the teacher plays selected recordings and talks about the composers. There is also some experience with rhythm and harmony instruments, some dancing, tapping, and perhaps some work with tonettes and paper keyboards. In the intermediate grades the string teacher and/or band director is introduced and volunteers are solicited to learn an instrument. If the director has a heavy schedule, these volunteers are screened by means of the office records and some form of musical aptitude test. The individual instruments are then chosen and the students meet for special instruction. Those who succeed drop their classroom music as soon as the opportunity arises and the weaker students slip back to the regular classroom.

This system has many weaknesses and something more constructive is clearly needed. Certainly, instrumental music can take a more vigorous part in elementary classroom instruction. Trial and experimentation with instruments can be provided here—in the classroom—without damage to the total program. A less artificial means of screening students for beginning instruction should be sought which does not overlook so many gifted students. Finally, the school's convenience should not be allowed to override an individual's need to begin instrumental study a bit earlier or later than the majority. Instrumental music cannot be safely handled on a production line basis.

If for no other reason, instrument playing needs to be articulated with classroom music because it is an efficient road to reading music. The following is one of the strongest statements we have seen:

> Very few children who are not learning to play an instrument ever learn to read music. . . . Any instrument, even the so-called "toy instruments," provides a medium for learning notation that far exceeds the voice. . . . It is possible, indeed, to spend six years in school music attempting to teach children to read notes using the voice as a medium and not achieve the success in this skill that can accompany six months of instruction on an instrument. [16]

This phenomenon needs further exploration, but the available evidence points to its probable truth. In too many instances, this possibility of teaching the mass of children to read music is overlooked because all energies and resources are being poured into building the performing groups. Happily, both goals can be accomplished. Fine high school performing groups are almost an automatic outcome of the broad, coordinated program of music instruction throughout the school.

Special Aspects of Instrumental Instruction

There is a need, here, to identify some of the persistent problems inherent in instrumental instruction. In the remainder of this book we will try to deal with these questions in terms of specific activities.

RECRUITMENT. Since instrumental music is still regarded as an elective, a student need never play more than triangle, woodblock, or tonette in the American schools. Thus a fundamental problem in instrumental music is to capture the interest of students to make them want to participate. One method is by example or demonstration, as when we show the young pupil our fine high school groups. Another method just discussed is through a more vigorous presentation and use of instrumental music in the elementary classroom.

The real key to recruitment, however, is the successful handling of those who are in the process of beginning instruction. If these students are

[16] Alfred Ellison, *Music With Children* (New York: McGraw-Hill Book Co., Inc., 1959), pp. 42-43.

playing and learning real music, their enthusiasm will be communicated to their acquaintances. If the volunteers are accepted wholeheartedly and given stimulating instruction, many more will become interested in the program.

EQUIPMENT. Instrumental teachers know the vital necessity for proper rehearsal rooms, good instruments, and related facilities. Financial support seems to follow results, but since it is really needed in advance, directors are forced to become money raisers and a levy is placed on the parents to start their child in instrumental music. But if every child is to have the opportunity to play through the system of free public education, the instrumental music facilities in our schools must improve. In the meantime, it may be wisest to drop the extras such as uniforms, trips, and awards, and buy the essentials, namely, space, acoustics, instruments, and music.

FINDING THE RIGHT INSTRUMENT. There are at least twenty different orchestral instruments in standard use, as well as the keyboard instruments and more informal instruments. Nearly everyone can learn to play one or more of these quite well, but may easily fail on the others. The greater part of our efforts may go unrewarded, unless we can match the instrument to the student. All present forms of instrument selection are comparatively ineffective. Enough instruments must be provided to allow pupils the needed trial and experimentation.

STAFFING. The typical instrumental teacher hasn't the time or energy to exert his knowledge fully, and although he is often a human dynamo, he cannot cover the entire task. While half the schools increased their music enrollments between 1956-57 and 1961-62, less than twenty percent increased the number of staff.[17] If there is to be more instrumental work in the classroom and instruction in strings and piano as well as band, more staff members must be found. Until the situation improves, part of the answer may lie in abandoning such items as private instruction and the show band in favor of more basic activities.

SCHEDULING. Scheduling is a constant problem for the instrumental director and he is forced into a parasitical position in the school, taking pupils out of every class and meeting with them at odd places and times. There should be less *pulling out* and more *going in* to the elementary class rooms, while beginning and advanced performing groups must be included in the daily class schedule. Schedules must be set up that favor these electives rather than penalize them.

PATTERNS OF INSTRUCTION. The instrumental teacher thinks in terms of large, fully instrumented groups and individual lessons, but it is well to consider a more diverse approach. Activities such as class instruction for beginners, sectional rehearsals, and small ensembles which involve groups of three to twenty players, can be a most fruitful means of instruction.

The greatest debate seems to center around the method of beginning

[17] NEA Research Division, *Music and Art in the Public Schools*, pp. 35-36.

instruction. Some feel that private study is the best way to develop proper habits. Others feel some form of class instruction is most effective. For instance, Fred Weber takes this position:

> Class lessons are not only economical and effective, but the group spirit fostered by them is of great importance. In the class the student learns to work with others and to play as a member of a group. He learns to compare pitches and tone quality, the importance of rhythmic activity and precision in ensemble. *From the beginning he learns what it takes to be a good band member.*[18]

He also favors the heterogeneous plan as demonstrated by the following statement:

> *The problem of dealing with classes of mixed abilities is much greater than that of dealing with different instruments.* The author's experience as a teacher makes him favor a school program based on mixed class instruction supplemented by encouraging as many students as possible to take private lessons.[19]

However, there are many more problems to be settled such as the kinds of musical literature that will provide the needed elements of instruction, what to do about scales, arpeggios, and warm-up drills, and how to best promote good playing position and embouchure. Such matters must never be treated as isolated problems, but rather in relation to the final objectives of the program.

PUBLIC APPEARANCES. Similarly, any public appearances to be sponsored by the school should be planned in terms of the desired outcomes. It is wrong to assume that performances must be given, if in process the desired values must be abandoned. The director must ask himself how much time he would spend on marching *if there were no shows to put on.* He should further consider the kinds of literature he would rehearse *if there were to be no concert or contest,* and how much time he would spend on certain numbers. The director should learn to regard a public performance as a regular occasion for educative experience, and particularly as a chance for the students and other observers to evaluate the regular work of the school. Public performance is a great help in securing motivation, but we should not be always preparing for the day when company comes.

THE INSTRUCTIONAL PROCESS

Objectives

Although an outline has been given of the objectives of music instruction in Europe and the United States and their relation to the true

---

[18] "The Elementary and Junior High School Band Program," *Building Better Bands* (Rockville Centre, L. I., N. Y.: Belwin, Inc., 1957), p. 6.
[19] *Loc. cit.*

values of music, it has not been possible to be specific because there is no set of universally applicable objectives. However, it is necessary to paint a broad picture of the goals of instrumental music in order to continue intelligently in this book, and help those who need to devise their own objectives. The instructional process depends upon the creation of a valid and coherent set of objectives. Failure in this task finds teachers trying to recreate their own childhood experiences and building up their groups despite all criticism, while wondering that so many of their graduates are poor musicians, and music teaching so unrewarding.

Objectives are definitions of the kinds of musical behavior to be sought. They are found by examining the musical needs of children and society and should be used in the planning and conducting of instruction, and in evaluating the results. Actually, whenever we teach or consider the effects of our teaching, we unconsciously refer to our objectives and our teaching will be no better than these objectives.

Objectives are of several kinds and levels—those for the school, for the total music program, and tactical objectives for each particular class which may apply for a week, a month, or a year. Those stated below are for the instrumental music program as a whole. They define the kinds of musical knowledge and understanding, the attitudes, appreciation, and musical habits which we seek for the students, and these are the goals largely associated with general musicianship:

Knowledge of:
  (1) musical literature from all periods and idioms,
  (2) basic musical patterns and usages,
  (3) musical vocabulary and meanings,
  (4) music's development as an art,
  (5) the principal forms and composers.

Understanding of:
  (1) problems in performing and learning to perform,
  (2) the elements of good musical interpretation,
  (3) the general methods by which music is constructed.

Skill in:
  (1) producing a rich tone with acceptable intonation,
  (2) playing with reasonable facility and accuracy,
  (3) performing by ear,
  (4) reading music of appropriate difficulty,
  (5) performing with others, independently, yet in proper relation to the ensemble,
  (6) hearing and following the main elements of musical compositions.

Attitudes of:
  (1) musical broadmindedness and the necessary discrimination of quality,
  (2) respect for music as an art and a profession,
  (3) intention to improve one's musicianship.

Appreciation of:
  (1) skilled and tasteful performance,
  (2) good music in any medium, style, or period.

Habits of:
  (1) frequent and efficient individual practice,
  (2) proper selection and care of instruments,
  (3) participating wholeheartedly in musical groups,
  (4) proper rehearsal attendance, deportment, and attention,
  (5) selecting good recordings, searching for more musically
      satisfying radio and TV programs, and attending worthwhile
      concerts.

The foregoing statements are intended as illustrations.[20] They can be revised, shortened, or amplified to meet individual convictions. Indeed, the student may develop his own special objectives, as perhaps, relating more specifically to a performing or teaching career in his field. Such a pupil, for example, might seek technical agility, a wide solo repertoire, skills in transposition, stage presence, conducting, or composition. It is our pleasure and responsibility to assist in this process, *so long as it does not seem to supersede the basic goals.*

The Preparatory Phase

If the objectives are valid, they may be promoted in every level and phase of the program. No utopian scheme of courses is necessary, since the normal instrumental activities—playing activities in the classroom, beginning lessons, large and small performing groups—all offer possibilities for productive experience. But it is necessary to organize a strong, well conceived and well taught program in all of these activities. Remember that outcomes vary greatly from school to school, even though the offerings are apparently equivalent.

It is very important to involve the student in musical investigation in the early grades, although the work at this stage is often desultory and haphazard. There should be more significant participation from instrumentalists in the planning and teaching than is usually the case. Careful introduction and use of the rhythm and melody instruments, as well as keyboard experience, produces some understanding of the problems of instrumental technique. The foundations of good eye, ear, and muscle coordination may be laid, as well as a proper basis for the development of the desired attitudes and appreciation of instrumental forms. Recordings should be selected with an eye to supplementing and reinforcing this process. By further demonstration and discussion, the pupils should have acquired a fair notion of the way instruments are learned, and combined into ensembles, before formal instruction is begun.

[20] For a full treatment of the process of establishing objectives see Charles Leonhard and Robert W. House, *Foundations and Principles of Music Education,* pp. 142-171.

Ideally, the individual decision to study an instrument should be almost spontaneous, so that a continuous flow of recruits will appear. Meanwhile, in the classroom, specific acquaintance with instruments should continue, at least through the junior high school years.

Learning to Play

The problems in choosing and acquiring instruments, grouping, and scheduling beginning players, have been noted and will be fully treated in later chapters. Probably the gravest mistake made in the instruction of these people is the abandonment of concern about general musicianship in favor of forced concentration on technical proficiency. Perhaps this is responsible for the many dropouts at this stage.

There are some necessary preliminaries involving instruction on proper care and assembling of the instruments, playing position, and basic elements of tone production. However, there cannot and should not be any attempt to perfect these matters at this point. As soon as the players can manage to play a few notes, they should start to produce real music. This ensures early attention to the problems of tonal balance, shading, phrasing, and style along with those of breathing, tonguing, fingering, and embouchure development. It has been found that improvement in these latter mechanical factors is often managed more easily when the requirements of the *music* suggest more bow or more breath, a cleaner attack, and the like. Instruction on such a basis is likely to seem more leisurely because there are so many occasions for learning in each number that it will not be *just* a matter of covering the notes and increasing the range and facility. As their technique develops, therefore, the students will be broadening their knowledge of literature, their understanding of musical interpretation and construction, and their appreciation and enthusiasm for music. It is this last factor which is so important in precluding dropouts.

Developing Finesse

Strictly speaking, the development of true finesse has its roots in the pattern of growth just outlined. But the student naturally progresses to finer and finer points in his last years of schooling, as he participates in the advanced performing groups.

Remembering the objectives of the program, it is necessary to foster as much independence as possible in completing the task of inculcating breadth of taste and appreciation, polishing various skills of performance, and strengthening the habits of musical participation and consumption. For example, the student needs freedom to try different interpretations, and he should have the opportunity to rehearse his section or small ensemble. There should be a chance to prepare and present solos, and perhaps to try composing. Thus, the good instrumental program at this level should not be conceived only as the process of rehearsing bands and orchestras for concerts. It should comprise a broad and flexible series of activities, in which there should be many small ensembles. If teachers with the necessary degree of specialization are available, several players should be induced to take individual instruction. The orchestra should be used not only as a complete ensemble, but also as a string choir, and to accompany soloists, choral groups, and stage productions. Also, it is fitting that the concert band become a strong, solid-sounding and precise marching unit. However, this implies drill on real marching evolutions and not a series of aimless tableaux.

Such a program will not be accomplished if the director imagines he is teaching robots. He must not finger every note and rehearse every change in dynamics and tempo. He must try to demonstrate musical principles, so that the students gradually learn to read and interpret with freedom and taste. He thus stimulates student initiative and guides its expression.

There is nothing revolutionary in the analysis we have made in this chapter nor in the outline of the role and process of instrumental instruction. Most teachers will agree in principle, but may contend that, for various reasons, it cannot be done in their schools. We believe, however, that when examination is made of the specific phases of instruction, the means will not seem insurmountable.

SUMMARY

The instrumental teacher is hampered by the old belief that instrumental music is a specialized trade concerned primarily with performing skill. This belief is rooted in European tradition and transferred to American popular education. However, successful music teaching and new educational forces led to the introduction of instrumental music in the Twentieth century schools. The basic patterns were firmly established in the period between the two world wars when the process was assisted by the method of class instruction, contests and festivals, and music educators' organizations. There was progress in teacher preparation, enrollments, technology, music literature, and facilities, although no universal, stable program has been achieved because of differences in school size and the free hand accorded directors. The public respects the place of school music but demands concrete results in the face of new curriculum pressures. Educators, also, grant the value of music in the curriculum but question its objectives and methodology.

The basic function of the public schools is to provide the appropriate tools for life in our time. Musicianship is an integral part of that scheme because, first, it is a universal and persistent phenomenon in daily activity and, second, it supplies a unique means of access to our inner feelings. Although instrumental music is an indispensable factor in achieving these values, it should be functionally and purposefully used in every level and phase of the music program. Problems inherent to this task include the securing of students and finding the right instruments for them; establishing practical teaching loads and schedules; and finding the proper approach to instruction and public performance.

The primary objectives of instrumental instruction are in keeping with the intrinsic values of music, including knowledge and understanding of musical literature and its uses, and skills useful to the average citizen. They should be approached through strong instrumental activity in the elementary music program and enlightened methods of beginning instruction. Many forms of musical experience should be sought in the final stage of schooling, which will lead to increasing independence and initiative on the part of the student.

QUESTIONS FOR DISCUSSION

1. When did instrumental music become a major force in the American schools? What factors helped in that development?

2. How extensive is instrumental music activity in today's schools? At what levels is it taught and how does it relate to the vocal music program?

3. Why is instrumental music sometimes considered a frill? On what basis must it stand in the curriculum?

4. What are some of the special values and characteristics of instrumental music? What are the problems to be faced?

5. Describe the instructional process. What are some objectives of instruction? What are the steps in individual development?

SELECTED REFERENCES

ANDREWS, FRANCES M., AND CLARA E. COCKERILLE, *Your School Music Program*. Englewood Cliffs, N. J.: Prentice-Hall, Inc., 1958.

Basic Concepts in Music Education, Fifty-Seventh Yearbook, Part I, of the National Society for the Study of Education. Chicago: University of Chicago Press, 1958.

DYKEMA, PETER AND HANNAH CUNDIFF, *School Music Handbook*. Evanston, Illinois: Summy-Birchard Co., 1955.

KUHN, WOLFGANG E., *Instrumental Music: Principles and Methods of Instruction*. Boston: Allyn and Bacon, Inc., 1962.

LEEDER, J. A. AND W. S. HAYNIE, *Music Education in the High School*. Englewood Cliffs, N. J.: Prentice-Hall, Inc., 1958.

LEONHARD, CHARLES AND ROBERT W. HOUSE, *Foundations and Principles of Music Education*. New York: McGraw-Hill Book Company, 1959.

MORGAN, HAZEL N., ED., *Music In American Education*. Washington, D. C.: Music Educators National Conference, 1955.

MURSELL, JAMES L., *Music Education: Principles and Programs*. Morristown, N. J.: Silver-Burdett Company, 1956.

The Music Curriculum in Secondary Schools. Washington, D. C.: Music Educators National Conference, 1959.

NEA RESEARCH DIVISION, *Music and Art in the Public Schools*, Research Monograph 1963-M3. Washington, D. C.: National Education Association, 1963.

NORMANN, THEODORE F., *Instrumental Music in the Public Schools*. Philadephia: Oliver Ditson Company, 1941.

SUR, WILLIAM R. AND C. F. SCHULLER, *Music Education for Teen Agers*. New York: Harper & Row, Publishers, 1958.

CHAPTER 2

Instrumental Music in the Classroom

The foundation of the school music program is the regular elementary classroom music period, supplemented and extended by the general music program of the junior high school. It is here that the minimum musicianship needed by all students is supposed to be acquired. By definition, such a program should be as balanced and *unspecialized* as possible. One of the basic weaknesses of school music is that this program often suffers from imbalance and lack of understanding, competence, and sincere intention.

This problem is partly a consequence of the organizational patterns of the American school. The idea has been to present the rudiments of all knowledge in a generalized and flexible fashion, followed by gradual separation and subdivision of the disciplines as the content becomes more technical and as the individual matures. In other words, we begin with the self-contained classroom and progress toward more departmentalization. Such versatility is required of classroom teachers that their preparation is necessarily spread very thinly and many of them receive only a superficial background to teach music.

It is easy to say that the job should therefore be turned over to music specialists. However, even if enough specialists could be prepared, this solution would only confirm the false idea that music is too technical for general education. After all, *if the simplest forms of musical activity are considered beyond the capacity of the classroom teacher, how can they be required of her pupils?*

Since there is no easy solution to this dilemma, schools have done their best with the available teachers. They have attempted to secure specialists and trade assignments in order to maintain at least a minimum course of study. In many instances, this has reduced classroom music to the bare essentials, which means that the chief emphasis is placed on singing and sight reading. Far from helping to improve this situation—having little understanding of it due to their specialized training—instrumental teachers who have tried to concern themselves actively with music in the classrooms have generally been considered meddlers. They find it more expedient to step in at the fourth- or fifth-grade level to take volunteers for instruction *outside* the classroom. Unfortunately, this sets up a two-track system that is quite injurious to the interests of students. Depending on local circumstances, the children learn to think of music in the classroom as either a sort of relaxation from intellectual strain, or dull drill with syllables and key signatures. The pupils find instrumental training a competition to meet proficiency requirements for the school band or orchestra. In such a climate it is very easy to form a distorted view of music.

In order to build musicianship, instrumental music should be a vital and integral part of the general program on its own merits, which is entirely possible within the framework of the American school system. This chapter will be devoted to showing how children in the classroom may be taught to play, understand, and appreciate instrumental forms, and how they may develop finer musicianship, even if they never elect the serious study of an orchestral instrument. Sustained instruction, leading to band and orchestra membership, is another topic, which will be treated in Chapter 3.

CLASSROOM ORGANIZATION AND OPERATION

The differing objectives of classroom teachers and their freedom to adjust the daily schedule of activity causes great variation in the time allotted to music. This ranges "from less than 20 minutes per week in some grades in some schools to more than 210 in others . . . the median number being 75 minutes in grades 1, 2, 3, and 4, and 80 minutes in grades 5 and 6."[1] Thus, in actual practice the time allotted to music compares unfavorably with the minimum of one hundred minutes per week usually prescribed, although the majority of students devote approximately three hundred hours to the various forms of musical activity during their elementary schooling. In addition to this phase, general music is sometimes offered, or required, in the junior high school (especially for those who have not become members of a performing group).

Whether this is enough time to accomplish a realistic set of goals depends upon the actual quality of instruction. Since these few hours constitute the complete musical schooling of the majority of our adult citizens, and because much of this instruction is handled by persons who

[1] NEA Research Division, *Music and Art in the Public Schools*, p. 12.

had a similarly meager background, it is understandable why the national level of musicianship is not exceptional. Fortunately, much can be done by re-examining the purpose and content of elementary school music, by more effective partnership of classroom teacher and music specialist, and by stronger teacher preparation.

Students

The usual elementary classroom (kindergarten through grade six) generally contains twenty to forty students, each of whom is a unique combination of physical, mental, and emotional characteristics. There is remarkable diversity of interests and motives. Each child can be understood only in terms of his particular background and environment and each has acquired individual perceptions and responses to the evolving classroom situation. For instance, the teacher's changed tone of voice may stimulate one pupil to greater efforts, evoke apprehension in another, and produce laughter or scorn in yet others.

Great variation in rate and direction of development is another marked characteristic of youngsters in the classroom. This is caused by pre-determined growth patterns (maturation) and changes in behavior resulting from cumulative experiences (learning). Thus readiness to master a particular idea or technique is not likely to be achieved simultaneously by all members of a class, although norms have been established for the skills and aptitudes of various age groups. The ability to achieve rudimentary keyboard facility, for example, ranges from pre-school to early 'teen years.

Music in the Elementary School Classroom

Wide variations in child development have led to a rather permissive handling of educative content in the elementary schools. The theory is that if an idea is presented several times and in different ways, each pupil will eventually be able to grasp it and incorporate it into his repertoire of knowledge or behavior. Thus, the child sings hundreds of songs and listens to compositions of gradually increasing complexity.

The general content of elementary school music, i.e., the skills and facts associated with a body of standard musical literature, is usually approached from these basic angles: singing, playing, listening, rhythm, and creativity. This procedure is supposed to produce a balanced understanding of music for the essential needs of future citizens.

Within each of the above categories, the school arranges a sequence based on the developmental levels of the students with a content which will create adequate concepts of rhythmic, melodic, harmonic, formal, and stylistic usage.

A typical course of study is outlined below:

Grade		Goals	Procedure
K	a)	Ability to sing many songs	Short length and range; geared to interest and ability
	b)	Sense of pitch	Matching; use of piano, bells
	c)	Improvement of non-singers	Individual work, for ear improvement
	d)	Sense of rhythm	Instrument and rhythm work, with and without music to establish pulse
	e)	Good tone	Demonstrate and strive for good tone
1	a)	More singing strength	Songs of greater length and scope
	b)	Better rhythm	Listening program and more use of rhythm emphasis
	c)	Good tone	Demonstrate; use outside help
	d)	Better pitch sense	Individual work; use of piano, bells, etc.
2	a)	Reading readiness	Introduce syllables; use syllable ladder
	b)	Read basic tonal patterns	Use of motives and simple tonal patterns in song book
	c)	Rhythmic sense	Continue instruments to stress pulse; use walking and running notes
	d)	Staff, signatures, and note recognition	Use board and cut-outs
3	a)	Development of reading ability	Locating *do;* triad sense; easy skips by syllables, rhythm reading; chanting words; rote-note; signatures
4	a)	Reading growth	Principle of dotted notes, accidentals
	b)	Keyboard knowledge	Learn rote melodies; use correct finger patterns
	c)	Feeling for major and minor modes	Recordings, scales, song materials
	d)	Two part singing	Rounds, descants; piano for harmonic feeling; all students try both parts
5	a)	Syllable ability	Introduce chromatic syllables
	b)	Keyboard experience	Stress scale patterns, use note names
	c)	Knowledge of orchestral instruments	Symphony concerts, pamphlets, drawings, etc.
	d)	More part singing ability	Numerous materials; reading parts at sight; hearing much harmony
	e)	Knowledge of pitch names	Use keyboards
6	a)	Knowledge of some opera, oratorio, artists, voices, and instruments	Recordings and unit work
	b)	Keyboard experience	Triads and simple accompaniment patterns
	c)	Three-part songs	Use rounds; improvise descants

The foregoing description of a standard elementary music program is not intended in either the spirit of criticism or approbation. It merely provides a background for our discussion of the instrumental phase of music in the classroom.

The Junior High School Program

General Music is a course commonly offered in grades seven and/or eight and/or nine. Theoretically, it should be an extension of the elementary school program, although taught on a departmentalized basis by a music specialist. Under normal circumstances, however, members of the performing groups are allowed to waive the class and the teachers' interest usually follows them. The class often becomes a second chorus or is devoted to review of music rudiments and listening to recordings.

This should not be the case for it is here that broad general musicianship can be solidified through comprehensive treatment of music literature. Practical experience with instrumental literature and technique is a basic feature of the general music course.

The content may be organized directly around functional categories, e.g., dance music, theatrical music, folk music, sacred music, chamber music, and symphonic music. The stiff chronological approach is thus nicely modified, and yet all styles, forms and appropriate subject matter may be introduced naturally, while singing and playing experience is readily managed. Similar results can be obtained by correlation with a concurrent sequence in geography or history. To secure the advantages of such a course, some junior high schools have developed it into a two year sequence synchronized with the performing groups. All students in grades seven and eight enroll in Music for five periods a week, but instead of choosing only one activity, each student is scheduled for two hours of general music and elects band, orchestra, chorus, or beginning instrumental classes during the remaining periods. This is an excellent transitional device to promote integration of the practical and theoretical phases of music while establishing the performing groups on a firm basis and encouraging the other students to try an instrument. General adoption of this plan would revolutionize the results of the school music program. A sample schedule for this pattern is illustrated in Chapter 8.

As a supplement to the nonspecialized general music sequence, some schools offer additional courses in theory and history of music. Instrumental music is an obvious ingredient of these courses but, strictly speaking, they are neither part of the instrumental music program nor part of the general music program, and are regarded chiefly as useful academic preparation for those intending to follow a musical career.

The Instrumental Phase

The inherent value of instrumental music in the classroom is recognized, but is usually neglected in actual practice. Because time is at a premium, singing, listening, and sight reading are given priority, without realizing that the periods devoted to playing can often reduce the time and effort needed for those activities. Without an effective approach to instrumental music the child grows in the state of musical malnutrition, for he lacks the necessary ingredients to stimulate and challenge him.

Basically, the classroom program is one of exploration, and its goal is not to develop triangle or wood block players, accordionists, or pianists. Its purpose is to promote some understanding of all kinds of instruments, to awaken interests, and especially to supply the means by which certain essential facets of musicianship may be acquired. For example, it is very difficult to establish any basis for sharps and flats without the use of instruments.

Of specific concern is the use of the simple rhythm instruments, melodic instruments such as bells and plastic flutes, harmonic instruments such as the Autoharp and ukulele, and the keyboard instruments. Of first importance is the development of an understanding of basic playing techniques and how to introduce them effectively and meaningfully.

Every pupil will not learn to play all of these instruments, and few will acquire any great playing facility through this level of instruction. The goal is not only the addition of instruments to the vocal ensemble (to help stress the principal beats and to signal the changes of harmony), but the more significant presentation of music in its natural setting, by employing instruments associated with the songs of a particular nation. It is also important to supply a challenge to those who are beyond the general music level of the class, as well as fresh stimulation for those who have fallen behind, and to seize the opportunities for introducing and clarifying general musical concepts. The playing of instruments is a primary means of introducing problems in notation, chordal function, rhythmic patterns, and the art of improvisation, and, in addition, these aspects should be supplemented by carefully chosen recordings involving instruments and instrumental forms.

The final result of this kind of activity should include the anticipation of serious study of an orchestral instrument.

THE INSTRUMENTS AND THEIR USES

The musical instruments ordinarily involved in classroom instruction are variously called pre-orchestral, rhythm and melody instruments, informal instruments, social instruments, and "easy-to-play instruments." Actually, the best description is probably *non-orchestral instruments*, for while, they are of varying use and difficulty, none is studied for the purpose of membership in the school performing groups.

The non-orchestral instruments may be classified as rhythmic, melodic, or harmonic, although all instruments have a rhythmic function and several can be employed to play melodies or to produce harmonic support. There is an infinite variety of instruments, and some confusion in nomenclature, but the following list includes those most commonly employed:

Rhythm Instruments	Homemade Substitutes
rhythm sticks	18 inch lengths of doweling, serrated
tone blocks	resonant blocks of wood or metal
wood blocks	
coconut shells	halved coconut shells
temple blocks	
clavés	short, thick, hardwood sticks
castanets	
snare drum	washboard
tomtom, tub drum	large can with stretched rubber cover
conga drums, bongos	oatmeal boxes
jingle sticks (clogs)	bottle caps loosely nailed to a stick
tambourines	pie tins with bottle caps attached
maracas	small cans filled with gravel or shot
sand blocks	sandpaper on blocks of wood
triangle	large nail suspended on string
cymbals, finger cymbals	pie tins, lids, etc.
chimes	pair of horseshoes
gong	
whistles	
warblers	

Melody Instruments	
song bells, marimba bells	tuned water glasses or bottles
resonator bells	tuned glasses or bottles
xylophone, marimba	redwood bars
Meloharp, etc.	
plastic flute (Tonette, Flutephone, etc.)	
ocarina	
recorder	

Harmony and Keyboard
    Instruments

Autoharp
Harmolin
piano
portable electric organ
harmonium (reed organ)
ukulele
guitar
harmonica
accordion
Melodica [2]

[2] Hohner Company has developed an instrument, the Melodica, combining features of the accordion and harmonica. It is fairly inexpensive and is finding use in some schools.

In view of the overlapping function of many of these instruments, it is apparent that a full instrumentation is not necessary. Of prime importance is an adequate supply of the basic types suited to each grade level. The underlying factor about instruments is the mechanical nature which each type possesses, relating it to a particular aspect and problem in music. That is, the playing of each type of instrument enables the performer to approach the music from a different angle, making possible new music insights and skills. Broadly speaking, the percussive instruments tend to promote a sense of timing and precision, the wind instruments an understanding of phrasing and tone control, and the keyboard instruments a feeling for structural and harmonic values.

Rhythm Instruments

Several basic instruments are included among the clickers—rhythm sticks, castanets, wood blocks, clavés, coconut shells, tone blocks, and temple blocks. All these are characterized by a hard, brittle tone of short duration, although they differ considerably in pitch and timbre.

Homemade instruments of the same type and function may be improvised from nearly any kind of hard wood.[3]

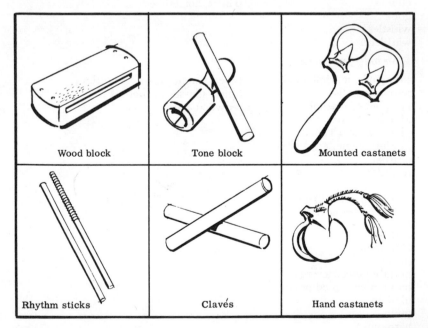

Wood block   Tone block   Mounted castanets

Rhythm sticks   Clavés   Hand castanets

Fig. 2-1.

[3] See Alfred Ellison, *Music with Children* (New York: McGraw-Hill Book Co., Inc., 1959), pp. 169-189.

Since the tone of the clickers is so clean and sharp, they are of great value in producing a sense of pulse and precision and are easily introduced at a very early stage, even during the first weeks of kindergarten. Primary classrooms should have access to several pairs of rhythm sticks. Wood blocks, tone blocks, and coconut shells are especially good for horses' hooves in western songs, while claves and castanets give an authentic touch to Latin songs.

One or two pairs of maracas, two or more tambourines, and several jingle sticks should be available to each class. These rattle type instruments produce sounds of longer duration than the clickers and are thus useful in achieving a cluster or drum roll effect, while the maracas and tambourines also have exotic connotations.

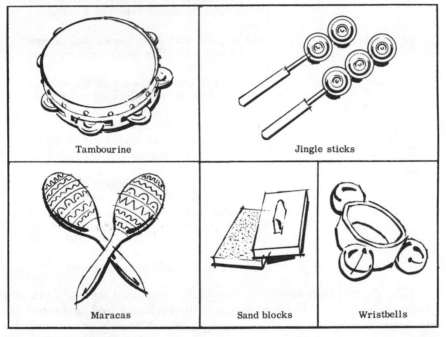

Tambourine   Jingle sticks

Maracas   Sand blocks   Wristbells

Fig. 2-2.

Sand blocks are similar to the rattles in having a long duration of tone. However, the effect is more precise and resembles the sound of walking or shuffling.

Two or three drums of different sizes are very useful for emphasizing the strong pulses and in giving sonority to the ensemble. At this stage they are more successfully played with hands and fingers than with sticks, although wire brushes can also be employed with good effect.

Triangles have great penetrating and sustaining powers and are consequently useful in helping to emphasize the melodic figures. Cymbals and gongs, on the other hand, are properly tied to the principal rhythmic stresses.

Some of these rhythm instruments are not to be played in the obvious fashion, but require a special technique which the teacher should know and demonstrate, as follows:

rhythm sticks	struck together, or scraped across ridges
wood blocks	struck with stick at different points for change in tone; sticks of various materials also produce different sounds
coconut shells	held in palms and clapped together or on table
clavés	one laid loosely on clenched knuckles and struck with the other held like a director's baton
castanets, hand	held in palm with cord looped over thumb and tapped with other fingers; roll by rapid shaking of wrist
castanets, mounted	held by stick and snapped with the wrist or struck against the palm; roll by rapid shaking of wrist
jingle sticks	played as mounted castanets
tambourine	struck sharply against other hand or lightly with thumb and fingers; rolled by shaking or rotating wrist
maracas, gourds	the wrists are snapped sharply downward, causing the shot to descend cleanly
triangle	suspended from a string and struck with a small metal beater; rolled by swinging the beater rapidly from side to side within one corner
cymbals, sand blocks	clashed together with glancing blow

The rhythm instruments are especially associated with the primary grades, since more mature endeavor with keyboard and orchestral instruments develops in the intermediate grades. Formerly, it was popular to create mass ensembles, even in kindergarten, which often produced little but a sort of generalized clicking and rattling.

The instruments are introduced one at a time, added to the vocal ensemble, and traded about so that every child acquires an understanding of the basic characteristics and techniques of each instrument. The instrumentation thus evolves in approximately the following sequence during two or three years and is used thereafter in any appropriate combination: 1) rhythm sticks, 2) tomtom, 3) jingle sticks, 4) sand blocks, 5) triangle, 6) tone block, 7) tambourine, 8) wood block, 9) cymbals, gong, 10) clavés, 11) maracas, 12) castanets.

As the more demanding and legitimate instruments are introduced, there is a natural lessening of interest in the simpler ones. This should not be resisted, for it is a sign that a readiness is developing for the more complex problems of keyboard, fretted, and orchestral instruments.

However, the children will establish certain specialties and techniques. One will have a knack with the maracas, while another will be particularly adept with the castanets, and so on. Printed orchestrations are, therefore, seldom useful except to suggest new patterns, since each class tends to create its own patterns for the songs being used. This is done first by rote and later by one-line metric notation on the blackboard, following directions by the teacher and experimentation by the children. For example:

Fig. 2-3.

The heavy, low pitched instruments usually play on the stressed beats, while those of lighter quality play the afterbeats or the melodic rhythmic patterns. However, this rule need not be taken too seriously if the children develop certain other patterns which happen to produce a good effect.

Nye and Nye list ten concepts to be achieved with percussion instruments:

Keeping time with the music (basic rhythmic response)

Differences in dynamics (degrees of loud and soft; strong beats and weak beats)

Musical form (the phrase; contrasting sections)

Mood in music expressed in terms of percussion instruments

Awareness of notation and its use

Tempi (slow and fast)

Pitch (high and low)

Relation of rhythmic patterns to appropriate instrumentation

The relatedness of tempo, dynamics, mood, melody, pitch, and instrumentation

Creative power on the child's level to invent and refine the percussion instrument score and to invent "sound effects" to accompany songs.[4]

[4] Robert Evans Nye and Vernice Trousdale Nye, *Music in the Elementary School* (2nd ed.) (Englewood Cliffs, N. J.: Prentice-Hall, Inc., 1964), p. 92.

Song Bells

At least one instrument with the keyboard layout, such as xylophone or marimba bells, is invaluable in the classroom as a transitional device to the study of keyboard and harmonic relationships. If possible, the chromatic type (of one and a half or two octaves) should be procured so that any melody sung by the children may be played.

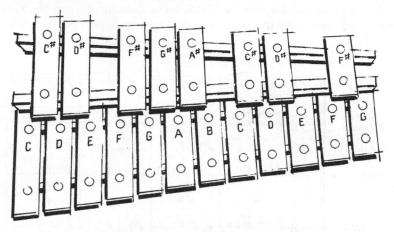

Fig. 2-4a. Chromatic Bells. Facsimile made by permission of Lyons Instrument Company, Chicago.

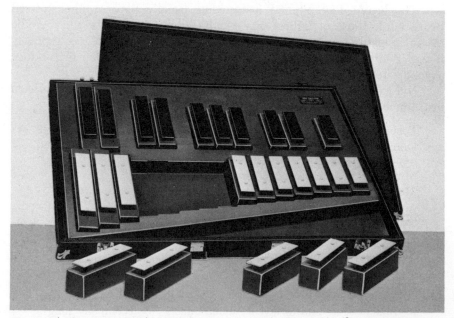

Fig. 2-4b. Resonator bells. Used by permission of David Wexler and Company, Chicago.

The individual resonator bells have a beautiful, sustaining tone which is very effective for chordal patterns. However, before the bells are introduced, it is well to experiment with tuned water glasses or bottles. As the children adjust pitches by varying the amount of liquid, as they label the containers, arrange them on racks, and test different sorts of mallets, they are learning how pitch, timbre, and amplitude are established and intervals are arranged. They discover that music is a more orderly art then they imagined.

Autoharp

The Autoharp is a zither type instrument which is played by depressing a button for the desired chord and strumming the strings with a pick. It is increasingly popular in the grades and the various song series have many songs with accompanying chord patterns indicated for the instrument. It is fairly inexpensive (about 28 dollars for the 12 bar model) and is of value in teaching the first principles of chord progression.

In playing the Autoharp, it is easy to press the levers and strum with the pick, but there is a certain abstractness in reading or choosing the right levers at the right times. Its use, therefore, is often postponed until late third grade. It is widely used as a simple substitute for the piano. Difficulty arises when it is not tuned carefully and frequently, in which case only an approximation of the proper effect is achieved. A good method of tuning the Autoharp is to tune each chord separately, adjusting to the common tones from chords tuned earlier and regulating the tension equally on both sides.

The Piano

Music teaching without a piano is unnatural. When a piano is not available in each classroom, a music room should be provided where the children can spend their music periods. If this is impossible due to lack of space or inconvenient scheduling, then an inexpensive portable electric organ or harmonium should be available for several classrooms, or a small piano can be fitted with a dolly allowing it to be rolled from room to room.

Teachers use the piano according to their capacity. Those who cannot play can learn to chord. The newer song series include simple accompaniments for many of the songs and indicate basic chord progression for the remainder by means of letter names or Roman numerals. See Fig. 2-6.

However, the piano must not be used incessantly, since too much piano is worse than none at all. The proper role of the piano is that of example and support. Thus, the teacher may introduce songs by playing through the melody or the parts, alone or with accompaniment, and then a short phrase or arpeggio may be used to establish the tonality for the group to begin singing. Later, certain difficult passages may need to

Fig. 2-5a. Portable electric organ. Used by permission of the Fred-Gretsch Mfg. Co., Brooklyn, N.Y.

Fig. 2-5b. Autoharp. Used by permission of Oscar-Schmidt International, Inc.

be rehearsed with the aid of the piano and, when the song is well learned, an accompaniment may be added to enhance the effect. However, constant reliance on the piano diverts the teacher's attention, inhibits natural phrasing and tone quality, and hampers the development of independent reading skill.

The piano is also useful as a means of illustration in listening sessions,

Fig. 2-6.

during which one may preview or review the principal themes and musical devices in the recording. It is even more indispensable as a medium for the various forms of rhythmic activity. Descriptive themes are played for marching, skipping, trotting, waltzing, swinging, swaying, bending, and other physical activities. These themes should all be directed at familiarity with the basic meters and rhythmic patterns. Some teachers use the piano as a signaling device, having music "for standing," "for resting," and "for getting wraps." Such music may also be furnished by phonograph or unaccompanied singing, but then it is not spontaneous, since the teacher cannot adjust the tempos and stresses with the required finesse. This use of the piano to accompany singing, for illustration, and as background for rhythmic activity, properly occurs at every grade level in the elementary school. When the teacher cannot play the piano, some students may be found in the intermediate grades who have developed sufficient piano skill to assist in this capacity.

Piano keyboard experience, which is needed by every child, is generally concentrated in the third or fourth grade and is primarily aimed at first, functional concepts of notation and intervallic relationships, and second, ability to execute simple melodic and chordal patterns. In other words, the children should be discovering about music staves, clefs, note values, and accidentals, and translating these into tones produced on the keyboard. They should also be learning about steps, half steps, and scale patterns and how these are built into melodies and chords to match them. Experience of this type is not "class piano" (which is discussed in Chapter 3) but is of critical importance in building a useful, general musicianship.

The teacher needs chalkboard, staff liner and chalk, a piano, and sufficient dummy keyboards for the entire class. Such keyboards may be purchased of flat cardboard or of formed plastic.[5] Two octave, life-size keyboards may also be constructed by students or teacher, using ink on cardboard. The silent keyboard work is directed by verbal and graphic

[5] More expensive models can be had with movable keys, and there is also an electronic piano with headphones as mentioned in Chapter 3.

illustration from the chalkboard and synchronized with live sounds produced at the piano. Each individual should have several opportunities for trial and testing at the piano.

Before introducing the keyboard it is wise to identify and explain the rudiments of notation by preliminary work with songbooks and at the chalkboard. The keyboards are then distributed, note names and fingering patterns are explained, and individual notes, tetrachords, and melodies are tentatively attempted en masse at keyboards and piano. The next step is to connect the notes on the staff with keys on the keyboard.

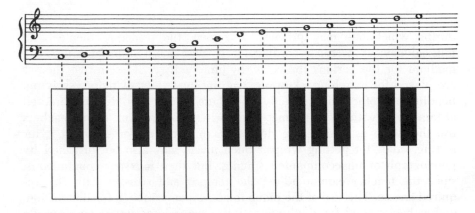

Fig. 2-7.

The teacher works with pointer and voice, while the students take their turns at the piano. Intensive drill is needed to establish prompt, accurate correlation of the keys on the keyboard to the written notes. The student is gradually presented with a variety of time values, accidentals, broken triads, solid chords, hands separately and together, and finally differing figures in either hand. Everything is introduced by rote and practiced by note. If aural imagery is cultivated, along with music reading, students will gradually learn to anticipate chord changes and thus develop rudimentary ability to improvise.

Neither theoretical principles nor their application should be stressed exclusively. The bases for clefs, scales and accidentals, chords and harmonic progression, and nomenclature should be explained naturally and simply, *as each concept is introduced.*

Such a process is obviously going to require considerable time, thus, the most efficient pattern could be to take two or three consecutive music periods for keyboard work and then allow three or four weeks before the next series. Ten or fifteen hours can well be given to this work in grades three and four.

Recorders and Plastic Flutes

The recorder is not really a pre-band instrument, but a solo and ensemble instrument of some complexity and cost. An ancient instrument which was largely superseded by the more powerful transverse flute, it has an extensive literature and is quite popular in Europe. There are four models—soprano, alto, tenor, and bass, and it is in this ensemble capacity that it can be most educationally valuable. A quartet of these instruments in the junior high school general music class will provide some practical performing experience and a natural avenue to direct acquaintance with Renaissance and Baroque forms.

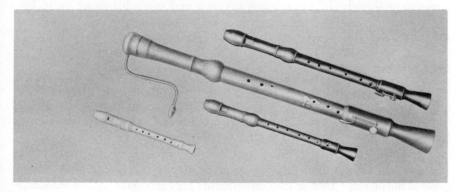

Fig. 2-8. A quartet of recorders. Used by permission of M. Hohner, Inc., Hicksville, N.Y.

Plastic adaptations of the recorder are now designed for mass use. The most common types are the song flute, tonette, flutophone, ocarina, symphonette, and melody flute. The compass of the first four is a ninth (above middle C), while the symphonette and melody flute extend two octaves. All fingering patterns, however, are similar to the flute, clarinet, and saxophone. The tonette is the most popular for use in third or fourth grades because of its practical range and adjustable tuning.

Plastic flute instruction is often regarded simply as a means of discovering and recruiting prospective band members, but such an outcome is really incidental. The chief value of the instruction is to provide generalized experience with the problems of wind instruments, regardless of whether a standard instrument is later studied. Furthermore, the process inherently lends itself to rapid mastery of the technique of music reading. Instruction should be carefully timed, therefore, to occur at the point where the children have grasped the idea of notation but are unsure of the application.

Because of its mechanical simplicity and soft tone, the plastic flute can be efficiently taught to groups of twenty or thirty. The practical plan is to devote four or five hours—i.e., the music period for two or three weeks, or once a week for a semester, to the mastery of a series of one, two, and three parts songs specifically adapted to the instrument. The standard instruction books have been found to be well designed for this approach. The teacher demonstrates how to produce the first few tones, directs and checks the children's execution, and identifies the written notes. Very quickly the students are doing simple exercises and tunes which can be alternately played and sung to help extend sight reading skill.

Since the cost of the instrument and instruction book is small, it is convenient if each child purchases his own and tapes his name on it, because when the school purchases a set for common use, a disinfectant solution must also be provided.

Folk Instruments

The fretted instruments—ukulele, guitar, banjo, mandolin, are seldom used in the elementary grades, because of their complexity and the fact that they are not related to the standard band and orchestra instruments. Nevertheless, they are useful and have good literature and a large following. The ukulele is the simplest and can be introduced into grades five and six, while the guitar is more appropriate to the junior high school general music class. One or two instruments for each class will be sufficient to give each student an opportunity to acquire basic techniques.

The ukulele strings may be tuned either to a, d', f' sharp, and b' (as illustrated in Fig. 2-9), or a step lower (g, c', e', a'). Small metal ridges (frets), fastened across the fingerboard and under the strings, serve to shorten the length of the string when the fingers are pressed firmly behind them. The frets are arranged to produce successive half steps. Notation for the ukulele is in *tablature* form, with the vertical lines representing the strings and the horizontal lines representing the frets; the black dots indicate the places to press the fingers to produce the desired chords.

Fig. 2-9.

The guitar is constructed and played similarly to the ukulele, but it has six strings. (See Fig. 2-10.)

Harmonica and accordion instruction has proved practicable on a commercial basis but generally it has been considered unsuited to school use because of the cost, technical difficulty, lack of usefulness in band or orchestra and until recently, inferior literature. However, any skills

Fig. 2-10.

which the pupils or teachers may have acquired can be employed by the use of judiciously arranged accompaniments and demonstrations.

INSTRUMENTAL FORMS IN THE LISTENING PROGRAM

Since instrumental music is commonly associated with active performance, the possible impact of the music listening program is often overlooked. Actually, a major portion of the recorded examples used in the classroom consists of instrumental forms, but are seldom clearly related to the unique functions of the instruments. Attention is usually directed toward formal structure, composers' lives, related historical events, national characteristics, the seasons, and stories associated with the compositions. However, some study must also be given to the characteristics of the instruments and their resultant influence upon the art of music so that the student, whether he plays or not, will have an insight into instrumental music which will last his lifetime. Knowledge of the following technical factors is needed to accomplish this task:

(1) Recognition of instruments by sight and sound

(2) Principles of construction and tone production—organ pipes and manuals, strings, sound posts and bow hair, air columns and reeds, and valve key mechanisms

(3) Special effects—vibrato, glissando, harmonics, bowings, triple tonguing, mutes, etc.

(4) Evolution of the modern instruments and their roles—from pipes, lyres, lutes, harpsichords, viols, and serpents, to pianos, violins, tubas, and electronic organs; and the gradual development of orchestras and bands

(5) Expanding musical resources—fugues, toccatas, dance suites, sonatas, and symphonic forms; and how increasing instrumental color, agility, and power allowed composers greater freedom and led to complexity of forms and more advanced idioms

(6) Composer, conductor, performer and score—score format and special markings; how the conductor reads and interprets scores; and players' responses

These factors are too complex for first graders, but can be introduced gradually over the years, by presenting the fundamental ideas first and the finer points later. However, the usual classroom teacher is not qualified to approach these matters unaided, and needs careful assistance from the music supervisor and the instrumental specialist. Wall charts, recorded solo passages, personal demonstrations, films, and dissemination of special materials and references are also helpful as well as coordination with local youth concerts, special TV broadcasts, and other sources. Broad comprehension is more valuable than specific details in educating students to be discriminating in their choice of concerts and records.

The amount of music a child hears on radio and TV and at church, and that which he plays or sings himself, is certain to outweigh that which is presented to him on records in the classroom. However, recordings of works heard elsewhere—such as *Peter and the Wolf,* the *Nutcracker Suite, Amahl and the Night Visitors,* and recent show tunes—will bring the student new insights when skillfully surrounded with appropriate information. Rare and esoteric items—from Bartok and Boccherini to Kenton and Clementi—must also be included if the student's acquaintance and tastes are to become sufficiently broad.

A suitable listening program for any specific age level depends upon the musical background of the listeners. It is not necessary to recapitulate the development of music, since it has been found that interest, understanding, and eventual appreciation depend upon the element of familiarity coupled with a trace of novelty. Thus, if a listener feels at ease with the regularity of Mozart, he is easily led to accept the occasional surprises of Prokofieff.

Usually, the young child is pre-conditioned to music through the qualities of folk songs or hymns, which have steady rhythm, regular phrases, and clear melodic line. However, he will accept complexity in contrapuntal and harmonic treatment and instrumentation so that the music most suited to the earliest grades is what musical adults would call obvious but not necessarily simple. This literature should be steadily expanded to include more subtle examples. The difficulty lies, of course, in determining just how obvious or subtle a given piece may be. The teacher's best guide is experience based on observation of students' reactions. The graded lists recommended by record companies and elementary music texts should be consulted.[6] However, these lists are likely to need further experimental supplementation.

Overcontrol of the children's listening materials is a danger to be avoided since this is an area of vast divergence in taste and capacity, and individual reactions are quite difficult to predict. It is better if record

---

[6] Some excellent suggestions are found in Raymond Elliott, *Teaching Music: Methods and Materials for the Elementary Schools* (Columbus, Ohio: Charles E. Merrill Books, Inc., 1960) pp. 95-99.

listening can be handled like English literature—i.e., by class study of a few leading examples accompanied by free choice of reading among selected works. To accomplish this purpose, many schools are finding success with a "listening corner." This consists of a record player and earphones, and should have an appropriate selection of recordings and a display of related factual material, both of which are changed at frequent intervals. Students listen on an assigned schedule during study periods. Results in terms of increased student knowledge seem to be equivalent to the traditional method, while attitude development seems to be more positive.[7]

BUILDING MUSICIANSHIP THROUGH INSTRUMENTS

Varied experience with instruments is indispensable to balanced musical growth, although mere exposure does not guarantee growth. It is necessary to seek the kinds of experiences in all instrumental activities that will actually produce stronger musicianship. Such results, in turn, largely depend upon the way in which the students' current needs and capacities are defined, the kinds of music they are given to study and perform, the facts and ideas that are presented to them, and the way in which the teacher proceeds to accomplish the task.

Musical Knowledge and Understanding

"Successful teaching of musical knowledge and understanding begins by providing affective experience with music".[8] The teacher centers attention upon melodic, harmonic, and rhythmic factors in the music being heard or performed which will clarify and enlarge the students' concepts, but to be most effective, any explanations should be made informally and in response to the students' own questions. For example, a tonette class may be encouraged to discover that uncovering each tone hole shortens the vibrating air column, producing a higher pitch, and that this same principle applies to the other woodwind instruments and also, by close analogy, to the brasses, strings, and percussion. Likewise, keyboard instruction naturally provides the occasion for considerable development of structural principles, including intervallic relationships and cadential formations and their evolution. It is preferable for the students to develop knowledge of accidentals and key signatures from the need to transpose scale patterns, than as an isolated convention to be memorized.

Preoccupation with factual matters, however, sometimes surrounds the music class with a facade of extrinsic detail:

[7] See Dorothy L. Andrews, "Comparative Study of Two Methods of Developing Music Listening Ability in Elementary School Children," *Journal of Research in Music Education,* Spring, 1962, pp. 59-64.

[8] Charles Leonhard and Robert W. House, *Foundations and Principles of Music Education* (New York: McGraw-Hill Book Co., 1959), p. 245.

> . . . information about the composer's life, the circumstances and
> reception of the first performance of the work and so on, although
> not essential, does have a place in musical learning. It must be em-
> phasized, however, that such knowledge is a means to the learner's
> heightened receptivity and not an end in itself. The utility of testing
> such knowledge is thus open to serious question.[9]

Thus, emphasis must always be placed upon the nature of the music
itself and the means of its production.

Musical Skills

Aural skill is largely a matter of perception and anticipation of
musical device. That is, the student is led to recognize musical themes
and their repetition and variation, as well as the interweaving of con-
sonance, dissonance, and modulation, and to perceive the general relationship of these factors within the fabric of a composition. He should become
aware of pure intonation, accurate tone placement, and clarity of style
and execution, and of any lapses which may occur. Such skills are not
achieved by contact alone. The students must be motivated to direct
their attention to these matters while playing and listening, and to practice
real discrimination. It is often effective to have the class tap beats, do
conducting patterns, hum chord roots, or invent descants. Another procedure is to stop the group without warning and ask an individual, "What
section is too weak?" "Can you hum *do?*" or "What is wrong with the
rhythm?"

Instrumental study is an obvious vehicle for the development of performance skill, but this skill is often conceived as mere agility to be
acquired through blind drill. To achieve an expressive musical result, the
learner should be led: first, to secure a concept of the way the music
should sound and the technical means to that end; second, to attempt the
execution and discover the points of greatest weakness; and third, to
consciously apply more effective movements and patterns to these passages
through concentrated practice. These factors are essential for learning to
play tunes on the song bells and tonette, to chord with Autoharp, piano,
and ukulele, and to read music.

Music reading is a form of performing skill tied intimately to the
requisite knowledge of fundamentals—tonality, notation, rhythm, and
structural design. The special value of the instruments as natural agents
for making the switch from rote to note has been previously observed.
The process is analyzed by Leonhard and House[10] as well as in various
texts on elementary school music. *The important factor is to make the
dependence on note reading easier and more effective than the imitative*

[9] *Ibid.*, pp. 116-117.
[10] *Ibid.*, pp. 240-243.

response, which is the natural role of instruments and should be fully exploited.

In the course of learning to read music, however, it is essential *not* to stamp out the ability to perform by ear. Improvisation, which is a creative skill, is too often a lost art among highly trained performers. Practice in chording and descanting should therefore be continued alongside music reading activity.

Appreciation, Attitudes, and Habits

Musical knowledge and skill are necessary for the development of appreciation, attitudes, and habits. Reference is made to the listing of objectives near the close of the first chapter. Unless the student develops these qualities of aesthetic enjoyment, positive reactions toward music, and independent pursuit of musical activity, his musicianship will be passive.

All experience in this realm is highly qualitative, i.e., results depend mostly upon the teacher's approach. A student's music appreciation, attitudes, and habits are determined by the *way* in which he acquired his knowledge and skill. It is possible, for example, to learn to play quite well but to acquire at the same time a dislike for playing because the process seemed to be strenuous and tiresome. It is likewise true that many graduates of our schools know much about music but fail to develop any interest in the art itself.

Nevertheless, it is the concrete musical facts and techniques that are the sinews of instruction. Leaving it at that, the "traditionalists" are likely to lose sight of the students' further reactions, while the "progressives" are wont to approach them directly with units on Record Collecting and Careers in Music. But the answer is to teach the facts and skills in a way that pupils will want to buy recordings and will consider the vocation of music.

Everyone knows the correct procedure for promoting desirable attitudes and habits: (1) appealing music rather than manufactured drills, (2) clear explanations instead of foggy generalizations, (3) enthusiastic approach rather than dull pedantry, and (4) bringing tasks to successful conclusion instead of abandoning them in a state of insecurity.

Instrumental study must be handled creatively. The teacher introduces the maracas, or the Autoharp, by demonstration and proceeds to supervised trials keyed to appropriate literature. Tonette and keyboard instruction is geared to produce real music without involving students in theories of embouchure formation and finger position. Information is wielded directly to produce better concepts, reading ability, and playing style.

The usual trouble is that the teacher is comparatively ill-prepared in this field and communicates this insecurity to the students, or else fails to make the effort at all. This problem is faced in the following section.

INSTRUCTIONAL ROLES

Most will agree that the kind of program we have outlined is desirable but not simple to install or sustain. It depends upon qualified teachers—both generalists and specialists working as a team.

The Classroom Teacher

The role of the classroom teacher in music instruction is still not defined. Most will agree that in the self-contained classroom the needs of young children are best met because of the teacher's understanding of the individual and the natural correlation of subject matter. On the other hand, the point is always reached in schooling where the nature of the subject matter demands a specialist. The argument centers around where that point is.

The most prevalent theory is that reasonably prepared classroom teachers (with supervisory assistance) are fitted to teach music in the primary grades and that the intermediate grades should be semi-departmentalized, thus, requiring that one of the intermediate grade teachers be enough of a musician to assume active leadership in developing music instruction among these classes. However, in some schools there are relatively effective music teachers in every room while others have practically none. The NEA Research reports cited in Chapter 1 indicate that about three quarters of the nation's classroom teachers *do* teach all or part of their music. Better instruction will be secured only by measures to prepare more specialists, greater efforts toward in-service education, and upgrading preparation to meet at least these standards. The following outline is recommended:

PREPARING THE CLASSROOM TEACHER TO TEACH MUSIC

It is still a moot point whether music in the elementary classroom is best taught by the classroom teachers or by music specialists. In view of the chronic short supply of the latter, however, it is clear that both groups will need to contribute their best efforts to the task during the foreseeable future. Establishing the musical competence of elementary teachers thus becomes a vital concern of collegiate music departments.

A MINIMAL PROGRAM

No single pattern of courses can possibly serve the needs of all candidates. Wisdom suggests that (1) basic qualifications be defined, (2) candidates be evaluated on those terms, and (3) those who prove sub-minimal be assigned to courses designed to meet their needs.

General Musicianship. The elementary classroom teacher should not possess less than the fundamental musicianship which the schools seek to produce. Briefly, this means:

(1) familiarity with a body of standard musical works
(2) broad but discriminating musical tastes
(3) awareness of basic musical design and the general outline of its evolution
(4) ability to perform by rote and by note
(5) participation in musical activities appropriate to one's interests and talents

Remedial work in these areas is usually provided in two courses:

INTRODUCTION TO MUSIC   2 semester (3 quarter) credits (music literature surveyed historically, structurally, and stylistically)

FUNDAMENTALS OF MUSIC   2 semester (3 quarter) credits (practical study of notation, keyboard, and sight singing)

Whether a candidate may need none, one, or both of these courses should be determined upon entrance into the elementary education program. A placement examination may be devised to ascertain depth and musical training and experience, to probe musical attitudes and tastes, and to sample knowledge of composers, works, and musical vocabulary.

Elementary School Music. Minimally-trained teachers will have, or should have, the aid and support of an experienced music consultant, but they should also possess:

(1) an understanding of music's role in the schools
(2) an acquaintance with essential materials and procedures for teaching music in the elementary classroom
(3) operational ability in musical instruction

To promote these ends, the following courses are considered essential for *all* elementary teaching candidates:

MUSIC IN THE ELEMENTARY SCHOOL   2 semester (3 quarter) credits
OBSERVATION AND PRACTICE TEACH-   5-10% of the total supervised teaching
ING IN MUSIC   experience

A FIELD OF CONCENTRATION IN MUSIC

Many future elementary teachers with relatively sound musicianship will find it advantageous to secure a minor or a field of concentration in music. This degree of specialization enables them to establish a stronger music program in their classrooms and to participate more effectively where team teaching is practiced.

Favorable attitudes and basic musical skills can be assumed on the part of those who elect such a concentration. Accordingly, a pattern of some professional depth is indicated. Such programs should comprise 16-24 semester credits (24-36 quarter credits) distributed among:

harmony and ear training (or music theory)
music history and literature
piano
voice and/or choral groups

music in the elementary school
observation and practice teaching in music (10-20% of the total supervised teaching experience)[11]

Whoever teaches music in the classroom undertakes to create the kind of educative environment which will produce the experiences needed by the children to develop broad musicianship. The teacher plans to do this by wise selection of music, an orderly progression of topics and assignments, and concrete procedures to present this material and evaluate the results. But the instructional process also involves daily and sometimes instant improvisation to meet the observed reactions of the students.

The Music Supervisor

The job of music supervisor or consultant varies greatly from school to school. It may include supervisory, administrative, and instructional functions, but the actual emphasis will depend upon the needs and traditions of the school as well as the supervisor's vision and capacity. In small schools the high school choral director usually supervises the elementary program and also assumes the role of special music teacher where needed. In the large city system, the elementary supervisor is more occupied in an administrative capacity and may have special assistants who maintain the needed contact with instructional activity. Whichever method is employed, the one to whom a classroom teacher looks for aid and assistance with music instruction is his real supervisor. The task is to facilitate and improve instruction by working directly with teachers and students toward well-defined goals, finer literature and equipment, improved teaching performance, and a more coordinated program.[12]

In instrumental music, however, the chief difficulty is that the majority of elementary school music supervisors are identified with the vocal program. These people generally attempt to assure proper emphasis on instrumental music, but are more at ease in their own specialty. This situation in general music indicates the need for more effective participation of the instrumental specialists.

Instrumental Specialists

Usually, band and orchestra directors become directly involved in the music program only at the point of beginning instruction on the orchestral instruments. They are seldom found in the classroom and rarely consulted on the general program in music. In other words, the instrumentalists are only concerned with the specialized forms of musical in-

[11] This outline was drafted in committee by the author for consideration by the National Association of Schools of Music and may or may not be adopted at some future date.

[12] The supervisory and administrative functions are discussed in detail in Leonhard and House, op. cit., pp. 269-331.

struction. This is probably due to the heavy demands of that task as well as habit and tradition, and is accepted as the instrumentalist's role.

However, if instrumental teachers were given more adequate preparation in the problems and techniques of instruction in the classroom, their efforts would have great effect in the general music program. They should participate directly in this instruction at the junior high school level, handling some of the sections, or, they should work on a team basis by rotating their specialties among the general music sections. At the elementary level they may assist in selecting good instruments and instruction books, in providing individual and group demonstrations, and in actual observation of instruction and consultation with the teachers. The stimulation to the instruction program far outweighs the effort.

Such cooperation requires some changes in attitude among instrumentalists, supervisors, and classroom teachers. The first step is to encourage better rapport among these individuals so that practical cooperation is extended until the instrumentalists are recognized as regular partners in developing the general music program.

SUMMARY

Generally, the instrumental music program is conceived as a separate entity concerned only with the school band and orchestra, and the necessary preparation of the playing members. However, the more vital aspects of instrumental music concerns its function in the elementary and junior high school classrooms in helping to secure the general musicianship of all pupils.

Students in the primary grades should be given extensive experience with the various rhythm instruments. A xylophone or set of bells and an Autoharp are vital aids in teaching melodic and harmonic relationships. With the student alternating on the various instruments, these are used in combinations to accompany singing.

The piano is used by the teacher to accompany singing, and also for direct keyboard acquaintance with chords, scales, and various notational functions.

Plastic flutes are quite useful on short term basis in making the transfer from rote to note, and for acquiring ensemble ability. The recorders are especially appropriate at the junior high school level. The use of fretted instruments should not be overlooked.

The listening program is a prerequisite for good results in instrumental music. It is important to present a wide variety of forms and idioms, gradually progressing from the obvious to the more subtle literature.

Aimless activity with instruments should be avoided. True knowledge and understanding comes from attention to and explanation of facts which will gradually clarify the pupils' concepts. Likewise, listening and performing skills depend upon proper example and analysis of the music *before* practice. If the musical understanding and skills are properly acquired, the likelihood of positive appreciation, attitudes, and habits is greatly enhanced.

The key to the entire process is proper preparation of the classroom teacher. Adequate measures need to be taken to ensure that they can read music and play some piano, and have the necessary acquaintance with the instruments and literature appropriate to their task. Additionally, music supervisors and instrumental specialists must involve themselves more actively in the instrumental program in the classroom.

QUESTIONS FOR DISCUSSION

1. What constitutes "the five-fold approach" to music in the elementary classroom? Why is playing activity so often underemphasized?

2. What is the proper role of general music in the junior high school? What part should instrumental music have in this course? How may the course be coordinated with the performing groups?

3. Describe the various rhythm and melody instruments and their uses. How are they introduced?

4. What are the functions of the piano in the elementary classroom? What keyboard skills should the child acquire, and how are these introduced?

5. How useful are the plastic flutes and fretted instruments? What is their purpose in instruction?

6. How should instrumental music be involved in the listening program? What are the objectives to be achieved through listening and playing?

7. What must the classroom teacher know about instrumental music and how may this preparation be accomplished? How may the supervisor and instrumental specialist best assist in the instructional process in the classroom?

SELECTED REFERENCES

ANDREWS, FRANCES M. AND JOSEPH A. LEEDER, *Guiding Junior High School Pupils in Musical Experiences.* Englewood Cliffs, N. J.: Prentice-Hall, Inc., 1953.

BECKLEY, W. OWEN, *Adventures in Instrumental Music.* Indianapolis, Indiana: W. Owen Beckley Publications, 1963.

DILLER, ANGELA AND KATE STEARNS PAGE, *Rote Pieces for Rhythm Bands, Teachers Book.* New York: G. Schirmer.

———, *How to Teach the Rhythm Band.* New York: G. Schirmer.

EGBERT, MARION S., *Keyboard Experiences, A Handbook for Classroom Teachers.* New York: Bourne, Inc.

———, *A Suggested Keyboard Experience Lesson Plan.* Chicago: American Music Conference.

ELLIOTT, RAYMOND, *Teaching Music: Methods and Materials for the Elementary School.* Columbus, Ohio: Charles E. Merrill Books, Inc., 1960.

ELLISON, ALFRED, *Music with Children.* New York: McGraw-Hill Book Company, 1959.

GRANT, PARKS, *Music for Elementary Teachers* (2nd ed.) New York: Appleton-Century-Crofts, 1960.

Keyboard Experience and Class Piano Instruction, William R. Sur, ed. Washington, D. C.: Music Educators National Conference, 1957.

MEYERS, LOUISE KIFER, *Teaching Children Music in the Elementary School* (3rd ed.). Englewood Cliffs, N. J.: Prentice-Hall, Inc., 1961.

MORALES, HUMBERT, *Latin American Rhythm Instruments.* New York: H. Adler Publishers Co., 1954.

NYE, ROBERT EVANS AND VERNICE TROUSDALE NYE, *Music in the Elementary School* (2nd ed.). Englewood Cliffs, N. J.: Prentice-Hall, Inc., 1964.

Pace, Robert, *Piano for Classroom Music*. Englewood Cliffs, N. J.: Prentice-Hall, Inc., 1956.

Winslow, Robert W. and Leon Dallin, *Music Skills for Classroom Teachers*. Dubuque, Iowa: William C. Brown Co., 1958.

Wisler, Gene C., *Music Fundamentals for the Classroom Teacher*. Boston: Allyn and Bacon, Inc., 1961.

CHAPTER 3

Beginning Instruction

In the previous chapter we have attempted to describe instrumental music as it functions within the general music program. Coinciding with this effort is a more specialized and intensive program of instruction on the standard instruments, which ranges from the beginning to the advanced levels and covers all forms of participation from individual work to large concert organizations.

This phase of instrumental instruction is properly elective (not compulsory), since every individual cannot be expected to possess this particular form of musicianship. However, every student should have the *opportunity* to participate, and each must be offered a chance to discover his potential as a player. Such a principle implies a program of great breadth and flexibility, particularly at the beginning level. For instance, we cannot claim universal opportunity, if a school offers no instruction on certain instruments, or if entrance is restricted to a single invitation at a particular grade level. Even greater restriction is caused by the policy of private purchase and permanent assignment of an instrument. The needs and capacities of very few are being met by such a system.

If the total instrumental program is to have breadth and quality, the foundations must be laid in the beginning stages. Here the student must have a fair chance to discover his aptitude and to achieve results commensurate with his efforts. His educational stance should be improved even if he does not elect further study. This chapter describes a beginning program designed for this purpose. It covers the period of introduction which is roughly equivalent to one year's study. Piano instruction is outlined first so that it will not be overlooked and because of its special nature. This is followed by procedures for the band and stringed instruments, which involves securing the students, determining what instruments they will play, and the organization and conduct of their instruction.

BEGINNING PIANO INSTRUCTION

Whatever keyboard familiarity is established in the elementary classroom does not complete the school's responsibility toward the piano. Keyboard experience implies mass instruction within the classroom (usually with artificial keyboards), to lead to a more intimate understanding of musical design. True piano study, on the other hand, aims principally at playing proficiency and a steadily enlarging repertoire.

This offering is a legitimate function of the school on an elective basis, just as is the study of clarinet or violin. It is strange that so few schools recognize the need for piano instruction, especially when many authorities insist on the advisability of piano study prior to any serious attempt at an orchestral instrument. Regardless of that opinion, it is certain that the piano is our most useful and popular instrument and cannot be lightly omitted from the curriculum. According to the American Music Conference, there are 9.2 million pianos in the country and 21.5 million who class themselves as players.[1] If any instrument deserves universal trial it is certainly the piano. Common observation tells us that few schools are making the attempt to teach piano; one estimate places it at 15%, although this figure includes only those who answered the questionnaire.[2] A more recent and extensive survey places the figure at 13.4%[3]

Obstacles usually cited are (1) lack of funds, (2) lack of instructors, (3) lack of space and pianos, (4) time conflicts, (5) tacit resistance from private teachers, (6) concentration needed on the other instruments and voice, and (7) teachers inadequately prepared.[4] The fundamental reason, however, is *lack of precedent,* stemming from the fact that the band and orchestra scores seldom call for the piano. The band director surely would produce pianists, if he needed them.

In any case, the job has largely been left in the hands of the private teachers, who operate on the basis of individual instruction and can reach only a fraction of the potential students. However, it is not suggested that the schools sponsor piano conservatories to meet this need. The possibility of providing the introductory phase on a mass basis should be explored since this is the function of the school in all legitimate fields of learning.

There are immediate problems in determining the proper mode of

[1] "Report of Amateur Music in the U. S. A.," *Music Journal*, October, 1963, p. 60.

[2] William R. Sur, ed., *Piano Instruction in the Schools* (Washington, D. C.: Music Educators National Conference, 1949), p. 23.

[3] NEA Research Division, *Music and Art in the Public Schools*, p. 16.

[4] Sur, *op. cit.*, p. 25.

instruction. The difficulty is that the piano is chiefly a vehicle for solo or accompaniment playing rather than ensemble use. A mass piano ensemble is unwieldy, noisy, often out of tune, and the mixture of parts and sounds is so pervasive that the individual player can scarcely identify his own part as it is played. Thus we cannot successfully handle piano in the same manner as beginning band and stringed instrument classes.

Individual instruction is not the answer to this dilemma for many of the reasons previously noted, i.e., it cannot reach enough students, it is expensive, and it does not hold the interest of most beginners.

Dummy keyboards will not carry the process far enough, because while they are useful in providing mass keyboard experience in the elementary classroom, a silent device provides no real check on the correct rendition of the material being performed.

The only practicable answer, therefore, is a form of individualized class instruction. Good results can be obtained with groups of ten to fifteen. A similar number of pianos are not required, since doubling or tripling at the piano is quite practical at this stage, and the quick learners can be placed with the slower learners to provide rhythmic stability. New material is sometimes essayed by the entire class, but prepared assignments are more commonly presented individually or by ensembles of two or three players. A favorite device is to have the members play in rotation, taking each phrase or stanza in turn, without pausing. These procedures give the young pianist an initial ensemble experience not achieved by ordinary methods, making the future development of accompanying skill much more natural.

A development holding some promise in this field is the electronic piano.[5] This instrument is permanently tuned, light in weight, and cheaper than the conventional upright piano. With the "Multi-Purpose Monitor System" each student may hear what he plays with earphones, while the teacher may speak, play, or listen to the individual, to groups, or to the entire class.

Classes of moderate size are suitably taught in this fashion for about sixty lessons, i.e., twice a week for thirty weeks. Thus, a skilled teacher can handle approximately 150 new students in a year. Promising students who complete this course should then be referred to qualified private teachers. A number of these students will eventually be able to re-enter the school music program as skilled accompanists and soloists.

Schools have offered class piano at various levels, but the most natural plan is to accept volunteers from grades three and four. In small schools, this additional teaching load can perhaps be assigned to the choral or instrumental teacher, although in most situations, one or more part time or full time instructors will need to be employed. Some schools have found it necessary to charge a nominal fee to cover this cost until the

[5] Made by The Wurlitzer Company, DeKalb, Illinois.

Fig. 3-1. An electronic piano class. Used by permission of The Wurlitzer Music Company, DeKalb, Illinois.

practicability of the offering is proven and its cost may be included in the regular school budget.

Staunch support must be offered by the band and orchestra directors in initiating this program. They must be convinced of its logical inclusion in any well rounded instrumental program and must take the lead in promoting and providing for the venture. Often, it is necessary for one of the directors to organize the first class and teach it himself in order to demonstrate its practicability. No great amount of pianistic ability is needed, but teaching skill and knowledge of piano class methods and materials are absolutely essential.

Class piano procedures are still in the experimental stage but some successful teachers have assembled their materials and outlined their systems in published class piano series. These are all more or less applicable to local situations if the teacher has imagination and ingenuity. Some class piano systems, however, almost require attendance at a workshop or master class with the originator, in order to understand and apply the techniques with freedom and confidence.

The piano presents musical problems in a somewhat different light from the other instruments. It responds instantly to the touch and the pitch can be trusted. Transposition is a natural process, and students are soon expected to read two clefs and several parts simultaneously, with continually shifting finger patterns. The learning process thus highlights intellectual concentration and motor coordination.

The students are seated at the piano and the hands placed so the wrists are straight and the fingers curved over the keys. The shoulder, not the keyboard, supports the arm. Natural action of hand and arm in tone production is sought.

It is well to select a beginning book which combines easy presentation of material with pieces of interest to the child. Some of the following materials will be found appropriate for the young beginner:

ALFRED D'AUBERGE, *Piano Course, Book I* (Alfred Music Co.)
BELA BARTOK, *Mikrokosmos, Vols. 1 and 2* (Boosey and Hawkes)
RAYMOND BURROWS AND ELLA MASON AHEARN, *The Young Explorer at the Piano* (Willis Music Co.)
ANGELA DILLER AND ELIZABETH QUAILE, *First Solo Book* (G. Schirmer)
SALLY MONSOUR AND MARY JARMAN NELSON, *Play!* (Marks Music Corporation)
ROBERT PACE, *Piano Series, Books 1, 2, and 3* (Theodore Presser Co.)
ADA RICHTER, *Piano Course, Book I* (M. Witmark and Sons)

The d'Auberge book has a two octave approach from middle C with freedom from any set finger patterns. It also has duet parts for the teacher or helper which add interest and rhythmic stability to the early tunes. The books by Burrows and Ahearn, Monsour and Nelson, and Pace all contain a wealth of examples as well as a practical approach to transposition. The Bartok books stress octave work and are useful in achieving versatility in several keys and with differing finger patterns.

As soon as the students have become oriented to the piano it is advisable to teach a few melodies by rote. These may be first sung and then played, employing either the black or the white keys. A regular part of every class session should be devoted to rote-learned material. Rote-learned melodies then become "observation songs," being replayed from the printed notes. Gradually it becomes possible to introduce new pieces by note with supplementary guidance by rote learning techniques, with the final stage being independent reading.

Beginning piano classes must be highly organized and streamlined in approach. The lesson agenda should be outlined on the chalkboard and students should be started playing when they enter the class. Regular routines should be established for seating and the playing of assignments, but these should be flexible enough to cover contingencies.

The natural procedure in each lesson is to hear material previously assigned with correction and possible reassignment, followed by explanation, demonstration, and preliminary trial of new material. Theoretical explanations should be avoided unless they are directly related to the music at hand. In this way, a practical knowledge of the musical rudiments is gradually established and this knowledge can later be consolidated and extended by a private teacher.

The characteristic process in learning to play the piano is coverage of a large and carefully graded repertoire. Technique and style are steadily improved by virtue of mastery of many and varied examples. By the end of the year's work the student should be able to read and play many simple tunes with both hands, and with accurate rhythm and good tone. He should also have acquired basic understanding of scales, triads, key signatures, rhythmic patterns, transposition, and some improvisatory skill.

Piano class teaching is a demanding task involving much more than assigning and hearing pieces but the results are probably greater in terms of student interest, understanding, and acceptance of music than could be evoked with any other use of the same amount of time and money. Prospective students are present everywhere in large numbers, waiting only for qualified teachers and the necessary pianos to be provided.

ORCHESTRAL INSTRUMENTS

The subject of beginning instruction on the orchestral instruments is complicated by the number of instruments and their unique problems. A vast lore has developed relating to promotional device, instrument selection and care, playing positions and tone production, literature, and teaching procedures from which each teacher may find techniques to meet his needs. Only those details which seem most indispensable and embody the most enlightened practice will be covered here.

One of the recurring questions a director must meet is "when to start and what to play." The answer will vary considerably but must not be based on simple expediency, i.e., *the director must not have his eye entirely on developing the players needed for his performing groups, but rather upon the means of creating the greatest number of successful players.* This means considerable flexibility in finding the proper time each student is to begin and the suitable instrument(s) for each.

Another question of prime importance is the mode of instruction. Many teachers insist that individual instruction is the ideal system, while others advocate some form of group instruction. The proper answer in each case will generally depend upon the number of players involved and the local patterns of scheduling.

In determining all these possibilities the director is caught between what he thinks he *ought* to do and what he *can* do at present. He must work in terms of local opinions and traditions, but he must not assume that these are immutable patterns. As local patterns change, or when he changes jobs, the director must seize the opportunity to move in the direction of the most progressive and enlightened form of music education.

When to Begin

No problem in this field is more difficult to solve than the optimum time for each child to begin an instrument. In part, it depends upon the maturity and motivation of the individual, coupled with the influences of home, school, and peer group. In a musically rich environment the child will tend to be ready sooner, while delay can actually inhibit a successful start. The proper time to start may thus range from between the ages of four and forty.

The condition of readiness can only be deduced by observation and individual consultation. Any child who is reasonably intelligent, successful in school subjects, sings accurately, possesses good motor control, and volunteers to play is probably ready to play an instrument regardless of age. A serious weakness in any of these points is generally grounds for delay.

Another factor to be determined is the instrument to be played. Violin, cello, flute, clarinet, alto saxophone, trumpet, trombone, and snare drum are the instruments favored for youngsters in the elementary schools, while other instruments are generally reserved for older beginners, or for those who learn to play a second instrument and thus become "switchers" or "doublers." However, the practical situation in the school also plays a part, in that it is difficult to schedule beginning classes to accommodate every age and grade level. The most likely time to begin is after a general musical foundation has been acquired but before other special interests are developed.

It is for these reasons that schools usually prefer to promote beginning instruction in grades four, five, six, and seven. The string program is often given a year's head start on the theory that this eases the recruitment competition with the band instruments, and it also gives the extra time that seems to be required in acquiring string technique.

A general plan for beginners, which offers practical stability along with the needed provision for early and late starters, can be outlined as follows:

Beginning string instruments

The basic group is formed of fourth or fifth graders and may include older students who were delayed and promising volunteers from lower grades if they can be scheduled. Most will play violin (some three-quarter and some full sized) and perhaps a few will elect the cello. As these players arrive at junior high school age those who either show awkwardness on the violin or have large hands and body frames will be transferred to viola, cello, or bass. A special effort will also be made at the junior high school level to interest band members and pianists in doubling on cello and bass.

Beginning band instruments

The basic group is formed of fifth or sixth graders, and any precocious volunteers from earlier grades who can be scheduled. The principal instruments will be flute, B–flat clarinet, alto saxophone, cornet or trumpet, trombone, and snare drum. Students who are determined but have embouchure problems will be switched once or twice to find a more promising instrument. Further conversions to horn, lower brasses, double reeds and lower single reeds will occur when practical, but especially at the junior high school level. New volunteers for beginning instruction will also be accepted from this latter age group.

Enlistment

There is no guaranteed procedure in enlisting students for beginning instruction. If the director is to succeed in interesting students whom he hopes to instruct, he will need to consider these five points:

(1) AN EFFECTIVE PROGRAM IN GENERAL MUSIC, INCLUDING SUCCESSFUL PLAYING EXPERIENCE. If the first few years of schooling have produced little musicianship, there is little hope of recruiting many promising students for specialized instrumental training. Volunteers are much more likely from groups which have learned to sing well, to play the rhythm and melody instruments, have acquired keyboard familiarity, and have a practical knowledge and appreciation of music. (These points were discussed in Chapter 2.) Effective class piano will further enhance the possibilities. The new director must proceed without this fund of talent where this program is not being followed, but he would be wise to concern himself with its development for the future.

(2) VIGOROUS, SUCCESSFUL INSTRUCTION. Where they have a choice, students will avoid the drab, ineffective, or tyrannical instructor in favor of the personable and effective teacher. Thus potential players will naturally elect choral music, art, or French instead of beginning instrumental classes if those teachers seem to offer more positive results. The new teacher must be sure his full personality is exerted, and that he succeeds with the material at hand.

(3) GOOD PERFORMING GROUPS. Few children will be interested in a program which is not visibly successful. Good high school bands and orchestras attract the needed replacements, and younger brothers, sisters, and friends of enthusiastic members will naturally be interested in joining.

(4) ADMINISTRATIVE SUPPORT. Much depends upon the attitude of the superintendent, principals, and counselors, and if favorable, a climate developes where membership in instrumental groups is encouraged. Thus, the director is advised to take every opportunity to present his philosophy to these individuals and to secure their advice and sanction for his procedural plans. This is particularly true at the recruiting point, since this is where a program is most readily encouraged or suppressed.

(5) CORDIAL INVITATION AND EFFECTIVE PUBLICITY. Every child should have advance knowledge on when and how he may volunteer for begin-

ning instruction. For best results, this campaign should be thorough and sustained, but noncoercive. Three or four of the following techniques should be employed:

(a) The director may announce the formation of beginning groups, following a performance of the band, orchestra, or small ensemble for a school assembly. Soloists on various instruments may be featured, or all the instruments may be identified and demonstrated. If the performing group is good and the director's personality engaging, considerable enthusiasm should be generated.

(b) The director may prefer to make a personal appearance in those classrooms where volunteers are sought. He may be accompanied by one or two advanced students to help demonstrate the instruments. The following is an example of the letter and form that should be given to each child to take to his parents:

April 15

Dear Parent:

Many of your child's classmates will be electing beginning instrumental instruction this fall or summer. We hope your child will also participate. Groups will be formed that will meet Monday through Friday this June 2–July 11. Other classes, meeting twice a week during school hours, will start in September. There is no charge for this instruction.

As soon as each pupil is ready he will be admitted to one of the performing organizations, provided there is an opening.

It is difficult to tell whether a child is musically talented. A general estimate is provided by the test we give all volunteers, but a more reliable guide is the child's general success in school. However, his actual desire to learn to play is the most important factor.

It is even more difficult to determine the instrument which will be most suitable for your child. Unless a particular instrument is desired, we would like to advise you on the choice, using general physique and future openings in our groups as a basis. In some instances it becomes apparent after a time that a change to another instrument is advisable.

For this reason it is not wise for you to purchase an instrument too soon. The school owns several which may be rented for one year at a moderate charge. The local music store will also arrange to rent you an instrument and any payments may be applied to a later purchase.

We believe that learning to play a musical instrument can be one of the most cherished experiences in your child's life. The knowledge and skill he acquires will be useful to him whether it becomes a vocation, an avocation, or a memory. Will you consider the matter carefully and return the following questionnaire?

Sincerely,

(Please mail or bring to the school music office by May 1st.)

Our child would like to participate in the groups starting
      ————this summer   ————next fall

Instrument choice,

————We would like to discuss the possibilities with you.

Our child has a strong desire to learn the————.

In procuring the instrument, we prefer

————to rent a school instrument, if available

————to arrange for an instrument independently

child's name	age

parent's signature	phone

(c) The announcement may be made by the classroom teachers who distribute letters and forms similar to the above. Of course, results will depend largely upon the enthusiasm exhibited by each teacher.

(d) As a preliminary to passing out letters and forms by the director or classroom teacher, the announcement may be made via office intercom.

(e) The bulletin board and/or special posters may be employed.

(f) The director may make brief talks to P.T.A., band parents' club, civic clubs, etc.

(g) Instrument displays in the schools may be arranged with local music stores.

(h) Announcements may be made via the school paper, local newspaper, radio or TV.

(i) Preliminary tests may be administered to all students (at the selected grade level) and results included in the letter and form mailed directly to parents.

Natural Selection of Students

There is no doubt that the director must adjust the number of students to fit his own time and energy, and to consider the future needs of his performing groups, whatever his philosophy may be. Unfortunately, this often means that he establishes a number (perhaps a score each of strings, woodwinds, and brass, with three or four drummers) to be started each fall, which is calculated to maintain a sufficient number of instruments for his advanced performing groups.

The selection is often done by means of so-called talent or aptitude tests.[6] However, no test yet developed is infallible in the separation of the good from the bad risks. Indeed, since grade averages are a rough index of intelligence and perseverance, there is some evidence that they offer a better correlation to success in instrumental study.[7]

The director should not be so unprofessional as to offer his services only to those whom *he* needs. He should remember that instrumentalists are not developed only for the school band and orchestra, but that bands

[6] See listing at end of chapter 8.

[7] Clarence M. Schultz, "A Prediction of Persistence of Study in Band at Duluth West Junior High School" (Master's thesis, University of Minnesota, Duluth, 1962).

and orchestras are formed to utilize the available players. Thus it is unwise to eliminate instrumental students just because there seems to be an
oversupply, and it is equally wrong to coerce unpromising recruits in
order to fill the chairs. If the director finds an insufficient number of
recruits, he should be sure that his invitation is properly disseminated,
and he should work harder with those he does have. If, on the other hand,
he finds too many volunteers, he should first advise the administration of
his need for assistance, and then expand the size of his classes in order
to quicken the pace of natural selection, so that the weaker students are
discovered and dropped more rapidly. This extra effort is not wasted,
because with keener competition, an abler and more easily taught group
will survive than if an artificial selection is made in advance.

Instrument Selection

Although there are many difficulties in determining the particular
instrument most suited to an individual, experienced directors have seen
instances of a miraculous transformation of an apparently dull student
into a veritable genius, caused by a fortunate shift of instruments. It
seems that each individual has special potential on one or two instruments,
which is over and above his general level of musicality. If the right choice
could be made in all instances, the present difficulties of instrumental
directors would largely evaporate, and music would indeed become a
flourishing art in America.

The following excerpt gives the general qualifications for the various
instruments:

1. *Stringed instruments*
   a. A keen sense of pitch is necessary.
   b. The left hand should be supple and large enough to reach the
      intervals needed for playing on all four strings.
   c. The right arm must be sufficiently long to enable the student
      to draw at least seven-eighths of the full length of the bow.
   d. Half- or three-quarter-size instruments should be recommended
      for smaller children. Three-quarter-size cellos and half-size
      basses are large enough for the elementary grades.

2. *Woodwind instruments*
   a. A good ear is essential.
   b. For single-reed instruments students should possess even lower
      teeth. An over-bite and protruding upper teeth are not serious
      handicaps.
   c. For the double-reed instruments irregular upper and lower
      teeth do not seriously impair good performance.
   d. Flute players should have even lower teeth.
   e. All woodwind instrument players need fingers long enough to
      cover the pads and holes completely, especially those parts

of the instrument which lie farthest from the mouthpiece. Bassoon players will need fairly large hands.

    f. Lips should not be excessively thick or flabby.

3. *Brass instruments*

    a. A good ear is necessary. This is absolutely essential for players of the French horn and trombone.

    b. Upper and lower teeth should be even. Trumpet and cornet players should not have an over-bite of more than one-sixteenth of an inch.

    c. Lips should set well against the teeth. The possession of a straight lip is an advantage.

    d. A strong, square jaw is an advantage for trombone, baritone, and tuba players.

    e. Trombone players should have a right arm long enough to reach the 7th position easily.

4. *Percussion*

    a. An excellent sense of rhythm is essential.

    b. A knowledge of some other instrument such as piano is decidedly helpful.

    c. Wrists should be supple and flexible.

    d. Possession of absolute pitch is a decided asset. The timpanist must possess a good ear.

Additionally

    larger instruments for larger students
    agile instruments for students of agile mind and hands
    difficult instruments for students of patience and extra talent [8]

The above list is a useful guide, although any experienced director will be able to cite many exceptions to the rule. There are apparently subtle points in a student's anatomy and psychology that are not revealed until actually put to the test. There is also the probability that an optimum time to start a particular instrument applies to each individual on a widely variable scale. Proper selection of an instrument thus rests on a student's physiology, interests, and opportunities.

We can only hope to consult the individual's interests, broadly interpret his physiological qualifications, and hold the door of opportunity open at all times. We must be humble in this process and admit our ignorance. When asked what one should play, it is better to suggest and advise rather than to prescribe.

Thus we should not be too alarmed if there exists an imbalance in the original instrumentation achieved by a group of beginners. If the instruments are not purchased, the surplus saxophonists will shift to the oboe, bassoon, and bass clarinet, while the extra trumpeters will become

[8] Theodore F. Normann, *Instrumental Music In the Public Schools* (Philadelphia: Copyright Oliver Ditson Company, 1941 used by permission), pp. 49-51.

baritone, tuba, and horn players. Parenthetically, it is wise to combat the usual feeling that "brasses are masculine" and "the strings and woodwinds are feminine." There is no basis for this idea and yet there are instances where instruction has been artificially limited in this way.

A word should be said here about the effect of doubling. Once a student has learned to play an instrument, it is relatively easy to transfer this knowledge and skill to another instrument, even though it is of a different family. Thus, the pianist learns to double on the bass violin, the horn player may try snare drum, and the clarinetist learns the cello. The process is especially suitable to the brilliant players and further enhances their musicianship, and is a natural step toward the vocation of music. Finally, doubling is of course extremely helpful to the school organizations.

Instrument Procurement

The key to a sound and flourishing beginning program often lies in the way instruments are procured and owned. If the people sanction a free, public education, and if promoting musicianship is a legitimate function of the schools, then school instruments should be provided to all instrumental students. Only in this way can equality of opportunity be insured. In typical American pragmatic fashion, however, the tendency is to rely on the parents to purchase the cheaper, more popular instruments while the school provides the other instruments needed to complete the instrumentation. A full complement is as follows:

C piccolo	1 or 2
flute	———*
oboe	2 to 4
English horn	1
E–flat clarinet	1
B–flat clarinet	———
A clarinet	2
alto clarinet	1 to 4
bass clarinet	1 to 4
contrabass clarinet	1 or 2
bassoon	2 to 4
alto saxophone	———
tenor saxophone	1 or 2
baritone saxophone	1 or 2
bass saxophone	1
French horn	4 to 8
cornet or trumpet	———

* Dashes indicate popular instruments which the students usually buy and are not purchased by the school.

trombone	— — —
bass trombone	1
baritone or euphonium	2 to 4
sousaphone	4 to 8
recording tuba	1 to 4
tympani	set of 2, 3, or 4
bass drum	1 or 2
cymbals	pair
field drums	4 to 6
concert snare	1 or 2
xylophone, gong, etc.	set
harp	1
violin	— — —
viola	6 to 12
cello	6 to 10
bass	4 to 8

Ordinarily, the majority of students arrange to rent or purchase their flutes, clarinets, saxophones, trumpets, trombones, and violins. If there are available instruments in the community, the director may assist the students by maintaining a list of prospective sellers. He can also arrange with local music dealers to establish a reasonable rent-purchase plan. He should advise students and parents about the desired size, model, and brands of instruments. For example, he might indicate that cornets should be purchased rather than trumpets and name two or three good brands that are available locally. The director should arrange to check all instruments before actual purchase and any instrument that is out of tune or mechanically defective should be rejected. No attempt should be made to appraise or set prices, but the fact that the director is to be consulted will tend to keep prices fair.

Many school officials are beginning to recognize that it is wise to devote additional funds to building the complete stock of the popular instruments necessary to supply each year's crop of new beginners. This policy is necessary if every student is to be given an opportunity, regardless of his parents' financial position, and it is imperative in arranging the necessary experimentation to find each student's best instrument. A stock of school instruments also ensures a more balanced instrumentation and usually upgrades the quality of instruments used in the performing groups. However, what is considered an adequate supply depends upon the size and extent of the beginning program. Since the instruments are usually acquired over a period of years, the answer will be found when the supply finally meets the demand. In general, it will look like this:

flutes	about 10% of beginning band group
clarinets	about 35% of beginning band group

alto saxophones	about 15% of beginning band group
cornets or trumpets	about 25% of beginning band group
trombones	about 10% of beginning band group
drums	about 5% of beginning band group
violins, half size	for students in grades 2-3
three-quarter size	for students in grades 4-5
full size	for those starting in grade 6 or later
cellos, half size	for students in grades 2-3
three-quarter size	for students in grades 4-5-6
basses, half size	for students in grades 6-7

other instruments needed would be available from the regular band and orchestra equipment

It is possible to reduce the number of instruments needed when there are many beginners in one building, and two or three students can be assigned to one instrument. This can be done by providing practice rooms, lockers, and extra mouthpieces. Under this system, the students often find more practice time, and instrument damage is also lessened. A rental fee is usually charged for these instruments, which can be refunded (depending on the condition) or used to amortise costs of future instruments. Generally, loan of the popular instruments should be limited to a year, when students should arrange to purchase their own, and the school instruments are then made available to a new class of beginners.

Instructional Patterns

The exact mode of instruction for beginners depends upon the director's philosophy, local traditions, and practical considerations. For example, the director may believe in group instruction but find that individual instruction has been the local custom and is easier to schedule. However, an unusually large registration of beginners will tend to alter the situation. The director should be flexible enough to adjust to whichever pattern suits the situation. Each method has its advantages and disadvantages.

(1) *The individual lesson* is the traditional mode of musical instruction wherein each student and his unique problems are subjected to the penetrating analysis of a specialist who is thoroughly familiar with the literature and techniques to be learned. It is the method used in private studios, conservatories, and collegiate music departments in order to produce skilled performers, but it is not suited to students who have not yet acquired the motivation for serious study. Few young students can be expected to practice only one page of music for a week, and it is also prohibitive in cost on a universal basis.

If individual instruction is overemphasized in some schools, it is because the teachers themselves are largely products of the system and are thoroughly familiar with its essential methodology. They regard any other form of instruction as a poor substitute.

Indeed, individual instruction has an important role in schooling, if it is carefully handled. It is very effective for older beginners and for those who have already become skilled on another instrument. It is also indispenable for advanced students who desire to refine their technique and acquire a solo repertoire. However, it needs to be accompanied by some form of ensemble experience. It also requires such a number of instrumental specialists that it may mean lesson fees, unless the school can subsidize the program for all deserving students.

(2) *Homogeneous classes* (group instruction on each kind of instrument). This system is really an expanded form of individual instruction. For example, the instructor forms a class of clarinets, another of trumpets, one of trombones, one of saxophones, and so on. Each class uses one method book and the problems and explanations all relate specifically to one instrument. Good ensemble literature in two or more parts may also be used. This method offers an excellent chance to develop good tone, intonation, balance, and individual accuracy, and also results in more interest and learning from one another's problems and solutions.

At first glance, this would seem to be the perfect answer for beginners—providing the benefits and economies of mass education without the complexities of mixed classes. However, the teacher often finds he has traded one set of problems for another, since scheduling is often quite difficult. While a single pupil may be easily excused from his study period for a weekly individual lesson, some members of a group may need to be released from regular classes, and this is especially true if pupils must come from different grades. There may also be an extra oboe, a French horn, or a baritone player to be accommodated. The director may find his students grouped on a very irregular basis, such as the following:

6 clarinets and 1 alto saxophone	2 thirty minute periods
7 trumpets	1 sixty minute period
3 flutes	2 forty-five minute periods
1 oboe	1 fifteen minute period
2 trombones and 1 baritone	2 thirty minute periods
4 alto saxophones	1 thirty minute period
3 clarinets	2 forty-five minute periods
3 snare drums	1 sixty minute period
1 trumpet and 1 French horn	2 twenty minute periods
1 flute	1 fifteen minute period
2 clarinets	2 forty-five minute periods

Obviously, this teacher would not be operating entirely on the homogeneous class plan but relying partly on mixed classes and partly on the individual lesson system. Such a director would do better to arrange thirty-six individual lessons or a few large mixed groups. In another and larger program, with good administrative support, the homogeneous plan will work quite well. It is also generally effective in the summer class plan in which all students come to one school and scheduling is simple:

6 flutes	2 forty-five minute periods
20 clarinets	"
9 saxophones	"
15 trumpets	"
6 trombones	"
3 snare drums	"

(3) *Family groups* (choirs of strings, woodwinds, brass, and percussion). This is a most practical plan for the medium size school. The technical problems within each family are closely related, and the differences seem to help the student grasp his own problems better as, for example, when the left-hand positions of the violin, the viola, the cello, and the bass are being considered. The music for such groups also provides a more characteristic part for each instrument, there is more original and worthwhile material available, and the tone color is more interesting to the student.

This pattern provides a good background for successful transfer of instruments, for in the early stages a student can often switch from trumpet to horn or saxophone to clarinet with a minimum of repeated material.

The size of the groups makes block scheduling possible:

beginning strings	10 violins	2 sixty-minute periods
	3 cellos	
	1 bass	
beginning woodwinds	5 flutes	2 sixty-minute periods
	1 oboe	
	12 clarinets	
	6 saxophones	
	1 bassoon	
beginning brass	10 trumpets	2 sixty-minute periods
	2 French horns	
	3 trombones	
	1 tuba	
beginning percussion	5 snare drums	2 thirty-minute periods

Each section within a class must be given a fair share of attention without overlooking the others. For example, it is easy to neglect the cellos and basses in favor of the violins, or to concentrate on the clarinets at the expense of the saxophones. This can be the result of the teacher's degree of understanding of the various instruments or his opinion that certain ones are less difficult to play or less critical to his groups. The best procedure is to know the special problems of each instrument, observe all players keenly, and include everyone in verbal directions:

> . . . Class, let's take Exercise 20 again. We need to listen more carefully to the pitch. Sally, you're flatting pretty badly. Cellos, be sure your left thumb is under your second finger, like this. . . Jerry, you're still grabbing that bass; keep your fingers arched and spread. Let's all take full bows and loosen up those wrists. . . Ready? . . . Play!

(4) *Heterogeneous groups.* When normal scheduling devices are not feasible, it is often necessary and desirable to include all instruments within the group. In effect, this group becomes a beginning band or, with strings, it becomes an orchestra. Rehearsal time may be found by alternating with another course (such as art or physical education), meeting during recess or study hall, or after school.

It is sometimes difficult to deal efficiently with a large group of beginners since they have a variety of technical problems. Progress is apparently slow, but it must not be forgotten that the students are acquiring more than just technical proficiency. It is wise not to hurry the preliminary stage where instrument care and assembly, playing position, and good tone production are taught. With a large mixed class, it is necessary to proceed systematically, for poor habits are later more difficult to detect and correct.

Organizing for Instruction

Having registered his beginners, found instruments for them, and considered the various modes of instruction, the director must schedule the lessons, provide the needed equipment and literature, and establish an effective plan of instruction. The actual type of grouping will largely depend upon the number of students and scheduling policy. Usually, the director is wise to arrange for classes of moderate size (five to twenty) of like or related instruments, but some find it most practical to combine two modes of instruction, i.e., individual lessons plus a weekly session with each family of instruments.

The types of groups will generally dictate the types of literature to be secured. Basic method books, studies, and collections of simple tunes are used for private instruction. Homogeneous classes may use the same or similar materials, with additional literature arranged in parts. Special instruction books are available for groups of mixed strings, woodwinds, and brasses, as well as a wealth of supplemental ensemble literature.

Heterogeneous groups need orchestra or band class methods supplemented by full arrangements of easy grade, and some material of each type should be available in order to anticipate changed circumstances. The choice of material is highly important, although a skilled instructor can do more with the wrong book than a poor instructor can do with the right book. Still, good literature is the life-blood of the music program and certainly makes teaching easier and more meaningful.

Among the weaknesses to avoid in beginning methods are: (1) artificial music, contrived only to introduce certain problems; (2) a scarcity of melodic material; (3) too rapid progress in the difficulty of material; (4) explanations either too subtle or grossly simplified; and (5) confusing or unattractive format. A good beginning method usually includes a clear explanation of basic techniques, appropriate drill material, and music selected from known composers and folk literature. We will include sample listings of such material later in this chapter.

Before commencing instruction, the director must of course arrange for the necessary rooms, racks, and chairs, and must make sure the instruments are in good playing order. These matters are discussed in later chapters.

Although each student must progress at his own pace and the various instruments require different periods of study to achieve equivalent facility, it is usually convenient to consider one year's study as the beginning phase. This amount of study is based on a program of about sixty lessons or assignments, and the practice necessary to master these. The average player will then have achieved basic technical powers, a certain facility in reading, some understanding of the music and his role in the ensemble, and an insight into the requirements for further study.

This preliminary stage can be extended or compressed, i.e., the normal twice weekly sessions can be cut to one, or intensified by daily sessions during a semester or summer session. While some directors favor slower assimilation and others favor the concentrated approach, a lot depends on the age of the beginner. The advantage probably lies with the concentrated summer plan, which simplifies many of the director's problems in scheduling and in obtaining sustained practice from his pupils. He is also less distracted by the business affairs of his regular organizations.

Teaching Procedure

The first task is to inculcate a practical notion of instrument assembly and care, playing position, tone production, and tuning, after which a half dozen notes needed for simple tunes and harmonies can be taught. Once music is being played, emphasis naturally shifts from mechanical points to problems of rhythm, phrasing, dynamics, and style while, at the same time, the students' range and facility are being gradually extended.

However, everything depends upon the *way* these matters are handled. It must be remembered that beginning instruction is not only a preliminary to the performing groups but is also an excellent avenue to general musicianship. Indeed, something besides sheer mechanical skill *must* be produced if the players are to continue beyond the beginning phase.

Therefore, it is necessary to devise a type of presentation which holds the players' interest and inspires their best efforts. The exact style of the class will vary with the personality of the director, but the following rules are generally applicable:

(1) Learn to know each pupil—his weaknesses and strengths and the kind of approach best suited to him.
(2) Establish a routine for everyday matters like checking roll, recording individual practice, checking out music, questions from the class, penalties, etc.
(3) Avoid a routine approach to the music by singling out the unique qualities in each piece, by lingering only on important points, and by searching for new ways of expressing old ideas.
(4) Choose music of the proper grade and then demand definite improvement—especially in terms of clarity and style.
(5) Work for overall coordination and easy fluency of technique rather than separate mechanical movements.

The director who applies the above rules will not proceed straight through the book but rather, by design, will skip one piece, read through another passage, and drill intensively on another. Warm-up and rhythmic problems will often be met with rote drills that can even be devised on the spot. The students should exhibit serious attention but not tension, and the teacher should demonstrate energy, tact, and a certain dramatic intensity.

Among the newer ideas for class instruction in strings is the one developed by Shinichi Suzuki of Japan and adapted for American schools by John Kendall. Much emphasis is placed upon rote learning, mnemonic devices, listening to recorded performances, and parental participation. The child hears the tune or rhythmic pattern, learns to sing or tap it, and then is guided to the necessary finger and bow movements. Rapid coverage of material is the result and, with skilled teaching, natural and fluent technique is achieved. The transfer to note reading is considerably delayed but is then comparatively easy to accomplish. If the system proves to be practical, there is no apparent reason why its essential principles could not be transferred to instruction in band instruments.

METHODS AND MATERIALS

The student who is preparing to teach instrumental music usually develops a familiarity with the technique and problems of several of the instruments. However, the beginning teacher soon discovers that he must achieve a much more comprehensive understanding of the instruments and their literature, and will find resource help in the many graded lists of materials, numerous books, articles, and pamphlets which detail the special approach to each instrument and methods for teaching it.

This book can assist him by pointing out some of the major similarities and differences in approach to the various instruments. These are the aspects which new teachers sometimes overlook, or underestimate, but attention to them will make study and experience much more productive in developing effective teaching methods. We will treat these matters by families: woodwinds, brasses, percussion, and strings.

The Woodwinds

The woodwinds consist of three groups—flutes, the single reed instruments, and the double reed instruments. These groups vary considerably in embouchure but are built on similar acoustical and mechanical principles.

Since one of the principal characteristics of the woodwind instruments is their relatively delicate mechanism, a good part of the development of players consists in acquiring an intimate knowledge of the instrument, its care and adjustment, and (except for flutists) reed selection and construction. The young beginner is, of course, not going to learn the finer points, but the following matters should be carefully handled:

(1) Show the student how to remove the instrument from the case; how to hold the keys down and twist the joints together without damaging the keys and joints; how to place and adjust the reed; and how to disassemble, swab out, and replace the instrument in the case. Supervise these trials carefully.
(2) Demonstrate the method for greasing joints and oiling keys and bore. Check their performance.
(3) Explain the effects of temperature and humidity changes.
(4) Caution the student not to attempt adjustments of key mechanism, of flute head joint, etc.
(5) Illustrate the principles for reed selection.

Instruction in pad replacement, corking, reed trimming and making, and mechanism adjustment should be reserved to later stages of instruction.

At first, the teacher will have to take considerable responsibility in adjusting the instruments, and selecting and trimming the reeds. He may also find it wise to do some experimenting with mouthpieces to find the most suitable ones for his players. However, the student learns much from observation, and gradually the teacher is able to trust the good student completely in these matters.

THE FLUTE. Production of the first tone is sometimes a bit difficult. Demonstrate carefully, give clear directions, and be patient.

(1) Take only the head joint of the instrument, and place it firmly against the lower lip so that only the edge of the hole is covered.
(2) Take a breath, set tongue back of teeth, close lips evenly, and stretch them lightly.
(3) Pull down slightly on the head joint of the flute, thus opening a small slit in the center of the mouth (about one-quarter inch wide).
(4) Lower the tongue quickly, directing the air at the outside edge of the hole; if a tone is not produced, try twisting the head joint forward or back and altering its angle to the lips.
(5) After a tone is dependably produced, assemble the flute, take the proper hand position and repeat the process to produce the tone.

Caution is necessary to keep the opening in the lips small enough to maintain pressure and control in back of the air stream. To overblow for an octave turn the instrument hole slightly toward the mouth, decrease the mouth opening, and increase the force of the air column.

THE SINGLE REED INSTRUMENTS. It is wise to make the first attempts with mouthpiece alone. The upper teeth rest lightly on top of the mouthpiece (about one-half inch from the tip) while the lower lip is drawn very slightly over the teeth. The lips are drawn around the mouthpiece as if sucking on a straw. Pressure of the lips must be in from the corners of the mouth so that the lower lip is contracted and drawn against the reed. The chin is kept down and flat and the cheeks must not puff out. The tongue strikes against the under side of reed, near the tip.

Squeaks are caused by: (1) worn or unseated pads, or cracks in the instrument; (2) a reed which is poorly made, chipped, or wrongly adjusted; (3) fingers not covering holes completely; (4) teeth touching reed or other maladjustment of embouchure.

Care is needed with beginning clarinetists in achieving the correct position of the left hand. The thumb must be adjusted at an angle permitting it to cover the thumb hole and control the register key but still allowing the index finger easy manipulation of the first tone hole, A, and A-flat keys. *The fingers should always be in contact with these keys*, and manipulation must be accomplished with the fingers alone. Maneuverability of the left hand and flexibility of embouchure are promoted when the clarinet is securely supported at the thumb rest by the right arm and thumb.

The saxophone requires a somewhat looser embouchure than the clarinet and is generally regarded as the easiest standard instrument to learn, but this fact should not lead to sloppy habits.

THE DOUBLE REEDS. The position of the reed in the mouth requires careful adjustment. Many will attempt to hold the oboe too low (like the clarinet), while some will try to hold the bassoon reed at right angles to the lips. Other common faults include putting too much lip over the teeth, putting the reed too far inside the mouth, biting or squeezing the reed too firmly, blowing too hard, and trying to finger at right angles rather than at a natural slant.

There is much individuality in woodwind playing. For example, it is too easily assumed that the mouthpiece which comes with the clarinet or saxophone is correct, whereas the mouthpiece must suit the individual as well as the instrument. The teacher is well advised to acquire four or five standard mouthpieces for clarinet and saxophone, and to allow the students adequate trial. Similarly, different brands and strengths of single and double reeds should be on hand.

Much cannot be determined by rule of thumb. One must present basic principles for holding the instrument, employing the breath, embouchure, and tongue, and then observe the results in terms of actual tone quality and intonation. As weaknesses are noted, the skillful teacher reviews the most likely causes and guides the student to refine his approach.

Since the fingerings are essentially repeated at the octave (although with much variation on the bassoon) or the twelfth (on the clarinet), and because exact intonation and embouchure adjustment are so delicate, this interval, which is a basic exercise, should be carefully practiced:

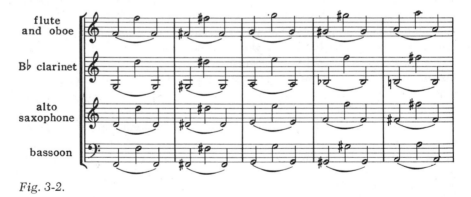

Fig. 3-2.

Other basic exercises include the chromatic scale and diatonic scales in various rhythms and articulations, and the long tone exercise for breath control:

Fig. 3-3.

The flutist especially must work to conserve the breath while the oboist needs to waste it and avoid deep breathing. Players of the single reed instruments must be carefully checked for incorrect breathing and tonguing, since the results seem less damaging at first, and the players easily develop poor habits.

Technical factors must never be allowed to take precedence over the musical problems. The basic mission of learning to play is to find the means to produce music, and the students' attention should not be entirely focused on the mechanics but more and more on the relative accuracy and beauty of the music he is producing. He should be encouraged to listen to and adjust the pitch and quality of his tone, produce the rhythmical patterns accurately, observe the proper dynamics, and achieve natural style and phrasing. Fortunately, these matters are universal to all music so the teacher needs no special prompting, for if he has developed sensitive musicianship, he will perceive what is wrong and sense the obvious remedies. It is in this area that too many instructors lack the patience and pedagogical skill necessary to the task. The specific error and its cause must be identified, the proper rendition explained and demonstrated, and the passage rehearsed until it is noticeably improved.

For example, automatic phrasing habits should be gradually established:

(1) Breathe at regular two, four, or eight measure intervals (depending upon the tempo) at the natural completion of the regular phrases of the music, and robbing a fraction of the final tone if necessary:

Fig. 3-4.

(2) Breathe during rests:

Fig. 3-5.

(3) Where phrases or rests do not conveniently occur, breathe at the end of long notes (especially ties or dotted notes):

Fig. 3-6.

(4) When the note values are equal, with no rests, breathe between any skips that do not occur over bar lines:

Fig. 3-7.

(5) As a last choice, when no other logical point for breathing is available, one can breathe just after reaching the top or bottom of a scale or arpeggio passage:

Fig. 3-8.

Following are some suggested materials suitable to the young beginner:

METHODS	SOLO COLLECTIONS
Flute	
Rex Elton Fair Method, Book I (M. M. Cole)	Album of Favorite Flute Solos (M. M. Cole)
Eck Flute Method, Book I (Belwin)	Everybody's Favorite Easy Flute Solos (Amsco, #83)
Oboe	
Gekeler-Hovey Method for Oboe, Book I (Belwin)	Oboist's Repertoire Album (C. Fischer)
Niemann-Labate Method for Oboe (C. Fischer)	
Clarinet	
Hendrickson Method for Clarinet, Book I (Belwin)	Album of Favorite Clarinet Solos (M. M. Cole)
Herfurth, A Tune A Day for Clarinet (Boston Music Co.)	Everybody's Favorite Easy Clarinet Solos (Amsco, #75)
Hetzel's Visual Method for Clarinet (Oliver Ditson)	Let Us Have Music for Clarinet (C. Fischer)
Bassoon	
Herfurth-Stuart, A Tune A Day for Bassoon (Boston Music Co.)	
Weissenborn Method for Bassoon (Cundy-Bettoney)	
Saxophone	
Herfurth, A Tune a Day for Saxophone (Boston Music Co.)	Album of Favorite Saxophone Solos (M. M. Cole)

Hovey, *Rubank Elementary Method for Saxophone* (Rubank)

Everybody's Favorite Easy Saxophone Solos (Amsco, #76)

Vereecken, *Foundation to Saxophone Playing* (C. Fischer)

Let Us Have Music for Saxophone (C. Fischer)

The Brasses

The French horn, cornet and trumpet, trombone, baritone and euphonium, and tuba are more reliable than the woodwinds and strings. That is, we expect the instrument to be ready to play and the student to play it, without a great deal of finesse and adjustment. Progress is often deceptively rapid, until further advancement requires persistent effort to develop secure attacks, accurate intonation, adequate range and endurance.

Just because the instruments themselves allow little adjustment, it is well to secure the best possible ones in advance. The teacher should be sure the instruments are clean, that the valves and slides work properly, and that the mouthpieces are suitable.

With the brasses it is better to start to play and not to treat instrument assembly and care too exhaustively. However, the trombonists must be shown how to assemble and oil their slides carefully, and some preliminary remarks should be made about the ill effects of jamming the mouthpieces, jerking the slides, etc. Then, in a few weeks, players should be shown how to disassemble their instruments, clean and flush them, and grease the valve slides. Young French horn players, of course, are not taught to disassemble their rotary valves.

HOLDING THE INSTRUMENTS. A few basic principles should be stressed. The torso should be erect, the arms held slightly away from the sides, and the instrument tilted to favor easy, natural fingering. Young tuba players will need bass stands or bass chairs. French horn players must be taught how to cup the right hand, with fingers on the far side of the bell. Trumpet and trombone players should be encouraged to hold their instruments as level as possible without raising the chin (thus tightening the throat). Flat fingering should be discouraged in favor of a natural arch over and down to the valve caps.

TONE PRODUCTION. There is a great deal of controversy on the subject of tone production, which stems from the individual patterns acquired by various successful players. Some prescribe varying amounts of lip under the mouthpiece, the "pucker" or the "smile" system for register control, and subtle variations in breathing and tonguing procedure. However, these are all interpretations of a few basic principles.

In any case, for the best results, beginners should be introduced to their instruments with the simplest directions possible. The teacher must then observe and curb any dangerous variations while allowing seemingly successful variations to proceed naturally.

The "buzz" system is useful but can be overdone. One moistens the lips, sets them, and blows to produce a light buzz. This should be attempted at higher and lower pitches. The process is then transferred to the mouthpiece before actually producing a tone on the instrument. Care should be taken to employ the tongue at this stage, or the student may tend to play the instrument without tonguing. A legato style of tonguing will help avoid movement of the jaw.

The main value of the buzz idea is to help ensure natural breathing and lip formation so the first trials on the instrument will actually be successful.

These are the general principles of the tone production:

(1) The player inhales quickly at the corners of the mouth, by expanding at the waist, and as the breath is completed the tongue is placed back of the teeth to hold the air as the diaphragm exerts pressure upward.

(2) The mouthpiece is set on the lips (usually moistened to promote flexibility) at the point of most natural support. With the trumpet and horn, the tendency is to set the upper rim of the mouthpiece so the pressure will be at the point where (under the lip) the gum stops and the teeth begin. Trombone, baritone, and the tuba mouthpieces will of course press beyond the gum line. It is hoped that the pressure will be at the center of the mouth, and on the skin rather than the mucous membrane, because the facial muscles coordinate better with a centered mouthpiece and there is no muscular support under the mucous membrane. For this reason, individuals with even teeth, straight jaws, and long upper lips are considered likely prospects for the trumpet. (Nevertheless, there are many successful trumpet players who would not seem qualified on those criteria.)

(3) The lips are tensed and slightly parted within the mouthpiece (as in the buzz) in order to produce the proper vibration when air is forced between them.

(4) The tone is produced when the tongue is withdrawn in a downward or backward direction, releasing the breath under pressure from the diaphragm through the lips and into the instrument.

(5) The tone ceases when the air pressure drops or is cut off by the tongue, when the lips relax their tension, or the mouthpiece is removed from them. In general, it is preferred to stop the tone by the first method—by releasing the air pressure.

The teacher should demonstrate these matters and then put the students to trial. A good note to start with is open concert F:

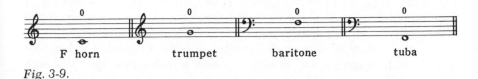

Fig. 3-9.

The teacher must not hurry this stage. He should carefully check the players' setting of the mouthpiece, their breathing, and tonguing procedures. Obviously, a good sound tends to confirm the fact that the student has found an acceptable method while a poor sound (splitting tone, pinched tone, unreliable attacks and releases) indicates trouble. The teacher points out the errors he thinks are responsible and recommends different and sounder procedures. Then, as soon as a reasonably reliable tone is produced the student should be taught the adjustments necessary to change register:

Fig. 3-10.

These are the principal methods for changing register:

(1) Arching and lowering the tongue (tah—ee—ah) as in whistling.

(2) Tightening and relaxing the lips and the aperture of the lips. This may be done by the "smile" or the "pucker." The smile system was formerly used, but in recent years it has been generally believed that the pucker system produces a better tone and helps endurance by putting more muscle under the mouthpiece.

(3) The "pivot system," whereby one tilts the instrument slightly in an upward or downward direction to direct the airstream toward the rim of the mouthpiece, thus increasing its intensity.

(4) Tightening or relaxing the throat, which has the same effect as arching and lowering the tongue, but is injurious to the general tone production.

(5) Increasing and decreasing the pressure of the mouthpiece upon the lips, which affects endurance adversely.

All of these methods are employed in varying degrees but dependence upon the first two or three should be developed, so the last two may be avoided as much as possible.

However, there is no real nonpressure system. The student works for the least possible pressure so that he will have some in reserve for the very top of his range. The director tries to establish the student's flexibility of the tongue and lips very early so that these habits may become refined and strengthened through the years.

As the student progresses and greater velocity is expected of him, the coordination of tongue and fingers becomes a major problem. Although reading ability, aural skill, and motor control are all involved, many fail to recognize that when tonguing and fingering patterns are each executed with rhythmic accuracy, coordination becomes automatic. This process can sometimes be facilitated by slurring a passage, then producing the same rhythmic pattern and tempo on an open tone, and finally combining the fingering and tonguing patterns.

The trombonist, of course, has certain special problems. At an early stage he must be taught legato tonguing to imitate slurring, and he should gradually be introduced to the alternate positions which will become an indispensable part of his technique.

As with the woodwinds, brass players should practice long tones (with crescendo and decrescendo) for better breath control and tone quality. When little improvement is achieved after persistent practice, it is because sufficient effort was not made to establish a true pianissimo at the beginning and end of each tone, or to continue always until the air is completely expelled.

All these technical matters should be kept subordinate to the musical problems of pitch, quality, dynamics, rhythmic accuracy, style, and phrasing. These are developed by effective rehearsal of the music being studied.

Some suggested beginning materials include:

METHODS

SOLO COLLECTIONS

French horn
  Hauser, *Foundations of French Horn Playing* (C. Fischer)
  Pottag-Hovey, *Method for French Horn, Book I* (Belwin)
  Skornika, *Rubank Elementary Method for French Horn* (Rubank)

Everybody's Favorite Easy French Horn Solos (Amsco, #81)

Cornet and Trumpet
  Edwards-Hovey Method for Cornet (Belwin)
  Lillya Cornet Method (M. M. Cole)
  Robinson, *Rubank Elementary Method for Cornet* (Rubank)

Album of Favorite Cornet Solos (M. M. Cole)
Everybody's Favorite Easy Trumpet Solos (Amsco, #77)

Trombone, Baritone

Herfurth, *A Tune A Day for Trombone or Baritone* (Boston Music Co.)

Long, *Rubank Elementary Method for Trombone* (Rubank)

Album of Favorite Trombone Solos (M. M. Cole)

Everybody's Favorite Easy Trombone Solos (Amsco #78)

Tuba

Endreson, *E–flat Tuba Method* (M. M. Cole)

———, *BB–flat Tuba Method* (M. M. Cole)

Herfurth-Miller, *A Tune A Day for Tuba or Sousaphone* (Boston Music Co.)

The Percussion

Many directors are dubious of their qualifications to teach beginning percussionists. Fortunately, this lack can be largely remedied by some self-instruction or by enrolling in a summer session for the instruction that was missed in college.

The beginning percussionists should be started on the snare drum. Drum pads may be secured for home practice, but regular drums should also be available for class practice.

First, show how to adjust the drum stand to the proper height, and then how the sticks are held. See Fig. 3-11.

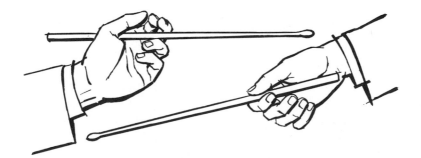

Fig. 3-11. From Robert Buggert, Teaching Techniques for the Percussions, *Belwin Inc., pp. 5 and 7. Used by permission.*

The first exercise is simply a series of single strokes, first with one hand, and then with the other. See Fig. 3-12.

Fig. 3-12.

As facility increases this pattern is gradually narrowed—R R R R L L L L, then R R R L L L, then R R L L R R L L—until the student can play the alternating single stroke evenly, i.e. R L R L R L R L R L R L.

These are formed into groups of three, four, five and six, starting each group with alternate hand:

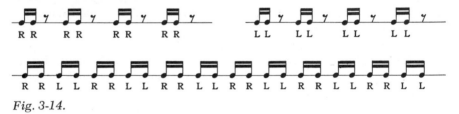

Fig. 3-13.

At this point the student is ready to repeat the above process, but rebounding each stroke:

Fig. 3-14.

One develops the flam similarly, up to this point:

Fig. 3-15.

These beats—the single stroke, rebound, and flam—are the foundation for all drumming, since they are the bases for every combination.

The rudiments are introduced one at a time, but not in the order illustrated in the "Twenty-Six Standard Rudiments." Instead, the simpler, less complicated ones are introduced first.[9]

Parallel with this rudimentary work an effort must be made to teach, first, accurate rhythmic reading, and second, application of the rudiments to the notation. Unfortunately, most drummers fail to become skilled on these latter points. The students must be led to understand that the basic rhythm of the music is defined by the longer and accented notes, and this

9 See Robert Buggert, *Teaching Techniques for the Percussions* (Rockville Centre, L. I., N. Y.: Belwin, Inc., 1960).

pattern must be clear and in tempo regardless of any subsidiary notes. The complicated stick work serves only to embellish and sustain the longer note values. The exact rendition will depend upon the tempo, the teacher's judgment, and the technical and interpretative powers of the drummer.

The remaining percussion instruments should be introduced to the drummer over a period of years. These include the cymbals, bass drum, tympani, the instruments played by mallet, and the various accessories. The tympani and xylophone are particularly difficult, but half of the task has already been accomplished by the well trained snare drummer.

Some suggested materials include:

Haskell W. Harr, *Drum Method* (M. M. Cole)
Very Easy Drum Solos (M. M. Cole)
Buggert Drum Method, Book I (Belwin)

For the combined band class (woodwinds, brass, and percussion) the following basic methods are suggested:

Buchtel, *Melody Time* (Kjos)
Douglas and Weber, *Belwin Band Builder* (Belwin)
Peters, *Master Method for Band, Book I* (Kjos)
Rusch, *Rote to Note* (Hal Leonard)
Sawhill and Erickson, *Guide to the Band, Book I* (Bourne, Inc.)
Skornika and Bergheim, *Boosey and Hawkes Band Method* (Boosey and Hawkes)
Smith, Yoder, and Bachman, *Ensemble Band Method* (Kjos)
Taylor, *Easy Steps to the Band* (Mills)
Weber, *First Division Band Method, Part I* (Belwin)

The Strings

Playing a string instrument involves sensitive physical coordination to the instrument and the demands of the music. Hence, teachers are greatly concerned with the specific nature of each player's instrument and its adjustment, and with establishing the basic playing motions which will lead to fluency and versatility. There can be no standardized approach, since individual differences produce natural variations in playing style. Consequently, long and diligent study is required to adapt to the technical demands of any stringed instrument and its literature. String instruction has thus been a stronghold of the private teachers, each of whom has his individual principles and methods.

This section will be devoted to a summary of the more fundamental aspects of the art of string playing.[10] Those instructors with a year or two

[10] The harp is not discussed here because it is such a specialized field that the players are normally developed by private teachers rather than by school directors.

of study should find it of help in establishing string programs, while advanced string players might be aided in their approach to the remaining string instruments.

THE PLAYERS AND THEIR INSTRUMENTS. Any beginners started before junior high school are likely to need smaller than standard size instruments. This table will be useful as a general guide:

Grade	Age	Violin size	Viola size	Cello size	Bass size
K	5	one-quarter		one-quarter	
1	6				one-eighth
2	7	one-half	junior (13¼ inch)	one-half	
3	8				one-quarter
4	9	three-quarter	intermediate	three-quarter	
5	10				
6	11	full	regular (15½ inch)		one-half
7	12			full	
8	13				
9	14				three-quarters
10	15		large (16½ inch)		
11	16				
12	17				

The above recommendations are, of course, based on averages. The instructor determines sizes more precisely by the following tests:

(1) The violinist or violist is ready for the larger instrument when he can hold it in position and reach his middle finger around the scroll and into the peg box. The viola is thus especially suited to those with large hands and long arms, and few are ever able to manage the large 16½ inch instrument.

(2) There is no simple formula for the cello. The estimation depends upon the teacher's judgment as he views the player at work. In general, the instrument (with six to eight inch end pin) should rest at midchest while in playing position. Also, test the player's ability to reach a major third in first position and to draw the bow in a straight line to the tip.

(3) Without end pin, and holding the bass perpendicular to the floor, the top of the fingerboard should be level with the player's eyes. The full size bass is only suited to very tall persons and is seldom used in the schools.

All string instruments should be carefully checked for cracks and openings, condition of strings, adjustment of pegs, fitting of bridge and sound post, and condition of bow stick and hair. Many instruments are poorly adjusted and can be greatly improved by some fine adjustment of

Fig. 3-16.

Fig. 3-17.

Fig. 3-18.

From Building Better Strings and Orchestras, *Belwin, Inc., Used by permission of the publishers.*

bridge and sound post. Teachers should at least be able to replace strings, to repair open edges, to reset a sound post properly, and to cut down a high bridge to the correct height. Details of these processes are included in Chapter 7.

Steel strings with tuners should be strongly considered for school use (at least E and A on the violin and complete sets on viola, cello, and bass), because they are long wearing, possess a strong tone, and are easier to tune and hold in pitch. The modern good quality steel string also has a very pleasant sound. The extra tension, however, can make them unsuitable for old or expensive instruments.

PLAYING POSITION. The violin and viola are held between the left side of the collarbone and the chin, usually with the aid of a shoulder pad or patented shoulder support. The fingerboard is pointed obliquely to the left, and the player's head is turned to face directly at the bridge and scroll. If the left hand is placed on the right shoulder the violin can easily and properly be held without further support. In playing, the hand is placed under the violin neck and the elbow is centered beneath the instrument.

a.

b.

Fig. 3-19a. From Building Better Strings and Orchestras, *Belwin, Inc. Used by permission of the publisher. Fig. 3-19b. From* Listen and Play, vol. I, *by John Kendall. Used by permission of Summy-Birchard Publishing Co., Evanston, Ill.*

The neck of the violin is supported within the top segment of the thumb and the lower joint of the index finger; the thumb joint should not be locked and the violin neck should not be squeezed. The fingers are then arched and the tips are placed on the strings with the necessary spacing to produce a tetrachord. The wrist adjusts to allow similar finger action for each string.

The teacher must be alert that: (1) The elbow remains centered beneath the instrument; (2) The arm does not rest against the body; (3) The violin neck does not slip to the bottom of the thumb.

The cellist sits well forward on his chair so his back does not touch the chair. He requires a chair which is secure against tipping and allows easy arrangement of his legs. It should be a flat-seated, non-folding type, and at least nineteen inches high for the full grown player. It is well to supply a firm pad or cushion, if the school chairs are not high enough.

The instrument rests on the end pin and slopes back diagonally across the body; it is cradled between the knees and rests lightly against the mid-chest. The neck of the instrument does *not* rest on the shoulder but remains close to the face. The end pin is adjusted so the bottom tuning peg just touches below the player's ear, but in playing he usually leans forward to clear this peg.

The left foot is slightly extended or retracted to lower the knee, and the right foot is tucked back so that the heel is raised. The cello is rotated clockwise a few inches to raise the A string side.

Girls wearing tight skirts will sometimes choose to swing both knees to their left and rest the cello against the right thigh. Obviously injurious to good playing, this practice can be avoided by providing a square yard of opaque material as a lap cloth.

A sharp end pin, T-bar, rug, or rubber mat is needed to keep the end pin from slipping on the floor.

The neck of the instrument rests on the left thumb along the inside corner of the thumbnail, while the fingers arch over and down to the fingerboard (the second finger should be about opposite the thumb). The wrist is flat and the forearm drops naturally away in line with the wrist. The fingers are evenly spaced to produce half steps. The entire arm is raised or lowered to accommodate the fingers to each of the various strings.

Whenever the cellist must encompass two whole steps without shifting, he learns to modify his position by extending the index finger upward and bringing his elbow forward to accommodate the move. He must *not* be allowed to reach forward with the other fingers, as a violinist does.

The usual errors to watch are: (1) The thumb is positioned opposite the index finger, or is turned to face upward, forcing the fingers to assume a twisted, violin position; (2) The finger joints do not remain curved but collapse; (3) The fingers are not spaced sufficiently to produce the half steps; (4) The elbow is unnaturally raised or lowered, thus twisting the wrist.

Fig. 3-20. Adapted by permission from Kay Instrument Co., Chicago.

The bass player stands with his feet comfortably apart and the left foot is slightly advanced. The bass rests on the end pin and leans back so the *side* of the instrument balances against the player's left groin and just inside of his left knee. Thus the instrument faces more to the player's right than does the cello.

The end pin is adjusted so the top of the fingerboard is level with the forehead.

Later, the player can be taught to play while seated on an adjustable stool with left foot hooked over the rung. In this position the tail pin should be shortened a couple of inches to accommodate the shortened height of the player. The instrument is now rested inside the left leg and the player is more around and in back of the instrument like a cellist.

Fig. 3-22.

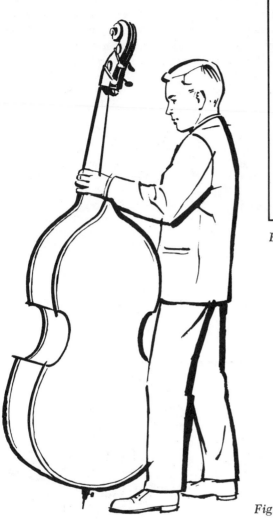

Fig. 3-21.

From Building Better Strings and Orchestras, *Belwin, Inc.; used by permission of the publishers.*

The left hand assumes a position similar to the cellist's extended position. That is, the thumb is almost opposite the second finger, the index finger is pointed upward, and the elbow is lowered. The fingers must be well spaced to produce half steps between the first and second, and the second and fourth, while remaining well arched and firmly pressed to the fingerboard.

The following should be observed:

(1) Be careful that the thumb does not oppose the index finger;

(2) Do not allow the hand to collapse against the neck of the bass; (3) Insist that the fingers do not clamp together but remain properly spaced.

BOWING. The art of bowing is too subtle to be covered in any detail at this point. It should be noted, however, that the violin-viola position is not quite the same as the cello-bass position. In general, these are the differences:

VIOLIN-VIOLA	CELLO-BASS
(1) The bow stick is grasped at the oblique, placing the index finger at the second joint and the little finger on top of the stick.	(1) The hand and arm are basically at right angles to the bow, and the fingers are well over the outside of the bow.
(2) The thumb is held perpendicular to the stick.	(2) The inside corner of the thumb is placed against the joint of frog and stick; the thumb is thus held obliquely to the stick.
(3) The fingers are in loose contact with one another.	(3) The fingers are somewhat spaced apart.
(4) The bow stick is leaned away from the player.	(4) The bow stick is leaned toward the player.

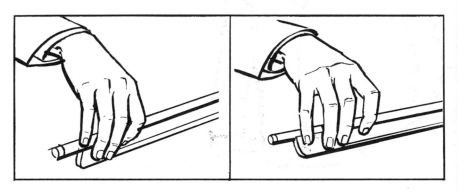

Fig. 3-23a. Bowing: violin–viola.   *Fig. 3-23b. Bowing: cello–bass.*

The German bass bow is quite different, as it is a survival from the old gamba tradition. It is held like a pencil with palm upward, and the arm remains almost straight while playing. Its use is not recommended because there is added difficulty in bowing on the lowest string, and because its special technique only adds to the problems of teaching heterogeneous classes.

Thus far, we have emphasized the essential differences in approach to the various string instruments—and they are critical—but the differences in position are actually required by the need to achieve an equivalent result on the violin, viola, cello, and bass in spite of the variation in size and playing angle. Thus, the mechanics of playing differ only in order to produce the needed finger spacing and dexterity in the left hand and the same type of bow motion on the strings. Instead of unduly stressing these differences, therefore, the wise teacher emphasizes the universal principles:

(1) Fundamentally, the bow travels parallel to the bridge. This means that the upper and lower arm, wrist, and fingers must operate at different angles and in different ways to produce a smooth, fluid stroke. Thus, starting at the frog, and holding the wrist rather high and the arm close to the body, the bow is pulled outward (while gradually flexing the thumb and fingers, and flattening the wrist), until at midbow the upper arm stops and the forearm continues the stroke while turning to increase the downward pressure on the stick. The process is reversed for the up bow.

(2) The bow travels midway between the bridge and fingerboard, adjusting toward the bridge to accommodate higher positions or added arm weight.

(3) The weight and force of the arm and the speed of the bow are varied to produce the necessary dynamics.

(4) Each string requires a different arm level and some adjustment of the bow angle and tilt.

However, the teacher should not attempt a detailed explanation of such matters for beginners. He illustrates and has them practice long bows while pointing out their most serious errors. He sets the pattern for the essential motion by manually controlling a few bowstrokes, and verbally corrects awkward position and movement. This must be done on each string, for the motions have a different feel. The cello and bass players are taught to pivot their instruments slightly when playing on the lowest string.

In developing good coordination, it is often helpful to have the students practice short strokes at each segment of the bow—at the frog, lower half, upper half, and tip—thus concentrating on the particular motions required at each point. Then bow changes involving change of string and different time values are attempted. All this may be done by rote.

TUNING. The young violinist can learn to tune acceptably within the first year. The A is struck on the piano or tuning bar while the player listens. Then he tries his A string and adjusts it with the tuner to the tone that he has just heard. Then he plays two strings (A and D), steadying the violin on the knee while twisting the D peg until the fifths are open and clear, and so on. The metal tuners should be used whenever possible.

The cellos and basses should be tuned by harmonics (lightly touching the strings), even before fingering patterns are learned. When tuners are used, the technique may be acquired during the first three or four lessons. After tuning the open A string, the cellist plays the harmonic at the middle of that string with his thumb, and the second partial (A) on the D string with his ring finger. He adjusts this pitch to unison by twisting the tuner. Then he moves over to the D and G, and then the G and C strings.

The bassist finds octave harmonics in third position with index and little fingers. He first tunes the middle strings to A, and then moves the hand across to adjust the other strings. The teacher may mark the proper spots on the cello and bass fingerboards with lead pencil, since the technique will be learned by the time the lead wears off.

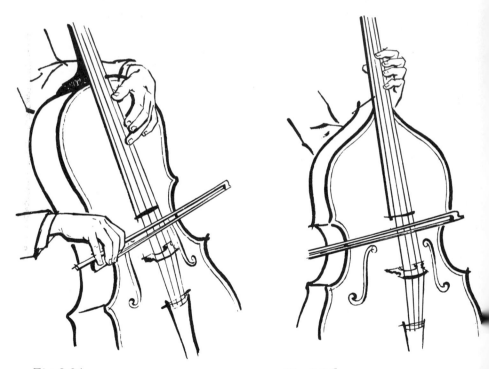

Fig. 3-24a.   Fig. 3-24b.

FINGERING PATTERNS. The very young player must attack one problem at a time. For this reason, the index finger is normally employed first and then the succeeding fingers are added one by one. The use of all fingers together should be attempted as soon as possible, however, as this tends to develop a more natural position. The descending scale pattern is particularly useful, since the complete hand position is established in advance.

Fig. 3-25.

Such an exercise can be taught by rote, using pizzicato (to avoid bowing problems). The teacher should first illustrate and then encourage the players to attempt the exercise, while he checks and corrects position, and as soon as some accuracy and facility is achieved the exercise should be bowed. Then the pattern is transposed to other strings, new finger patterns are introduced, the notes are named and read from score, and various skips and rhythms are employed.

A regular instruction book develops these patterns in a systematic fashion, although the teacher should not hesitate to construct his own exercises to supplement the course wherever he feels that special clarification is necessary. For example, simple measured trills are of great value in the early stages, to develop strength and sure finger action.

ADVANCED TECHNIQUES. The well-constructed books may also be relied upon to introduce the standard positions and bowings in a logical order. However, the teacher can only trust himself to make certain that the indicated movements are correctly executed. The basic principles may be summarized as follows:

(1) Work for bowing versatility. Students should develop not only a smooth legato, but also a light staccato and martelé, at any point of the bow. The young student should also be introduced to slurred staccato.

Fig. 3-26.

The secret on all these staccato strokes is that the pressure of the bow on the strings is actually *increased* between the notes to stop the bow, and then lessened to allow the bow stroke to proceed.

Bowing facility can be speeded by practicing a la Sevcík; that is, by applying several different bowing patterns one by one to an appropriate exercise.

The thrown strokes, ricochét, tremolo, spiccato, and other such bowings are not taught until the student is more advanced.

(2) Shifting is accomplished on the following basis: a) Anticipate the new pitch and distance to be covered; b) Move the entire forearm and hand as a unit, and hold down the current finger combination, while gliding as quickly as possible to the new position; c) At the new position, add or release the necessary fingers. Shifting is soon necessary on the bass, and rather soon on the cello, if any music is to be played. By the end of a year's study, the cellist and bassist should be rather well acquainted with half, first, second, third, and fourth positions, while the violinist might still be confined to the first position.

(3) Fingered, consecutive double stops are seldom practical on the bass, and are reserved to the advanced cellist. They are very useful, however, on the violin and viola at an earlier stage to help form the proper hand position.

(4) Vibrato can be taught when finger habits become well established. The technique is simpler on the cello and bass than on violin and viola. The entire forearm moves as a unit on the cello and bass, while the violinist and violist must depend more upon wrist movement. Because the thumb and vibrating finger must function as fixed pivots, and since each finger is at a different distance from the thumb, vibrato motion must vary with each finger. However, the student finds it easier to place the thumb directly across from the vibrating finger, and this tendency must be firmly corrected. As soon as the proper motion is established, the vibrato should be practiced slowly and regularly, and then increased in speed as it becomes natural.

Some suggested beginning materials:

VIOLIN METHODS

Best, *All the Strings, Books I and II* (Belwin)

Gordon, *Visual Method, Book I* (Highland Music Co.)

Herfurth, *A Tune A Day, Book I* (Boston Music Co.)

Hermann, *Bow and Strings, Books I and II* (Belwin)

Kendall, *Listen and Play, Books I and II* (Summy-Birchard Co.)

COLLECTIONS

Kelley, *Graded Pieces for Violin and Piano, Books I and II* (Oliver Ditson)

Koch, *Folk Tunes in Fiddle Finger Forms* (Boston Music Co.)

Palmer and Best, *Twenty Tunes for Beginners* (Oxford)

Webber, *Fiddle Fun for the Young Violinist* (Belwin)

VIOLA METHODS

Best, *All the Strings, Books I and II* (Varitone)

Gordon, *Visual Method, Book I* (Highland Music Co.)

Sopkin, *Basic Method for Viola* (C. Fischer)

COLLECTIONS

Kritch, *First Book of Viola Pieces* (Witmark)

Whistler, *Solos for Strings* (Rubank)

CELLO METHODS

Kummer, *Cello Method*
(G. Schirmer)

COLLECTIONS

Moffatt, *Old Master Melodies for Young Cellists* (Associated)

Moffatt, *Old Masters for Young Players* (Associated)

Trew, *Primary Pieces for Violoncello Classes, Book I* (Oxford University Press)

BASS METHODS

Marcello, *Basic Method for String Bass, Books I and II* (C. Fischer)

COLLECTIONS

Lesinsky, *Thirty-four Solos for Bass* (Belwin)

STRING CLASS METHODS

Applebaum, *Belwin String Builder, Part I* (Belwin)

Isaac, *String Class Method* (M. M. Cole)

Hermann, *Bow and Strings, Book I* (Belwin)

Waller, *String Class Method, Book I* (Kjos)

COLLECTIONS

Findlay, *The Junior String Choir* (Summy-Birchard)

Preston, *String Ensemble Favorites* (Belwin)

FULL ORCHESTRA METHODS

Weber-Mueller, *Belwin Orchestra Builder, Part I* (Belwin)

COLLECTIONS

Fischel, *Beginners Orchestra Folio, 3 vols.* (Gamble-Hinged)

Taylor, *Classroom Concert Folio* (Belwin)

SUMMARY

Beginning instruction on instruments should be calculated to give each student an opportunity to find and cultivate any talent he may have. This means, first, the widest possible variety of offerings, second, a policy of some latitude in accepting volunteers, and third, an experimental approach to the choice of instruments.

The piano class offering properly follows the basic keyboard familiarity established within the classroom. Pianos, rather than dummy keyboards, should be used. Systematic coverage of materials is the key to establishing the needed facility with basic patterns.

Readiness to play an orchestral instrument is difficult to determine, and starts should not be arbitrarily limited to one age level. Enlistment of volunteers depends upon the quality of the total program and also on effective promotion. To avoid mistakes, natural selection of students (by trial and attrition) is wiser than artificial selection. Similarly, instruments cannot be assigned by arbitrary judgment, but must depend upon the students' expressed interests, qualified by any obvious malformations; freedom to switch instruments is a great help in this selection. In turn, this policy requires access to a number of the popular instruments for beginners.

Instruction may be by individual lessons, or classes of like instruments, families of instruments, or heterogeneous groupings. Most directors employ all of these methods in varying degrees. The introductory phase is usually completed in about sixty sessions. The teacher must first establish practical habits of instrument assembly and care, playing position, and tone production. The first notes are employed in simple tunes and exercises, which lead to further range and facility, and gradual refinement of expression. Attention to the special mechanical problems, while critical, always takes a secondary position to regular rehearsal procedures for musical results.

The young teacher must know the unique features of each instrument in order to teach it adequately. The woodwinds are characterized by a delicately adjusted mechanism and subtle variations in embouchure. The brasses are less complicated but require much care with the embouchure. Percussion playing is approached quite systematically. Natural position and fluid movement must be established on the string instruments in order to achieve the needed facility and style.

Good instruction books may be relied upon to present the problems and techniques in proper order. Only the teacher, however, can guarantee that the movements are properly executed and the music decently played.

QUESTIONS FOR DISCUSSION

1. What are some of the reasons for and against piano instruction in the schools? How could such instruction be organized and conducted?

2. How may we determine when a student is ready to begin to play an orchestral instrument? How is he enlisted?

3. Is there a reliable method for determining the best instrument to play? What about "switching" or "doubling?"

4. What are the best means of procuring needed instruments? Which should the school own?

5. What are some advantages and disadvantages of the various types of class groupings? How are the classes organized?

6. What are some of the essentials to be taught to the beginning woodwind, brass, percussion, and string players?

SELECTED REFERENCES

ARNOLD, PAULINE EDKIN, VERA BROWN LEWIS, AND JOHN SHELBY RICHARDSON, *Piano Teachers Guide.* Mount Pleasant, Michigan: Michigan Music Teachers Association, n.d.

AUTREY, BYRON L., *Basic Guide to Trumpet Playing.* Chicago: M. M. Cole Publishing Co., 1963.

BUGGERT, ROBERT, *Teaching Techniques for the Percussions.* Rockville Centre, L. I., N. Y.: Belwin, Inc., 1960.

CHAPMAN, F. B., *Flute Technique.* New York: Oxford University Press, 1958.

EDWARDS, ARTHUR C., *String Ensemble Method for Teacher Education.* Dubuque, Iowa: Wm. C. Brown Co., 1959.

FARKAS, PHILIP, *The Art of French Horn Playing.* Evanston, Illinois: Summy-Birchard Co., 1958.

Handbook for Teaching Piano Classes. Washington, D. C.: Music Educators National Conference, 1952.

HODGSON, PERCIVAL, *Motion Study and Violin Bowing.* Urbana, Illinois: American String Teachers Association, 1958.

KLEINHEIMER, EDWARD, *The Art of Trombone Playing.* Evanston, Illinois: Summy-Birchard Co., 1962.

KROLICK, EDWARD, *Basic Principles of Double Bass Playing.* Washington, D. C.: Music Educators National Conference, 1957.

MANTON-MYATT, BRIAN, *Woodwind Book.* London: Boosey and Hawkes, Ltd., 1957.

MOORE, E. C., *The Brass Book.* Kenosha, Wisconsin: LeBlanc Corporation, 1954.

PALMER, H. G., *Teaching Techniques of the Woodwinds.* Rockville Centre, L. I., N. Y.: Belwin, Inc., 1952.

PERNECKY, JACK M., *Basic Guide to Violin Playing.* Chicago: M. M. Cole Publishing Co., 1963.

POTTER, LOUIS JR., *Basic Principles of Cello Playing.* Washington, D. C.: Music Educators National Conference, 1957.

ROLLAND, PAUL, *Basic Principles of Violin Playing.* Washington, D. C.: Music Educators National Conference, 1959.

ROTHWELL, EVELYN, *Oboe Technique.* New York: Oxford University Press, 1953.

SPENCER, WILLIAM G., *The Art of Bassoon Playing.* Evanston, Illinois: Summy-Birchard Co., 1958.

SPRENKLE, ROBERT AND DAVID LEDET, *The Art of Oboe Playing.* Evanston, Illinois: Summy-Birchard Co., 1961.

STEIN, KEITH, *The Art of Clarinet Playing.* Evanston, Illinois: Summy-Birchard Co., 1958.

SUR, WILLIAM R., *Piano Instruction in the Schools.* Washington, D. C.: Music Educators National Conference, 1949.

SWEENEY, L., *Teaching Techniques for the Brasses.* Rockville Centre, L. I., N. Y.: Belwin, Inc., 1953.

THURSTON, FREDERICK, *Clarinet Technique.* New York: Oxford University Press, 1953.

WEBER, FRED, ET AL., *Building Better Bands.* Rockville Centre, L. I., N. Y.: Belwin, Inc., 1957.

CHAPTER 4

The School Band and Orchestra

It is commonly assumed that the school program of instrumental music exists in order to create and sustain the band and orchestra. These are the groups that are musically most complete, that the public comes to hear, and that the students aspire to join. The instrumental teacher can easily devote so much energy simply to building these groups that he becomes conditioned to the idea that this is his true role.

Undoubtedly, the school band and orchestra are primary agencies of instruction. Good groups are necessary in any effective music program and poor ones betray a weak program. It does not follow that the achievement of an impressive performing group always guarantees good educative results. *A school band or orchestra must be regarded as a laboratory for the study of a special class of music literature and the concepts which derive from it.* No other educative activity can fulfill this function so intimately and practically.

Any book on instrumental music, therefore, must deal with these ensembles as thoroughly as possible, while keeping them carefully within the overall picture of the program. They should be merely a natural result of teaching many students to play and a further means of advancing and refining the musicianship of these players.

The band and orchestra are each unique in certain respects yet retain many common elements. It is difficult to treat each one separately and completely, without much repetition, but they cannot be treated as a unit, either.

Accordingly, we will attempt to characterize the differences first (in role, organization, and literature) followed by the technical and musical factors which have general application to any large instrumental group. Rehearsal management, as such, will be taken up in the succeeding chapter and other related matters (mass groups, sectionals, individual instruction, programming, equipment, etc.) are treated in yet later chapters. Here we are concerned only with the function and organization of the school band and orchestra.

THE BAND PROGRAM

The band, unlike the orchestra, is almost a universal institution in the American high school. This position is not of long standing, having been achieved largely in the period between the two world wars, and coinciding with the decline of the professional and community bands. The probable significance of this is that the school bands are able to fulfill the functions formerly discharged by the nonschool groups.

Bands originated as military units for parades and ceremonials, hence the reliance upon loud instruments capable of being played while marching. The next step was to expand the basic repertoire (marches) by borrowing lighter works from other sources. Gradually the band became a primary medium of popular musical culture. In recent years even this position has been largely taken over by the dance band. Meanwhile, the band became established in the schools and acquired an original repertoire.

Probably the underlying reason for the powerful hold of the school band is the relative speed with which concrete results may be obtained. The academic disciplines can claim progress toward ultimate performance, but active performance is an essential characteristic of bands. This very fact easily leads to the exploitation of the school band for public entertainment. Directors know that these pressures are very strong.

The educational purists are quick to point out that mere ability to play and march are of little future use to the individual and society, since these skills are seldom used after graduation. Only a few succeed in transferring to symphonies or professional dance bands, or become school band directors. Thus, the inherent mission of the school band must be to provide for the general musical education of its members, and it must help to secure the kind of musical understanding, wide knowledge of literature, and good taste which will be of use to the player when he puts away his instrument.

The task of the band director is thus many sided. He must be enough of a promoter and organizer to capitalize on the inherent appeal of his field; enough of a perfectionist to create the best possible musical performing group; and enough of an educator to remember the real values for which he is working.

The Junior Bands

Except in the smallest schools there is usually more than one band in the school system. The youngest band is an assembling of students who started individually or in classes, a few months or a year previously. The group may be activated at the grade school level or in junior high school, depending upon the age of the beginners. These students may then progress into one or more other bands before they reach the most advanced group.

Compared with the school's concert band, the usual junior band has rather rudimentary low brass and reed sections. Along the way some of the players are converted to the needed instruments and new members are recruited. The literature is also quite different, for the young band members have rather limited technical capabilities. Unfortunately, suitable music is quite difficult to find for these groups, and this fact is partially responsible for a certain musical insensitivity in many older bandsmen.

The secret of working with these junior bands is to consider them full fledged musical units in their own right. Their activity should not encroach on the advanced groups to the extent of marching drill, a repertoire beyond their years, numerous trips, and so on, but they are not just "feeder" groups either. Unless the individual player can get a few musical thrills out of the experience he is not going to be very promising material for the advanced groups.

Care must be taken to develop smoothness and flexibility of the group as well as the range, velocity, and proper habits of the individual players. Too often, the director is content to rap out the beats and keep the players approximately together. The theory is that mere exposure will eventually polish the players. However, deliberate attack on basic problems must not be postponed.

(1) Good habits of rehearsal deportment and responsible membership must be established, i.e., acute listening to the ensemble, attention to the director, prompt attendance, home practice on difficult passages, etc.

(2) Any poor habits in posture and playing position need to be corrected.

(3) Any faults in the mechanism of tone production should be located and remedied.

(4) Rhythmic and tonal accuracy are to be demanded at all times. Faking cannot be allowed. If sloppy playing continues to occur, the music is too hard or the director is too soft.

(5) The quest for purer intonation, tone quality, and dynamic control is unending.

(6) Players are now ready to begin mastering the special techniques involved in their instruments, i.e., alternate fingerings, double and triple tonguing, muting, transposition, and vibrato, etc.

(7) A definite beginning should be made to establish good sense of style and phrasing. A player should learn when to play staccato and when to play legato, which notes should be stressed, meaningful dynamic shading, natural phrasing, and so on.

(8) The musical vocabulary of the player should be extended to include all markings found in the music and common musical terminology. The player's insight into the formal and structural elements of the compositions should be steadily increased.

(9) Better ensemble is a constant goal. The players must *not* be allowed to proceed without reference to the director's attempts to alter speed and dynamics. Melodies and important parts must not be buried.

(10) Great effort is needed to improve the group's ability to do everything with less repetition and prompting. In other words, sight reading skill is sought.

(11) There should be further refinement of the players' ability to adjust and care for their instruments. The director can teach the woodwind players to select and trim their own reeds, and replace pads. Players should test and compare different mouthpieces. Frequent instrument inspections should be held. The goal is more and more student independence.

The Concert Band

As the players advance toward the senior high school concert band, attention to the above mentioned problems is not relaxed. More and more effort should be devoted to the finer points and more difficult music can be used.

Policy on advancing the players depends on the number of players and the flexibility of local arrangements (which factors relate to the size and location of schools).

(1) In very small school systems there is usually one band, and players are immediately admitted following beginning instruction.

(2) Schools of medium size tend to have a junior band and a senior band. Players are transferred when ready and an opening occurs, without reference to grade level.

(3) In larger systems, the line between elementary, junior high school, and senior high school tends to be strict. The bands are formed at each level, and the players transfer automatically.

(4) In a large and thriving program, the number of available players may exceed full instrumentation. In such cases it is normal to form a prep band and a select band.

INSTRUMENTATION. Fashion in band instrumentation has varied considerably through the years. Unlike the orchestra, the music is written to fit full instrumentation, and every player generally has a part. Skillful doubling and cross cuing takes care of incomplete instrumentations.

Changes in instrumentation have reflected changes in the band's role, in the construction of instruments, and in the concept of tone. Twentieth century bands have experimented with circular and upright alto horns, F, B flat, and double French horns, helicons, sousaphones in E flat and

BB flat, upright and recording tubas, tenor horns, E flat and B flat cornets and clarinets, trumpets, flügelhorns, baritones and euphoniums, heckelphones, bassett horns, sarrousaphones, alto, bass, and contrabass clarinets, D flat and C piccolos and flutes, and all varieties of saxophone. (We now have the fiberglass sousaphone.)

In general, the movement has been toward separating the concert and marching functions. Thus, some bands possess a set of recording tubas for concert work, and a set of sousaphones for marching. Brass is wanted for marching, while the ideal instrumentation for concert work includes about two thirds woodwinds. Some concert groups contain harp, string bass, and even cello. The tendency has been to strengthen the top and bottom parts.

The table below shows three traditional instrumentations for different size bands plus experimental trends exemplified by the Eastman Wind Ensemble and the recommendation of the College Band Directors National Association.

	Small Band	Full Band	Symphonic Band	Wind Ensemble	CBDNA Report
C piccolo		1	1		
flute	2	4	7	3	6
oboe	1	2	2	3	2
English horn			1		1
E flat clarinet			1	1	1
B flat clarinet	8	15	22	8	18
E flat alto clarinet		2	4	1	6
B flat bass clarinet		2	4	1	3
contrabass clarinet			1	1	2
bassoon	1	2	3	2	2
contrabassoon				1	
B flat soprano saxophone			1		1
E flat alto saxophone	2	2	2	2	1
B flat tenor saxophone	1	1	1	1	1
E flat baritone saxophone		1	1	1	1
B flat bass saxophone			1		1
French horn	2	4	8	5	4
E flat cornet					1
B flat cornet	3	6	8		3
B flat trumpet	2	2	4	6	3
trombone	3	4	5	4	3
bass trombone		1	1		1
euphonium	1	3	4	2	3
tuba	2	4	6	2	3
percussion	2	4	6	6	5
string bass			1	1	
harp			1	1	
	30	60	96	52	72

As any director knows, the instrumentation must be a compromise between his ideal and the number of players actually at his disposal. In order to stay within a preconceived instrumentation, he will not actually turn away those promising new trumpet and tuba players in favor of adding unprepared flute and horn players. Of course not.

More important than the specific number in each section is the strength of the individual players and the effective depth of the sections. The basic balance of the high school band is predetermined by the composition of the earlier beginning groups and the ensuing conversions and dropouts.

Because band scores already exhibit considerable doubling, substitution of parts is not such a heinous crime. Parts must occasionally be substituted or written in for groups with incomplete or special instrumentation. Following are some common substitutions.

piccolo = flute (played 8va)
flute = oboe = muted trumpet (played up a step)
English horn = oboe (played down 3½ steps)
E–flat clarinet = B–flat clarinet (played up 2½ steps)
B–flat clarinet = soprano saxophone = trumpet or cornet
alto clarinet = alto saxophone
tenor saxophone = bass clarinet = baritone (treble clef)
bassoon = trombone = euphonium = baritone sax (using treble clef and three more sharps)
F horn = E–flat alto (played up a step)
harp = piano
celeste = bells = piano (played 8va)

Seating plans are by no means standardized. In general, the higher pitched instruments are to the conductor's left and the brasses are in the rear.

Plan A (Fig. 4-1a) is a natural seating plan for small groups. It gives a certain prominence to the cornets who must carry the lead. Plans B (Fig. 4-1b) and C (Fig. 4-1c) are variations for typical concert bands.

All the best players should not be at the top of their sections. In fact, some good players have embouchures that suit them especially for the lower parts. Thus the French horn players with good high range would be assigned to the first and third parts and those with better low range to fourth and second horn. Further reshuffling should be accomplished periodically by the director's reassignment, student challenges, or general auditions. This process keeps the players on their toes, and helps them learn from one another.

THE BAND SOUND. Closely related to the band's instrumentation is the conception of proper sound. The band has traditionally sounded brassy and percussive, but as the band has become more of a concert unit, the feeling has grown that a symphonic sound should be achieved, while not

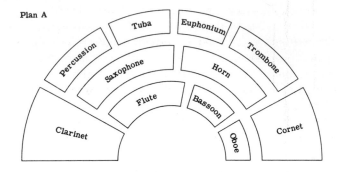

Fig. 4-1a.

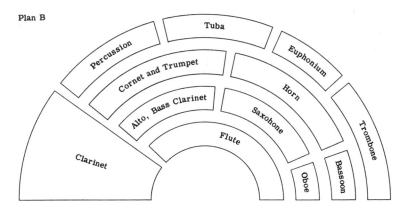

Fig. 4-1b.

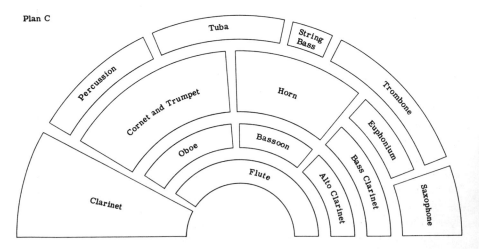

Fig. 4-1c.

attempting to imitate the orchestra. Carried to extreme, this style is termed the *sotto voce* band. The ideal is great smoothness and dynamic control. The effect is achieved by:

(1) Carrying a larger proportion of woodwind instruments, especially flutes and low reeds; (2) stressing the softer range of dynamics (*fortissimo* becomes *forté*, *forté* becomes *mezzo forté*, and so on); (3) avoiding violent attacks and crisp staccato; (4) emphasizing rich, dark tone quality and blend, i.e., cornets and euphoniums are used in preference to trumpets and baritones (which have smaller bores), and high clarinet parts are often transposed downward; (5) careful balance within sections for full chords.

Admirable as all these qualities are in themselves, they can be carried to an extreme which reduces the natural buoyancy and range of expression. The players are actually repressed from the true expression of the feeling in the music, and listeners easily tire of the smooth sound.

Another style of playing might be termed "pit style." This is aimed at brilliancy and extravagant effect:

(1) Only one or two players on a part, for clarity (wind ensemble instrumentation); (2) exaggerated dynamic contrasts and stylistic treatment (highlighting accents, staccatos, legato, etc.); (3) contrasting tone quality between sections, i.e., brilliant trumpets and trombones, smooth clarinets, mellow saxophones, rich euphoniums and horns, sharp percussion, etc.; (4) great care in precision.

One cannot have everything but would prefer a certain mixture of these two styles, depending upon the style of composition. A good band is trained as a *sotto voce* band which is capable of letting off the wraps at the proper times.

THE SCHOOL ORCHESTRA

It is no secret that the majority of school systems have no orchestra at all and that many others exist on a marginal basis. This situation occurs in spite of the acknowledged preeminence of the orchestra as a musical unit, and some band directors are even rather apologetic for their own mission. Yet few directors seem able to lend a helping hand to create a better climate for strings and orchestras. More universal efforts should be made to prepare college wind instrument majors adequately in string techniques so they may be able to assist in launching string programs in their schools.

Some of the more pessimistic see the school orchestra as a dying institution and even despair that America will be able to staff the string sections of the existing professional and semiprofessional symphonies. But such a trend would be difficult to document. One survey, based on rather limited data, seems to indicate that the larger schools manage to maintain a fair enrollment in strings.[1] This factor should be of more effect as our urban population expands and school consolidation is extended. The simple fact is, however, that we would all be surprised to see any dramatic growth in the school orchestra movement during our lifetimes. We know that creation of a good school orchestra requires a skilled and dedicated teacher, a number of far seeing students and parents, and an enlightened school administration, but it is difficult to find and keep such people in one place.

That is to say, any school orchestra necessarily requires careful nurture, and any change in directors or policy must be cautiously undertaken. It is quite difficult to re-establish the program after a serious interruption has occurred. These shifts do not seem so critical in the case of band and choral programs, for the lost momentum can be regained much more quickly.

The individual preparing to be a school orchestra director does not have to worry too much about this situation. He is entering a profession that is in short supply. There will be a place for him where he can exert his full talents. Only the cumulative efforts of many such individuals will finally bring the orchestra to its rightful place in school music.

The Role of the School Orchestra

"Orchestra" is often taken to mean strings alone, without winds and percussion. This is because an orchestra depends principally upon strings and the teacher's efforts are concentrated upon them. The wind and percussion players are largely identified with the band and tend to be added to strings to produce an orchestra. This fact is a complicating one in the instructional process, as we shall see.

The metamorphosis from beginning string class to school orchestra is usually accomplished by steps. The basic corps of young violinists who started in fourth or fifth grade eventually graduate to full size instruments and some of these players may transfer to viola, cello, and bass. A dozen or so wind and percussion players will be brought in from the band to augment the group for special occasions. Other players will often be recruited from the band to double on cello and bass. If all goes well, by senior high school the string choir has achieved a comparatively full instrumentation and is supported by the necessary complement of winds and percussion.

The orchestra thus evolves from successive beginning string classes into a senior high school group of more or less symphonic proportions. The instrumentation may be adjusted to fit the requirements of a Mozart divertimento, the accompaniment for a Broadway musical, or a symphony by Dvôrák.

[1] See *A Study of Instrumental Music in 322 School Systems* (Chicago: American Music Conference, 1957).

This flexibility is not an unmixed blessing. The director is faced with the problem of a constantly expanding and contracting instrumentation. He therefore must arrange to secure the extra percussion and trombones needed for one number and to excuse the horns and trumpet which become surplus in the next one, or he must arrange some judicious substitution and doubling which will employ these players. Usually he plans to rehearse numbers at specific times so that he can add or release certain players by appointment. This particular problem is seldom faced to any extent by band directors.

The inherent function of the school orchestra is to rehearse and to perform the kind of music suited to the available instrumentation and the capabilities of the players, thus securing the utmost improvement in the musicianship of its members. The grade of difficulty is primarily determined by the advancement of the string players, since the major burden of the music is carried by that section.

Unfortunately, the string group as a whole is normally less advanced than the wind group since the latter are selected players. The effect is heightened by the comparatively simple wind parts and thin scoring of Baroque and Classical works. This easily becomes a morale factor. Conductors sometimes feel compelled to combat it by, first, choosing large orchestrations with more interesting wind parts and accepting comparatively poor execution from the strings, second, by excusing the wind players while the strings develop the needed facility on their parts, or third, by choosing arrangements which in effect provide simplified string parts.

This situation may be faced with more equanimity if the director is forewarned. He must seek to create a balanced organization which *sounds* like an orchestra (not a band) and can learn to play the music he puts before it without undue pressure. Regardless of its size and advancement, such a group can fulfill its role, with honor, in concert and as an accompanying group for soloists, choir, and staged presentations.

Organization of the Orchestra

Membership of the string section is more or less determined by the number of beginners started in earlier years and the kind of job that was done with them. Many times there is difficulty, however, when the players enroll in seventh grade and again when they enter senior high school. Dropouts may be expected if morale is poor, or if unsympathetic counseling and scheduling policy are encountered. The director should consider these steps:

(1) Establish an early understanding with students and parents so that after a couple of years' instruction the players may be counted on to continue through school.

(2) If there are different instructors at elementary, junior high school,

and senior high school levels, be sure to establish good liaison so the program has continuity and the players transfer schools and directors automatically.

(3) Establish an understanding with principals and counselors regarding the enrollment of the players. Provide specific listing of the players and the periods they are to be scheduled in orchestra.

Completion of the instrumentation with wind and percussion players depends upon the basic scheduling policy. If the groups meet at different periods, the director chooses from band volunteers who report to orchestra on a regular or irregular schedule—or a full wind complement is enrolled for daily participation in orchestra.

When the two groups meet at the same period, however, with different directors, certain wind players must either be enrolled exclusively with the orchestra or else the necessary band members must be selected from the band and report to orchestra as per arrangement between the directors. In other words, these particular players become *part time* members of both band and orchestra.

As anyone can see, the scheduling relationship between orchestra and band is critical. Personally, we deplore the tendency to schedule the two groups at the same period. Although it does ensure the needed instrumentation for concerts, we suspect that in many cases it is an administrative arrangement to avoid the issue of students wishing to elect both groups. It hampers the program because, first, the full instrumentation is too seldom available, second, the players may not double on string and wind instruments, and third, it disrupts rehearsals of both groups and so becomes a possible cause of friction between directors. When this plan is in force, the directors are advised to establish a systematic schedule for full orchestra rehearsals under administrative sanction.

Some schools try to solve the problem by meeting band and orchestra on alternate days, but this robs both groups of valuable rehearsal time. Adequate progress seems to require about two hundred minutes of rehearsal per week.

This problem can be admirably solved where an extra half period can be scheduled before school (see Fig. 4-2), or after school (see Fig. 4-3).

	M	T	W	TH	F
Before School	Orchestra		Orchestra		Orchestra
1st Period	Band | Strings	Band	Band | Strings	Band	Band | Strings

Fig. 4-2.

With bus transportation and school cafeterias becoming more the rule than the exception, some schools are finding the time at lunch period (see Fig. 4-4).

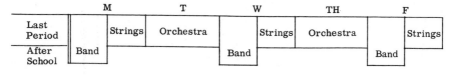

	M		T		W		TH		F	
Last Period		Strings	Orchestra			Strings	Orchestra			Strings
After School	Band				Band				Band	

Fig. 4-3

	M	T	W	TH	F
3rd Period	Band	Band	Band	Band	Band
Lunch Period A	Orchestra	Orchestra	Orchestra	Orchestra	Orchestra
B	Strings	Strings	Strings	Strings	Strings
C					

Fig. 4-4.

Instrumentation and Seating

Every director naturally works to build a capable group of symphonic proportions. But there is nothing magic in mere figures. Younger and weaker players in one section will not balance older and stronger players in another section. So the idea is to adjust the instrumentation to achieve balance between strings and winds, and between the upper and lower voices.

Following are typical proportions of school orchestras:

	SYMPHONETTE	STANDARD	SYMPHONIC
flute	2	2	2
piccolo-flute		1	1
oboe	1	2	2
English horn			1
clarinet	2	2	2
bass clarinet			1
bassoon	1	2	2
French horn	2	4	4
trumpet	2	3	3
trombone	1	3	3
tuba			1
percussion	1	2	3
harp			1
first violin	4	10	16
second violin	4	8	14
viola	2	6	10
cello	2	6	8
bass	1	4	6
	25	55	80

Plan A

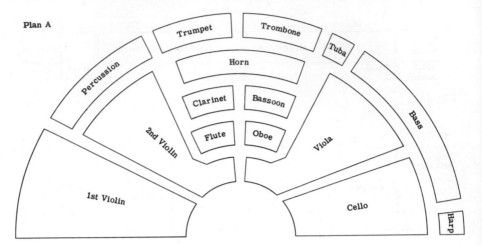

Fig. 4-5a.

Plan B

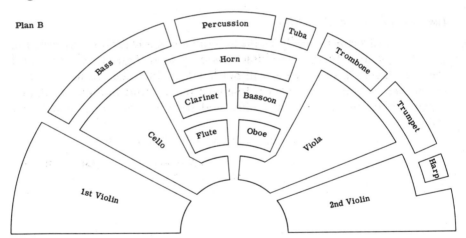

Fig. 4-5b.

Plan C

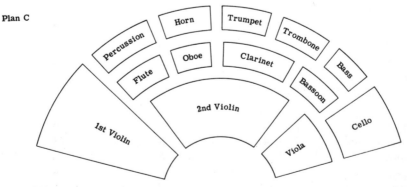

Fig. 4-5c.

Typical seating arrangements for these groups are shown in Fig. 4-5a, 4-5b, and 4-5c.

Plans A and B (Fig. 4-5a and 4-5b) are favorite seating patterns for standard and symphonic size orchestras. Plan A probably gives better tonal contrast and precision in the strings. Plan B is usually favored if the lower strings are few or weak, for their tone is directed more favorably toward the listener. Plan C (Fig. 4-5c) can be adapted for three or four rows of players, and some variation of it is usually successful with groups of twenty-five to fifty players.

It is often wise to distribute the better players among the string section as is shown in Fig. 4-6 (numbered according to advancement).

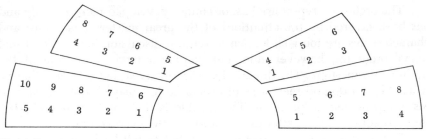

Fig. 4-6.

This tends to help the precision and unity of the group, looks better from the audience (because the better players are exposed), keeps up the strength during page turns, gives the more difficult *divisi* parts to the right players, and helps the weaker players to develop (by pairing them with the better players).

Other directors prefer to rotate the posts of responsibility by reshuffling the seating two or three times a year. Still others allow the seating to adjust by means of the challenge system, whereby the players may try out against one another on specified passages.

Some rotation should occur between violin sections. In general, violinists enter the second violin section and are switched to first as they acquire the needed velocity and facility in higher positions. Later, they may be switched back to provide section stability.

Unless the viola section is fully manned, certain violinists (especially those who take their music rather seriously) should be given a tour of duty in this section. The practicability of this sort of doubling between cello and bass is also becoming recognized.

LITERATURE

Taken collectively, all the numbers played by a school band or orchestra over the years actually constitute the textbook for the course. The outcomes can extend no further than the artistic problems inherent in the music that is attempted. The critical role of the director in making this selection is obvious, and any persistent gap or weakness in the chosen repertoire will be mirrored in his players.

The literature for band and orchestra is somewhat overlapping in type and function. The same forms (marches, overtures, suites, symphonies, and so on) are scored for either combination of instruments. Many composers have written for both groups and some works written for the one have later been transcribed or arranged for the other. Yet, the fact that the two ensembles are really unique has resulted in a gradual divergence of repertoire so that today neither group can totally fulfill the function of the large instrumental ensemble alone.

The orchestral repertoire has, of course, developed more steadily and has been favored by the attentions of the great masters (its extent and characteristics are too well known to require discussion here). The usual school orchestra, however, does not employ a large proportion of the traditional repertoire. The director has recordings of master works that he would like to do and memories of others he has played, but knows that his group cannot tackle them. The trouble is that most great orchestral music is suited to the better groups and not the average ones.

In this situation, the director is tempted to fall back upon the commercial grade of literature, which is replete with simplified arrangements of the classics and new compositions of unknown merit. If, in addition, he restricts his choice to examples with supposed audience appeal, the director will make certain that his players suffer from musical malnutrition.

Because of the evolving function and instrumentation of the band, the director faces an even more perplexing problem in choosing its literature. The chief categories follow.

(1) Early original band material, including the standard marches by Sousa, King, *et al;* the cornet and trombone solos (polka style); and a few early works for winds by Gabrieli, Mozart, Berlioz, Mendelssohn, and other masters.[2] This literature can be used sparingly with good effect.

(2) "Park band" literature (well known to older generations), including the von Suppé overtures, operatic medleys, and the like. This material is chiefly usable for junior high school groups and outdoor pop concerts.

(3) Transcriptions of orchestral masterpieces, ranging from relatively straightforward Baroque and Classical material to complex late Romantic and Twentieth century compositions. Much of this literature is entirely unsuitable and formerly was used only because the supply of original works for band was so limited. If chosen with great care, some may still be used, but generally these are the numbers of a more sustained, uncom-

---

[2] See the discussion by Richard Franko Goldman, *The Wind Band: Its Literature and Techniques* (Boston: Allyn and Bacon, Inc., 1961), pp. 205-24.

plicated texture, without characteristic string passages. The tonal conception of organ works usually transcribes beautifully for band, since both are basically wind instruments. Most transcriptions of Bach, Mendelssohn, Franck, and the modern masters of the organ are quite successful and this literature should be extended.

(4) Adaptations of popular hits, Latin numbers, and Broadway show music. Such material can be used sparingly for its educational value and audience appeal, but the concert band is not especially suited to these styles.

(5) Educational music, which includes music of easy and medium grades, usually written by less distinguished composers to meet the technical requirements of school bands. Unfortunately, most of this music has little expressive message, which fact is recognized by players and audience alike. So, it is here today and gone tomorrow like much popular music. By necessity, some of this material must at present be employed for junior groups.

(6) Serious, original band music of contemporary composers. This list has widened considerably since 1940 and as still newer works are added and these all become more familiar, a great deal of the band director's problem will be solved. Meanwhile, much of this literature is too avantgarde, dissonant, and difficult for the average school band. Care must be exercised in choosing among these works.

In spite of the problems we have outlined, more and better music is available today than ever before. Enough usable material can be found for any school band or orchestra if the necessary effort is made, and if proper criteria are kept well in mind.

Each number chosen should have intrinsic merit. This does not mean that the choice is limited to Bach, Beethoven, and Brahms, for many good pieces are quite simple and light. But it does mean that there must be something musical, something fresh and original about the music that captures the imagination. The trite and banal must be avoided in favor of that which possesses natural style and feeling.

The director must be the judge of the music's worth, supported by his observation of the students' off-hand comments and expressions. After all, the director must appreciate a piece of music if he is to do a decent job of interpretation and carry its expressive qualities to the students. The director must guard against using numbers that he feels he *ought* to like but really doesn't, since this merely creates a good looking program on paper.

By and large, one expects to find the better numbers written by recognized composers. New composers, of course, must have their chance, but the average school group is not the most likely agency to give premiere performances.

Similarly, arrangements and transcriptions are seldom as effective as the original scores. After all, new versions are only suggested by the merits of the original. It is wise, therefore, to view the original score before buying an arrangement. In many cases, the arrangement is chosen because it has been carefully simplified without destroying too much of the original effect. The younger and weaker the band or orchestra, the more it must rely upon arrangements and/or new works especially written with its limitations in mind.

Works should be representative of the principal forms and idioms. A school band should avoid specializing in any era or style in favor of a mixed diet. Standard marches, serious contemporary numbers, light popular style tunes, and suitable works from the Classical and Romantic eras should all find a place in the year's repertoire. Orchestral materials should likewise include a fair balance of Eighteenth, Nineteenth, and Twentieth century works. Dissonant idioms should be neither avoided nor overemphasized. The student is helped, in this way, to achieve the desired acquaintance with the range of musical literature and a good basis for the development of taste. Furthermore, the various sections are given their rightful opportunity to meet the special techniques and responsibilities required of band and orchestra players.

To put it more concretely, if the orchestra is to participate in a Broadway musical, scheduled for the spring, this should be balanced by a diet of more traditional styles during the fall and winter. A planned performance of the *Messiah* at Easter would tend to rule out Bach at Christmastime in favor of some Tschaikovsky, Copland, and Leroy Anderson. The band's repertoire for the year similarly contrasts music fitted to marching season with traditional contest type numbers and other more piquant, experimental works.

All the music that is chosen should be suited to the ability of the players. This means skillful selection to challenge the players without overextending them. It also means careful attention to the particular strengths and weaknesses of the group so that the pieces chosen will demand more of the better players. This cannot be accomplished consistently, but the director who knows his literature can do much, in this way, to increase the educational impact of his effort and the effectiveness of his programs.

Usually if a number can be read with no trouble, it is too easy, and if the group bogs down every few bars, then it is too difficult. Selections with the most educative possibilities are those that can be read with some raggedness and stops, and the director senses that he can retain the group's interest for the period necessary to clear up the notes and polish the work.

The process of choosing promising literature is constant. One remembers numbers he has played or conducted in earlier years; he attends concerts of other school groups and special sight reading clinics; he notes numbers heard on radio and television; he checks catalogs and contest listings, and orders music on approval. Some can evaluate unfamiliar numbers by viewing the scores. However, others require aural acquaintance that can be provided only at the piano, or by recording, and finally, from a reading by the ensemble itself.

It is a wise practice to retain concert programs and to keep a notebook, listing every promising number brought to one's attention. Each work should be catalogued by composer, title, and publisher, and with some estimate of length and relative difficulty.

To sum up, the director must choose music for the welfare of the players, not the audience. He is naturally aware of a number's suitability for the coming concert or contest, but he does not make his decision entirely on this basis. Public performance only provides an excuse to rehearse. The audience reaction is incidental, although it is well known that a poor performance and critical reception can wreck the potential of any group. The point is, that a good performance will almost automatically follow twenty or thirty hours of rehearsal if the music is suited to the needs of the students, and if they have learned all they can from it.

DEVELOPMENT OF THE PLAYERS

The function of the school band and orchestra is to extend the musicianship of its members to the highest degree consonant with the general purposes of schooling. The shape of this effort has just been outlined, but it is clear that specific steps must be taken to actually produce better musicianship. Every player must develop surer command of his instrument and its possibilities while, at the same time, the ensemble is welded into a more musically expressive unit. Such results are necessary to increase the general musical competence of students and are not achieved by merely playing music together.

Technical Progress

In too many instances, we have seen rather promising trumpet players who were completely ignorant of the technique of triple tonguing, cellists who shifted to every note beyond first position (and then immediately back again), and hornists who could not transpose. Such players, having passed beyond the beginning stage, have been wrongfully left to develop further on their own, while the director's energies are devoted entirely to the new crop of beginners. Following are some of the problems to be faced.

BOWINGS. Mark them sufficiently to set the pattern for any passage. Do not be afraid to change the printed bowings. Be aware that young players cannot manage as many notes per bow as more advanced ones. Also be aware that rapid string crossings on cello and bass are usually taken in a reverse direction from the violin and viola (because the string order is reversed). (See Fig. 4-7.)

Fig. 4-7.

FINGERINGS. Mark sparingly, but sufficiently to clear up any doubts as to the proper position. Be aware that each student goes through a certain evolution in acquiring the advanced fingering technique so that the same fingering is not always applicable to all the players. Thumb position should be taught to cellists and bassists when the need arises. Chromatic fingerings should be practiced by all.

Neither should the teacher overlook the alternate fingerings, slide positions, and trill fingerings for the brass and woodwinds. A good set of wall charts for fingerings is a great help.

DOUBLE STOPS AND CHORDS. In the early stages, it is well to instruct the players to play double stops and chords *divisi*. As the players advance, the director may work in more and more of the fingerings necessary to produce all the notes.

TRANSPOSITION. It may be necessary to prepare transposed parts for inexperienced trumpet and horn players according to the following formula.

TRUMPET	TRANSPOSITION	HORN
F to B flat	3½ steps up	
E to B flat	3 steps up	
E flat to B flat	2½ steps up	B flat to F
D to B flat	2 steps up	A to F
	1½ steps up	A flat to F
C to B flat	1 step up	G to F
A to B flat	½ step down	E to F
	1 step down	E flat to F
G to B flat	1½ steps down	D to F
	2½ steps down	C to F
	3½ steps down	B flat basso to F

Soon, it is possible to write the above formula on the music folders and merely mark certain key notes in difficult passages (by written notes or letter names). Finally, one is able to trust the players to do the transpositions independently.[3]

A similar process must occur when these instruments meet new clefs:

bassoon	(tenor and treble)
trombone	(tenor and alto)
viola	(treble)
cello	(tenor and treble)

VIBRATO. At the proper time, string players should be encouraged to develop a vibrato. All are not ready at the same time, but whenever a player achieves the necessary freedom and facility with the left hand, the proper method for vibrato can be explained and demonstrated, and he can be set to practicing the required drill. When the oscillation approaches six per second, he is asked to apply it in the music, first to the longer notes and then the shorter ones. At first, it may help to mark these longer notes *vib* as a reminder.

The woodwinds and brasses should also be encouraged to develop and use vibrato when appropriate. Flutes, oboes, bassoons, and saxophones use vibrato rather constantly (as string players do), but it is considered out of character for clarinets except in popular style playing. Some teachers favor a vibrato produced by the diaphragm or breath, while others prefer a lip vibrato. Vibrato tends to be more sparingly used on the brasses, being confined to melodic or solo passages, and hornists use little or none. It may be produced by the breath, the lip, or by a slight oscillation of the hand or trombone slide.

double tonguing

tuh   tuh kuh tuh   tuh kuh   tuh

triple tonguing

tuh tuh tuh kuh tuh   tuh tuh kuh tuh

Fig. 4-8.

tuh tuh kuh tuh kuh

tuh tuh tuh kuh tuh tuh kuh

Fig. 4-9.

[3] The player can learn to think the necessary interval above or below, or devise the necessary clef and key signature to produce the needed interval, or make the original transposition and then proceed from note to note by *melodic* interval.

TONGUING. Whenever the brasses and flutes meet parts requiring rapid tonguing, the technique for double and triple tonguing should be explained and demonstrated. A few simple exercises may be taught by rote, progressing from single figures (see Fig. 4-8) to double figures (see Fig. 4-9).

A continuous pattern may be achieved within a few weeks.[4] The serious player is then capable of applying the technique to any needed passage.

Even more important is the acquisition of single tonguing techniques appropriate to various types of passages. The brasses need the militaristic, marcato attack, the crisp staccato, and the smooth legato style. But they also need the symphonic style which can best be described as a powerful push, produced with more air and less decisive tongue, and when well done the effect can be compared to strong, well spaced organ chords.

SPECIAL EFFECTS. Some of the more common effects are explained and illustrated below and should be taught as the need arises.

(1) Natural harmonics are produced by lightly touching the string according to simple mathematical division of its length, which causes the string to vibrate in equal segments when bowed (see Fig. 4-10).

Fig. 4-10.

(2) Artificial harmonics, on the other hand, are produced by using one finger to stop the string and another to secure the harmonic (see Fig. 4-11).

Fig. 4-11.

(3) Flutter tongue is produced on the flute and brasses by exerting air pressure against the tongue so that the tip flutters against the roof of the mouth.

(4) Stopped horn is produced by completely closing the bell of the horn with the right hand. The pitch will be a half step higher than fingered. The confusing thing is that some editions give the note already transposed, while others allow the hornist to make the transposition. The conductor must know in advance by studying his score.

---

[4] It must be recognized that a few authorities advocate different triple tonguing patterns: Tuh-kuh-tuh Tuh-kuh-tuh . . . and Tuh-kuh-tuh Kuh-tuh-kuh . . .

(5) Glissando is of course no great problem on the trombone or stringed instruments. On other instruments it is produced by partially depressed pistons or keys combined with well coordinated embouchure adjustment. The technique is so touchy, however, that many must substitute a rapid chromatic figure.

(6) Percussion effects are too numerous to mention in any detail. The successful director, however, is quite positive in determining and coaching the players on the proper effects. For example: (a) Cymbals are most often clashed together with a glancing, off center blow, and swung outward to face the audience. But they may be crushed together, clashed and then choked against the body, tapped lightly together near the edge, struck with a mallet, rolled continuously with tympani or snare sticks, or played with foot pedal and snare stick or brushes (in dance band fashion). (b) Bass drums, snare drums, tympani, and gongs are usually struck a glancing blow (off center), for best reverberation. But a blow to the center produces a dull thud, while strokes near the rim are softer and less reverberant. (c) The characteristic timbre of the snare drum is created by snares of metal or gut stretched across the drum head. The tomtom effect is produced when the snares are released from contact with the drum head, and still different sounds are produced by muffling or choking the drum head with hand or cloth. Even further variation is made possible by striking the drum head with padded tympani sticks or only with the hands (instead of employing the standard wooden sticks). The explosive rim shot results when drum head and rim are struck simultaneously.

This is enough to give the idea. There are standard techniques and several variations, for every percussion instrument, which should be learned by the director and passed on to his players.

INSTRUMENT CARE AND REPAIR. The rudimentary knowledge acquired by the player at the beginning level must be gradually extended. Following are some basic procedures.

(1) Provide a set of tools, supplies, and repair bench.
(2) Post mimeographed materials explaining the basic techniques.
(3) Have manuals available on reed making and repairs.
(4) Conduct special classes, especially in summer, arranging for professional assistance as necessary.
(5) Encourage those students who become more expert to pass on their skills to incoming players.

This topic is discussed in more detail in Chapter 7.

Musical Finesse

We have just discussed several technical matters to be cared for in the unfolding development of the players. But much more is at stake in fostering the musical qualities which are a reflection of the ultimate tastes and skills we seek. These include rhythmic and tonal accuracy, intonation, quality of tone, dynamic balance, style, and ensemble. These items are goals of every rehearsal, but in a larger sense they depend upon long term planning.

RHYTHMIC AND TONAL ACCURACY. The ability to play the right notes at the right times is a product of habits and conceptions developed through long experience. The player is first presented with very simple tonal combinations and is coached in triggering the proper muscular responses to reproduce those combinations. Since each new tonal pattern is closely related to familiar ones, the player is more and more able to conceive what he must do and whether he has, in fact, done it. This is possible by virtue of the feedback of the patterns to the player's ear and brain.

Eventually, the process can become so automatic that the player seems to play almost without thought. What happens, of course, is that such a player has command of basic patterns and his concentration is so unconscious, that the rendition is comparatively effortless. It is in this hope that we cause students to practice scales and études and to do much sight reading.

On the other hand, intensive practice without definitive understanding of the proper results is absolutely miseducative. Fortunately, our western system of harmony and notation has evolved in a conventional fashion, providing many factors around which to organize our playing responses. For example, we have a stable twelve tone scale, bar lines and specific note values, more or less regular phrase lengths, and more or less systematic chordal formations. The trick is to train the player to relate the musical patterns he encounters to these constant factors.

One with faulty rhythm is not relating the time values to the beat. First of all, he must establish the tempo and pulse—a foot tap is generally found useful to help provide a sense of timed duration. Then the player must be led to see *within* the beat, i.e., to conceive the subdivisions and intricate combinations of subdivision which carry him forward to the next beat. Each beat must be *numbered* in his mind. It is not simply *beat, beat, beat,* but an inexorable *one, two, three.* Only in this way can the player rectify his mistakes en route.

There are several ordinary procedures to help in this task. One is the foot tap (which we have just mentioned), another is counting aloud (both beats and subdivisions), and still another is to introduce new rhythms by equivalent notation, which gives insight into the mathematical division.

But the basic tools to rhythmic accuracy are simply, first, slow practice and second, repetition. Nearly any rhythmic problem can be solved, if it is first attacked at a slow enough tempo so the basic relationships can be pondered and executed safely, and then the tempo can be stepped up. If, in addition, the figure is presented over and over in a changing musical

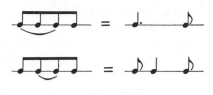

Fig. 4-12.

context, the player will secure full command *unless he is too distracted by many other problems.*

Of course, we have been speaking about establishing stable rhythmic responses. Subtle and deliberate alterations in tempo for expressive purposes is another topic—part of the art of interpretation.

Getting the right notes is a closely related problem but it depends largely upon hearing the interval in advance and controlling the movements to produce it. This is where scales, arpeggios, and appropriate études or studies are so helpful. Systematic practice on these can give the player the needed aural and mechanical facility.

INTONATION. Accurate pitch or intonation is a refinement of the right notes. That is, one may get the right notes but be somewhat off pitch. Good intonation is essentially a matter of finer perception and control of intervals.

Musicians realize that pitch is not absolutely constant. The proper frequency of a tone varies according to the key and degree of the scale. Even A 440 is not so constant as many believe. Complications arise when instruments such as the strings and trombone (which can be played in true temperament) are mixed with the other brasses and woodwinds (which are essentially tuned to favor certain keys), with the piano (which is tuned to equal temperament), and with percussion instruments of indeterminate pitch. The picture is even more disturbed by the addition of vibrato and human error.

Fortunately, we are saved by the sense of tonality. We listen to the movement of the bass line and the related melodic and harmonic formations to acquire a sense of *prevailing* pitch to which we can then relate our own part. Granted a well tuned instrument, the one who plays noticeably out of tune is simply lost, i.e., he has no stable point of reference.

Some individuals may possibly be found who possess an inherently poor sense of pitch. But by and large, the fault stems from lack of musical experience, lack of attention, or both. The teacher's job is to provide the experience and secure the attention.

In this connection, practice of simple chord progressions and chorales can be a great help, for they highlight the sense of tonality. Pitch impurities, which are bound to occur, will merely cause the player's sense of pure intonation to become further dulled, however, unless there is a process of correction to prove the beauty of pure intonation. By words and signals, the director points out the worst offenders and gradually achieves habitual attention to the adjustment of pitch. The goal is *self-correction.*

TONE QUALITY. A beautiful tone is closely related to purity of intonation, depending as it does on a good quality instrument, an adequate conception of tonal beauty, and fine control of the mechanism of tone production.

First, the teacher must make sure of the quality of the players' equipment and then he must attempt to establish or improve their concept of a good tone. It is for this reason that teachers despair of the shallow, flimsy tone so often exhibited in popular and commercial music. To combat this, one must try to provide good recordings with rich, warm tone for the students to hear, to encourage concert attendance, to demonstrate personally, and to point up any good examples one can find in the group (avoiding odious comparisons). Even further, the teacher must note changes in an individual's tone, complimenting him on the improvement or warning him of deterioration.

However, it is necessary to provide specific measures for the player to try. The string player's bowing technique and the wind player's breathing, tonguing, and embouchure should be constantly under observation, and remedial measures should be suggested and checked.

Overall tone quality of a group is also a matter of instrumentation and dynamics. If these are properly adjusted, the players will tend to conform to the norm.

DYNAMIC BALANCE. Like pitch, tone quality, and most things musical, dynamics are relative. We have judged contestants who have played every note and observed every dynamic and tempo marking to such perfection that the performance was starved of all natural feeling. Needless to say, the performers were probably quite perplexed at the judge's comments. But utter disregard of dynamic markings and the inability to handle the changes artistically is a much more common sin.

The first requirement is that students be trained to produce a real pianissimo and fortissimo. Many seem to have very little dynamic elasticity. Some good can be done by simply practicing long crescendos and decrescendos in unison, to develop breath control, and a sense of gradation. Dynamic level as applied to music is largely a matter of habit, which may need considerable effort to change.

A good trick is to take a tone, pianissimo, with one player (or a section) that can do it properly, and then add players or sections one by one—still maintaining a relative pianissimo. With this method, the careless students are easily spotted, and they also may perceive how they are harming the ensemble. The same procedure may be followed at piano, mezzo forté, forté, and fortissimo, which helps define these levels for the players in very concrete terms.

Of course, the real test of dynamics is in achieving balance within and between sections. It must be remembered that important parts (melodies, special figures, and moving parts) need a slight emphasis in relation to subsidiary parts. On the other hand, full and balanced chords within sections must be maintained. It is for this reason that the dynamics indicated by the composer or arranger must be adjusted to a considerable extent. That is, the total *effect* of a pianissimo should be very soft, even though certain individuals may need to play more strongly than others. Such changes should be marked by the players as the director indicates, but gradually the process should be accomplished more by skilled conducting and the good taste of the players.

Indeed, the natural prominence of certain notes and the dynamic shading of phrases can hardly be indicated in notation. This phase of dynamics is intimately connected with style.

STYLE AND INTERPRETATION. Music style is that form of presentation which makes a performance seem in or out of focus. Technically, style is a matter of subtle differences in accent and duration, in dynamic shading, nuance, intensity of vibrato, speed of glissando, and the like. These are matters of choice, and are often unconsciously executed. They are the chief carriers of expressive meaning in music. Since it is such a crucial matter, artists are at great pains to produce an authentic and moving style in their performances. That the results vary considerably, can be proved by listening to recordings of the same work by different artists.

Yet there are certain conventions to be taught. Composer, medium, tempo, and inherent qualities in the music tend to dictate the general approach. At least we have been conditioned to believe this. For instance, the Classical masters are generally supposed to be played with more restraint than the Romantics; when playing Haydn or Mozart, therefore, one neither accents so heavily, nor accomplishes such obvious rubatos, and is careful to shift positions more quickly and cleanly. On the other hand, jazz and modern popular styles are characterized by a certain deliberate laxness and exaggeration.

Certain illustrations may make this clearer.

(1) In any passage, the longer tones tend to receive more stress than the shorter ones, while short notes are generally treated as auxiliary notes (see Fig. 4-13). Unless directed otherwise by composer or conductor,

Fig. 4-13.

therefore, the advanced player almost automatically lightens up on the sixteenth notes.

(2) Unless marked to the contrary, high notes tend to be stressed and ascending passages acquire a natural crescendo. This is the *natural* thing to do, because more effort is required, and it has become conventional. It is indeed difficult to achieve a decrescendo in passages moving upward to a high note.

(3) Unslurred notes in passages of angular (skipping) or military character tend to be spaced apart, or detached. Again, this convention has its origin in the need for time to change embouchure or position, and the need for such notes to *speak*.

We hasten to add that numerous exceptions are obvious. The composer may wish to bring a certain figure *through* the ensemble that would otherwise be blurred, so he marks accents on the short notes to be sure it is done (see Fig. 4-14). But the conductor or player may do this anyway,

Fig. 4-14.

because he senses that this needs to be done.

We do not mean to imply that everything that seems natural is right. The natural desire to gain speed on crescendos, to accent the beats in rapid passages, and to push the tied note are normally to be resisted.

So, the director needs to be wise in establishing in his players a distinction between *normal* style and exceptions. He needs to teach them that syncopes are usually played as in Fig. 4-15, but in popular style music

Fig. 4-15.

they are played approximately as shown in Fig. 4-16. In fact, most popular

Fig. 4-16.

music is characterized by legato style and stress remains on the beat. In the case of series of eighths, this gives almost the effect of six-eight meter (see Fig. 4-17).

Fig. 4-17.

The student also needs to develop true march style which is characterized by slight spacing between notes (see Fig. 4-18) and to acquire the

Fig. 4-18.

subtle difference in execution of afterbeats as between regular waltz and
Viennese style (see Fig. 4-19).

Fig. 4-19.

Stylistic considerations are a major factor in the art of interpretation.
A conductor interprets a number in terms of its thematic development,
tempos, dynamic and tonal qualities, and style inherent to such a setting.
Interpretation is thus the working out of the total concept of a piece of
music. We shall discuss this in the following chapter as a phase of the
conducting-rehearsal situation.

ENSEMBLE. Similarly, ensemble is not so much a specific goal as it is
the result of success in achieving the matters we have been discussing.
That is, it is the product of rhythmic and tonal accuracy, good intonation
and tone quality, dynamic balance, and successful style, all achieved in
terms of a common conception. A musical group with good ensemble has
the same effect of coordinated complexity as the playing of a fine organist.

No school group can hope to approach the musical finesse of our
better professional organizations. The immaturity of the players, the lack
of rehearsal time, and the turnover of membership will not allow it. This
is by no means tragic if the quest is stimulating to the players and truly
helps them to understand and appreciate the music. Whether a group
sounds better or worse does not necessarily determine its educational impact. It is the process by which they became as good as they are. This
forms the topic of the next chapter.

SUMMARY

The vast popularity of bands rests largely upon the entertainment value
and the relative ease of learning to play the instruments. Conversely, little op-

portunity exists for a graduate to be a performing bandsman. The chief function of such instruction must be the development of general musicianship.

The instrumental classes generally evolve into junior bands, and finally the school concert band. Good results depend upon carefully guiding the individual players to the necessary habits of mature musicianship.

Band instrumentation is still evolving from the "street" to the concert conception. This generally means more woodwinds, and increasing emphasis on the highest and lowest pitched instruments. The desired sound is either rich and woody, or brilliant (or some happy combination of the two) but not so brassy and thick as formerly. Seating plans have evolved to meet these conceptions.

The band literature has greatly expanded in recent years but great care is still required to achieve a practical, balanced repertoire.

Professionally, the qualified orchestral musician has a bright future, but the orchestra is not so well established in the schools as the band. Administrative and instructional continuity is imperative to the development of orchestras.

The orchestra is basically conceived as a string choir with added winds and percussion. This causes some problems in recruitment, scheduling, and rehearsal planning. Good literature of simple and medium difficulty is comparatively scarce.

The technical progress of wind, percussion, and string players does not occur without careful attention. Players must be instructed in the finer points of bowing, fingering, tonguing, vibrato, transposition, and special effects of various sorts. Also, the players must gradually learn to assume responsibility for the care and minor adjustment of their instruments. Even more important, the musical finesse of the players must be fostered through attention to tonal and rhythmic accuracy, intonation, tone quality, balance, style, and good ensemble habits. Public performance is at once the motivation and the means of evaluating all of this development.

QUESTIONS FOR DISCUSSION

1. Describe the unique qualities of the school band program as contrasted with the orchestra. What are the common factors?

2. What are the basic concepts of the band sound and how are these achieved?

3. What are the problems in selecting repertoire for either organization?

4. Describe some of the technical matters to be taught. How do these relate to the musical expression of the group? What qualities of performance are to be sought?

SELECTED REFERENCES

Band and Orchestra Handbook. Elkhart, Indiana: Pan-American Band Instruments, 1951.

Band Music Guide. Evanston, Illinois: The Instrumentalist Co., 1961.

FENNELL, FREDERICK, *Time and the Winds.* Kenosha, Wisconsin: G. LeBlanc Corporation, 1954.

GOLDMAN, RICHARD FRANKO, *The Wind Band: Its Literature and Techniques.* Boston: Allyn and Bacon, Inc., 1961.

List of Contemporary String Music, 2nd ed. Urbana, Illinois: American String Teachers Association.

Moore, E. C., *The Band Book*. Kenosha, Wisconsin: G. LeBlanc Corporation, 1954.

NIMAC Selection Committee, *Selective Music Lists for Chorus, Orchestra, Band*. Washington, D. C.: Music Educators National Conference, 1962 and alternate years.

Prescott, Gerald R. and Lawrence W. Chidester, *Getting Results with School Bands*. Minneapolis: Schmitt, Hall and McCreary Company, and New York: Carl Fischer, Inc., 1938.

CHAPTER 5

Rehearsal Management

The principal point of contact between the instrumental music teacher and his pupils is ordinarily in rehearsal. It is by no means the entire story of teaching, but it is the keystone. The director recruits his beginners, helps secure the instruments, builds their basic playing techniques, sets up teaching schedules, and selects musical literature so he may assemble the players and teach them (through playing), in rehearsal. All other activities—individual lessons and conferences, sectional rehearsals, small ensembles, public appearances, and so on—are more or less coordinated with the regular group rehearsal.

Unless the director does a good job in rehearsal, therefore, the entire program will falter. The usual traps include, first, pursuit of false objectives, second, weakness in preparation, third, unfortunate approach to the players, and fourth, tendency to waste time. The director must try at all costs to use his rehearsal time (so dearly won) in the most efficient and effective way to achieve his purposes. His true goal, as always, is the musical welfare of the individual players. This means that every action must be calculated to improve the player's musical understanding and insight. The chosen literature is to be mastered to the point where its musical values and subtleties are revealed to the players. Impending public performance is an incentive in this process but its immediate result is *not* the measure of success.

Likewise, teaching methods must be judged by the needs of the students. If forbearance produces only laxness, it must be abandoned, and if firmness produces only sullen compliance, it must be relaxed or enlivened with purpose and humor.

The previous chapter has dealt with the special organization and function of school bands and orchestras, including their literature and the technical and musical results to be sought. This chapter will cover the operational phase of rehearsal—rehearsal preparation, rehearsal activity, and student management. By necessity, material pertaining to the fields of conducting, orchestration, and methodology must be included, but only as specifically related to our topic.

REHEARSAL PLANNING

Preparation for rehearsals of band or orchestra begins with score study. This is not necessarily intensive, but extends over a long period of time. That is, one studies the score, as necessary, before he selects the number for his group, and then ordinarily, he does some more detailed analysis before he puts out the parts, while tentatively determining tempos and identifying important passages and problems that are likely to occur. If the number is to be seriously attacked after the first reading, he really gets down to business, transposing parts as needed, readjusting his tempos and dynamics, rebowing and fingering parts, determining stylistic treatment, and identifying the passages which will need especially intensive rehearsal. This process continues from rehearsal to rehearsal as new weaknesses are revealed and more subtle judgment is required. As the performance nears (when he cannot stop the group to explain and correct) the director begins to study the score more with an eye to his own role with the baton.

So, score study is not a *one shot* affair. It may not always be so formidable as we seem to make it, since it depends upon the complexity of the score and the proficiency of the group. But one thing is certain, no rendition of a work can ever exceed the conductor's conception of it.

Musical Scores

There are essentially two types of score provided with musical works—the full score and a condensed or reduced version. The full score includes all the players' parts exactly as written. Trumpets are in B flat and horns in F, or whatever keys are chosen by the composer. However, parts having long rests are often omitted from the score to save page space and then returned to the score at the next entrance. Parts are arranged on each page (one staff for each part) according to a traditional pattern—woodwinds at the top, then the brasses, the percussion and keyboard instruments, and finally the strings.

The pocket score (or miniature score) is simply a full score reduced in size for economy and convenience in study. The notation is often too small for easy use in rehearsal.

Many compositions, particularly those of easier grade, are published with both full and condensed scores, or condensed score alone. The condensed score is really an expanded piano score. All parts are written in concert pitch and combined on three or four staves, and important entrances are cued. But the exact distribution of parts within a section and the doubling of octaves, etc., must be inferred by the reader. Also, the exit of parts is not clearly defined.

The condensed score is easier to follow. That is, the director's eye can comprehend at a glance the total development of the melody and supporting parts, and he can easily compare the sounds being produced with the notation in concert pitch. Since more music can be included on the page, the director is less occupied with keeping his place and turning pages, and therefore can direct more attention to his players.

Where both kinds of score are available, therefore, some directors prefer to use the full score in early rehearsals, until they are sure of the players' accuracy, and then switch to the condensed score as a less distracting prompting device.

A compromise between the full score and condensed score is produced by reduced, compact, and compressed scores. In essence, these attempt to include all the parts but to combine them logically on fewer staves.

Transposition

In interpreting any score, the director cannot escape the necessity for thorough facility in transposition. With the full score, he must be able to translate the parts into concert pitch for aural purposes, while if the score is in concert pitch, he needs to know what notes the players are charged to execute. For convenience, this matter is summarized graphically below.

A INSTRUMENTS

written
sounding a minor 3rd lower   A clarinet

F INSTRUMENTS

written   English horn
sounding a perfect 5th lower   French horn
                                    basset horn

Eb INSTRUMENTS

sounding a minor 3rd higher   Eb clarinet
written
                                    Eb cornet

Fig. 5-1.

written
sounding a major 6th lower

alto clarinet

alto saxophone

alto horn

 written

sounding an octave and
a major 6th lower

E♭ contra-alto clarinet

baritone saxophone

D♭ INSTRUMENTS

 sounding a minor 9th higher   D♭ piccolo

written

C INSTRUMENTS

 sounding as written

flute, oboe, bassoon

trombone and baritone in bass clef

tubas (E♭ and BB♭)

tympani, xylophone

piano, harp

violin, viola, cello

sounding an octave higher

written

C piccolo

bells

celeste

written

sounding an octave lower

contrabassoon

string bass

B♭ INSTRUMENTS

written
sounding a step lower

clarinet, soprano saxophone

trumpet, cornet fluegelhorn

written

sounding an octave and
a step lower

bass clarinet

tenor saxophone

trombone and baritone
treble clef

Fig. 5-1 (cont.).

written

bass saxophone

sounding 2 octaves and   BB♭ contrabass clarinet
a step lower

Fig. 5-1 (cont.).

To make the picture more complicated, horn, trumpet, and even clarinet parts are occasionally written in other keys (which point was noted in the previous chapter). The basic rules to remember are:

1) The *player* transposes the interval between the key of his instrument and the key named (e.g., F horn to D horn = 1½ steps down).

2) The *director* thinks in terms of transposition from concert pitch (e.g., D horn sounds a minor seventh lower than written).

Such knowledge of transposition is imperative if the director is to be able to analyze chords and mistakes, and to make corrections on the spot. It is also needed in arranging for substitution of parts, or transposed manuscripts where the instrumentation is incomplete, or when certain passages must be simplified for inexperienced players.

Interpretation

Every experienced conductor knows that the selection of a proper tempo and the subtle bending of tempo requires critical judgment. Not only must he know how to interpret the marked tempos, but also how to hold tempos and when to deviate from them, and how to faithfully retain these concepts in performance.

The young director should practice selecting various tempos and estimating the timing against the second hand of his watch. That is, he learns to space fifteen counts to occupy precisely a quarter of a minute (for a metronomic marking of sixty), then twenty beats in the same period (for a marking of eighty), and so on. When the metronome marking is given on the score, such training should guarantee accuracy at sight (within three or four percent). Even at the performance, if the director becomes doubtful of the precise speed that he rehearsed, the marking will serve to steady him. The director, so trained, can also determine the exact tempos he wishes to assign to more general markings such as *allegretto* and *vivace,* or to what degree he wishes to change the marked tempo—say from sixty to sixty-eight.

The exact determination of tempo, of course, depends upon a composite of first, the composer's recommendations, second, any traditions established by famous conductors (one must check recordings), third, the capabilities of the group, and fourth, the inherent tempo dictated by the style and texture of the music as interpreted by the director himself. To put it plainly, the conductor should trust himself most, *if* he has taken pains to consult the other authorities as well.

So, noting the marked tempo and knowing what Bernstein or Szell do, the director should hum the melody and imagine the movement of parts at a certain tempo. Does it get a *little* frantic here to bring out the rapid chord changes? Or a bit slow for natural phrasing? How would it feel if one were actually playing the trumpet part or the bass part? After adjusting the tempo to feel just right, the director should check this metronomically and so mark the score. He may later change his mind, of course.

It should be noted that the trend in professional circles is toward more and more rapid tempos. This is possibly due to improvements in instruments and playing techniques and/or a modern respect for brilliance and sheer proficiency. On the other hand, school groups often play at much reduced tempos in order to achieve greater tonal and rhythmic accuracy. Either extreme should be avoided. The tempo should be what the conductor feels is inherently right.

But one must guard against rigid tempos, too. Only music of certain types (marches and dances) are properly performed in strict tempo, and even these are often to be bent slightly here and there, for expressive purposes. Most tempos should be more or less plastic. Again, the director consults the score markings and recordings, but he must interpret these things to suit his ideas of the music. The more drastic changes may be explained or demonstrated to the players, but the subtler ones are accomplished with the baton.

Other elements in interpretation include dynamics, balance, and style—which cover all the factors of relative stress, duration, tone quality, phrasing, nuance, and the like. So the director must search the score for the principal melodies and motives, and their relation to the supporting parts. What is the appropriate dynamic level here, here, and here? Which part must come out at this point? How would one play this or that tune to secure just the right character? Would one naturally breathe here? Or there? Such concepts must be clear in the director's mind before the first rehearsal, if he is to avoid being conditioned by haphazard reading of the parts.

Marking the Score

As part of the process of determining interpretation, the conductor is well advised to mark his score with colored pencil before the first rehearsal and later, as additional points come to mind. In the stress of the moment, it is easy to miss a repeat, a time change, or an important cue. Following are some of the matters to be considered.

(1) Any aspect of format that is likely to be confusing should be clearly marked. For example, lines may be drawn in the margins or across the page when a thinly scored passage is continued below, instead of

progressing normally to the next page. Some scores do not identify the separate parts after page one, and these will need to be marked on ensuing pages. D. S., D. C., and repeats may need to be circled. Sometimes rehearsal letters are missing and will have to be determined.

(2) Changes in meter and tempo (including ritards and accelerandos, holds, etc.) should be clearly marked.

(3) Any sudden or surprising changes in dynamics should be made clear.

(4) Important cues should be marked by abbreviation (fl., ob., tpt., hn., and so on).

(5) Any unfamiliar musical term should be looked up in a musical dictionary and the translation used in the score.

(6) The director's stylistic intentions should be indicated where necessary—by means of dots, legato dashes, accents, commas for breathing, bowing signs, and the like—to serve as a cue for the necessary gestures and explanations.

All such markings merely say, "Do what you will, but don't forget this." As such, they should not be so detailed as to become commonplace. The director knows which line his eye will be following at any moment, and he should make his notations in that vicinity.

Another sensible preliminary is to run through the score—at least any complex sections of it—while humming it to the appropriate conducting gestures. Essentially, this is one's rehearsal in communicating his predetermined subdivisions, meter changes, cutoffs, cues, dynamic and stylistic patterns, and so on.

For the reader's convenience, full score instrumentation and foreign equivalents are listed below:

ENGLISH	GERMAN	FRENCH	ITALIAN
Piccolo	Kleine Flöte	Petite Flute	Flauto piccolo
Flute	Flöte	Flute Gross	Flauto
Oboe	Hoboe	Hautbois	Oboe
English Horn	Althoboe	Cor Anglais	Corno Inglese
Clarinet	Klarinette	Clarinette	Clarinetto
Bass Clarinet	Bass Klarinette	Clarinette Basse	Clarinetto Basso
Bassoon	Fagott	Basson	Fagotto
Saxophone	Saxophon	Saxphone	Sassophone
French Horn	Horn (Ventilhorn)	Cor	Corno
Trumpet	Trumpete	Trompette	Tromba
Cornet	Cornett	Cornet-à-pistons	Cornetto
Trombone	Posaune	Trombone	Trombone
Tuba	Bass Tuba	Tuba Basse	Tuba Bassa
Tympani	Pauken	Timbales	Timpani

ENGLISH	GERMAN	FRENCH	ITALIAN
Snare Drum	Kleine Trommel	Tambour	Tamburo
Bass Drum	Grosse Trommel	Grosse Caisse	Gran Cassa
Cymbals	Becken	Cymbales	Piatti
Gong	Tam-tam	Tam-tam	Tam-tam
Triangle	Triangel	Triangle	Triangolo
Xylophone	Sylophon	Sylophon	Xilofone
Tambourine	Tambourin	Tambour de Basque	Tamburino
Castanets	Kastagnetten	Castagnettes	Castagnett
Chimes	Glocken	Cloches	Campane
Bells	Glockenspiel	Carillon	Campanetta
Harp	Harfe	Harpe	Arpa
Violin	Violine	Violon	Violino
Viola	Bratsche	Viole (Alto)	Viola
Violoncello	Violoncell	Violoncelle	Violoncello
Double bass	Kontrabass	Contre-basse	Contrabasso

Marking the Parts

All parts should be checked to acquire greater familiarity with the problems to be faced by the players. In the wind parts, certain phrase markings, alterations in dynamics, etc., may need to be inserted, and needed simplifications, substitutions, or transpositions should be made. But the big job is with the string parts. Unless his section leaders are qualified to do the job, the director himself must mark the necessary bowings and any critical fingerings on one part for each section (first violin, second violin, viola, cello, and bass) and rely on the orchestra librarian to transfer them to the remaining parts. We need not explain this process here because only an experienced string player can hope to do the job properly, and, indeed, many of these fail to do equally well with both the upper and lower string parts. Six or eight bowing marks per page, and the shifts necessary to facilitate any high or awkward passages are usually enough to clarify the patterns. All markings should be large and clear, with the fingerings placed near the heads of the notes, where the player reads.

Rehearsal Follow-Up

Many directors do a good job of preparation for the first rehearsal but fail to follow through. In rehearsal, unexpected difficulties arise, which are attacked on the spot, and afterwards the director should review these matters, making notes on the score or on another paper, to guide him in the next session. Any new interpretative ideas should also be incorporated in the score markings.

Physical Arrangements

The physical and mechanical preparations for rehearsal are of much importance, but are obvious enough to require little discussion. The director should rely upon the custodial staff and upon his assistants, but *he will have to establish the routines and see that the tasks are properly handled.*

Lighting, heating, and ventilation conditions must be regularly observed and adjusted. These matters are treated in Chapter 7.

Before each rehearsal all music racks and chairs, percussion equipment, piano, harp, and so on, should be properly placed. If different groups use the same room (so that the rehearsal arrangement is disturbed), the seating plan must be charted or demonstrated for those who are responsible for setting up the equipment. Some directors go so far as to paint the seating plan on the floor, while others have used masking tape for this purpose.

With the assistance of the band or orchestra librarian, the parts to be played must be in the music folders, and these must be placed on the proper racks or in a large multiple rack where the players can secure them. Folders must be returned or collected after rehearsal.

To affix responsibility, a definite system for checking out music is usually necessary. This the player may do by initialing a wall chart, signing a list, leaving a note on the rack, etc. Generally it is wise to require that folders, not single parts, be checked out.

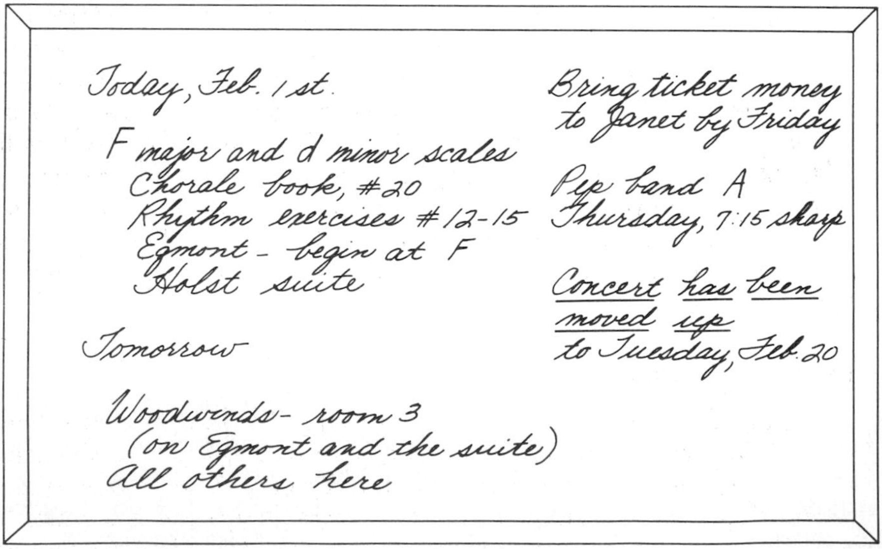

Today, Feb. 1st.

F major and d minor scales
Chorale book, #20
Rhythm exercises #12-15
Egmont – begin at F
Holst suite

Tomorrow

Woodwinds – room 3
(on Egmont and the suite)
All others here

Bring ticket money
to Janet by Friday

Pep band A
Thursday, 7:15 sharp

Concert has been
moved up
to Tuesday, Feb. 20

Fig. 5-2.

Announcements should be carefully planned. A fixed or portable chalkboard in front of the group is a great help. It serves to outline the sequence of the rehearsal and to make any special functions clear.

CONDUCTING REHEARSAL

Each rehearsal must be as musically exciting and productive of improvement as possible. To carry out this principle implies a certain routine combined with flexibility and variety.

Tuning

An electronic tuner should be employed if one is available; otherwise, the tuning bar, piano, oboe, etc., may be used to establish a standard. Many orchestra directors find it necessary to tune all the string instruments just before rehearsal, in which case it is advisable to work by bowed fifths and harmonics rather than pizzicato. As soon as possible, the players should be weaned to accomplish their own tuning. In any case, the first order of business when the players report to rehearsal should be to check and adjust their tuning (which makes a good first step in warming up). About midway in rehearsal another A or B flat should be sounded and a half minute allowed for readjustment of tuning. The director can aid in the process of finer adjustment by causing the group to sound various unisons, intervals, and triads.

Business Affairs

Roll should be taken after or during tuning, preferably by the director (by checking off empty seats). Only in this way will the director know each individual's record and the students will be aware that this is a matter of personal concern to him. But excuses and tardy slips, etc., should be handled by someone designated by the director. No extraneous factor should be allowed to distract the director's attention during active rehearsal. Any necessary verbal announcements should be made at the conclusion of tuning and roll check.

Warm Up and Technical Drill

Some groups spend too much time on conscientious coverage of several scales, chorales, and rhythmic drills; too often, these are done rather prosaically.

The warm up period is simply a chance to warm up the instruments and to reestablish the players' coordination without stress. It also offers the opportunity for some generalized instruction in areas which may not appear in the particular compositions at hand. If the material can be presented by rote, it will secure the players' undistracted attention and thus improve control and flexibility of the group. For example:

> "Today, let's do everything in A–flat major. Brass, let's hear your concert A–flat . . . Okay, now add the woodwinds . . . Flutes, up an octave . . . Oboes, you seem a bit sharp . . . That's better . . . Now, all together, up the scale as I direct (doing some notes longer, louder, decrescendo and crescendo, etc.) . . . and back . . . Too heavy in the trombones . . . Now, let's do it again this way (the director sings, to demonstrate the pattern).

Fig. 5-3.

Same rhythm, drums . . . Ready? Play! . . . Trumpets are rushing . . . and don't accent the beat so much . . . That's it . . . Now build the chord, like this

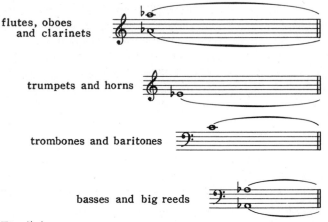

Fig. 5-4.

Okay . . . but attack together . . . Now . . . Watch the decrescendo . . . but keep up the pitch . . . All right, now get up the overture."

Such a process (so glibly outlined above) is of course not easily achieved. The players are gradually inducted into the necessary transpositions, the various chord spellings, their own place in the chord formations, and the various fingerings, rhythms, and other techniques involved in this process. This is precisely the kind of learning the director wishes to promote. To accomplish this, he establishes basic procedures, keeps varying and expanding the patterns, and always maintains a careful scrutiny of the players' rendition.

These rote learned drills can be supplemented by published chordal and rhythmic patterns.

The remainder of the rehearsal is devoted to the introduction of new literature and/or more or less detailed study of previously read works, usually for a planned performance.

New Material

Sight reading skill is one of the chief marks of musicianship. Unfortunately, it is often placed in a special category, whereas it actually involves the application of the complete range of musical knowledge and skill. So one should avoid sterile procedures—either running through numbers without halt or comment, or introducing them too carefully phrase by phrase and part by part.

All familiar literature was once new material to the players. The point of first acquaintance is critical, since very lasting impressions are formed. The inherent purposes of the director are: (1) to expose the players to a new and worthwhile composition and thus widen their comprehension of stylistic and formal matters; (2) to meet the specific technical and musical problems therein, thus sharpening the students' performing skills and understanding; (3) to determine the suitability of the work for possible programming; and (4) to awaken the students' interest in further study of the work.

In order to do all this, it is not enough to get through it. The trick is to dwell sufficiently on the difficulties and subtleties in order to provide tentative facility, while acquiring perspective through an overall view of the work. This is done by a process of trial and error, discussion, and repetition.

The procedure depends somewhat upon the complexity of the work in relation to the players' understanding and proficiency. Some numbers can be read through at an easy pace, followed by a few verbal comments and retrial of the weaker passages, and then read again at full tempo. Others require a more painstaking approach, with stops here and there as the ensemble breaks down, quick remedy of the gross errors, and a sort of rehearsal by overlapping, until the end is reached and a full reading can be attempted. Still other numbers may be spot rehearsed, i.e., the difficult passages or important themes are explained and "set" first, followed by a full reading.

The director is constantly comparing the actual rendition with his ideal rendition. Whenever any passage becomes seriously out of focus, he stops the group and attempts to make the needed correction. It may be either a matter of wrong notes, inaccurate rhythm, poor intonation or balance, inappropriate style, or simple lack of velocity. So the remedy will vary with the circumstances.

Expediency is a good rule in sight reading. One does what he can and leaves the rest to later, more systematic methods. He illustrates the proper execution of the phrase, prescribes the necessary modification in dynamics, supplies the necessary fingering, or tries the passage a couple of times at a slow pace, as the case may suggest.

Where such measures fail to secure results, the director has several choices. (1) If the ensemble is secure, he may ignore the problem for the time and proceed. (2) He may simplify the part temporarily, by instructing the player or players to leave out the figure that seems to be at the root of the difficulty. (3) He may ask another player or section to play the cue. (4) He may skip over the next section, or rehearsal letter, and proceed. (5) If several serious breakdowns have occurred, he may decide to abandon the number (although this is self defeating and should not occur if care was taken in the selection). But it is usually wise to avoid announcing this decision, or castigating the players. One can return, for a moment, to one of the more successfully played sections before turning to another number.

The whole process is a failure unless it stimulates the players' interest in the number and a desire to improve their performance of it. They must get their teeth into it but not enough to feel they have mastered it. The director should try to forestall any feeling of inadequacy on the one hand, or any false sense of security on the other. He must guard his own attitude very carefully, and give way to no undue pessimism or optimism.

Above all, the director should avoid dullness. He must approach the reading with imagination and enthusiasm. He must watch the players carefully and imagine his reactions if he were a player in the group. What is the *reason* for their inadequacies? Are they confused as to his intentions? If so, he must slow down and patiently clear up the misunderstanding. Are they impatient with his many stops and long discussions? If so, he must read on and do more talking with the baton. Are they becoming noisy and inattentive? Then he must sharply recall their attention to the music, change his pace, and proceed more forcefully.

Old Material

Much of what we have said about reading applies to later rehearsals as well, although, the process is much more detailed and systematic. The goal is to do as expressive and polished a job as possible, and thus increase the players' sensitivity to the music.

In order to do this, it is usually necessary to set up public appearances to provide the students and director with the incentive to sustain them through the period of intensive study. While this is fitting and proper, the director must not sacrifice sound educative principles on the altar of public appearance. He must diligently rehearse each programmed number to the point where further gains are becoming too costly of the time and energy that could be spent more profitably on other numbers. All that we say must be interpreted in this light.

Rehearsal implies correction, repetition, and further correction. Most things that the band or orchestra director selects for intensive rehearsal will demand several readings in detail, combined with individual practice and perhaps sectional rehearsals. So, after the original reading, the director reassesses his problems. How did the rendition fail to measure up to his conception? In what ways did the reading change his ideas? What are the likely remedies?

The sensible policy is to attack the big problems first, and gradually work down to the finer points. For, how can we deal with section balance, rubato, and phrasing until the notes and rhythms are generally correct? A great deal of time is often wasted in trying to put on the finishing touches first.

So, work is begun in individual lessons and/or sectionals to correct basic misunderstandings about the number and to achieve a degree of facility. The individual players are expected to learn their parts, starting always with the most difficult passages and crucial solos. These can be done at a slow tempo and gradually worked up to speed, since the original reading established some conception of the composition. If this conception is weak, it is a good time to employ professional recordings.

In full rehearsal we gradually tighten the requirements. After several rehearsals, if a player or section still fails to execute a passage reasonably we must consider these possibilities: (1) arrange special coaching sessions; (2) give the part to another player in the section; (3) rescore the passage for another section.

Each rehearsal need not start at the beginning and go on to the end of the work. It is quite effective to start slow drill on the difficult runs at K, work on the intonation of the chords at G, develop better spacing on the massive chords at R, and then reread the entire number.

Needless to say, all corrections made by the director should be noted on the parts by the players. Nothing is so impertinent of a player or so discouraging to a director, as to see his corrections ignored and forgotten at the next rehearsal.

Throughout this process of detailed study, the director must work to avoid the loss of the anticipation and interest in the work that was achieved at first reading. Indeed, this should be enhanced by the students' growing realization that this is a challenging composition that has great possibilities. The director must increasingly devote his attention to the expressive components of the music, in order to bring out the unique flavor and striking effects inherent in it. This becomes more and more possible as the players develop facility and familiarity.

Then, as the final performance approaches, the director becomes very careful with pacing the final polishing. He may tape the rehearsal and play it back, while pointing out the remaining weaknesses. He may schedule further sectionals and individual work to correct stubborn problems. Or he may find it wise to *mark time* with the work (with an occasional reading) if he feels that further attention will only cause this work to become stale. He wishes to present the work at the peak of perfection, not just because the audience will applaud the effort, but because this is the way he wanted his players to hear and feel it.

Promoting Musicianship

Over and above the development of ability to play specific works, stands the ultimate goal of rehearsal—deeper musicianship. This comprehends everything affecting the students' reaction to music—sightreading skill, ability to hear and comprehend musical device, acquaintance with literature, familiarity with musical origins and vocabulary, informed taste, and so on.

It is clear that these ends are best achieved in rehearsal of real music. It is equally clear that it is possible to concentrate too heavily upon concrete results, thus missing the opportunity to illuminate the study of the notes with observations and comparisons, which would enhance musicianship.

There are two principal ways to approach this task. One is the method of improvised comment upon points which naturally arise in dealing with the music. The director must be alert to the significance of the material at hand. He does not simply call for a crescendo, but explains that this is a "Rossini crescendo," for which that composer was justly noted. He not only secures a properly executed grace note, but takes the time to explain how the Classical appogiatura is handled and how this convention originated. He calls not just for the chord at G, but speaks of the pedal point beginning the coda at G. Such an approach requires an apparent relaxation of efficiency, but is actually repaid by added values.

The other method of promoting broader musicianship is the planned introduction of recorded examples, appropriate anecdotes, and background information on the composers whose compositions are currently in rehearsal. In this way, the director attempts to inculcate an understanding of the idiomatic devices and their derivation, and to broaden and deepen the horizons of the student. If something like this is not done, the student is likely to remain entirely unaware of the musical significance of the works he has studied, and remember them vaguely in terms of certain difficult or pleasing passages in his own part. Instead of a dry recital of textbook facts, originality and spontaneity are needed.

PERSONNEL MANAGEMENT

Remembering that school rehearsals are supposed to foster meaningful educative experiences, the director needs to take measures for an effective environment. He must produce stimulation, attention, and a sense of active participation in his players, which involves a certain amount of organization. The incidental results are good discipline and morale.

Student Leadership

Regardless of the titles used and the method of selection, there are three or four natural posts of responsibility that should be filled by students.

(1) THE STUDENT CONDUCTOR assists in tuning and warm up; takes rehearsal when the director must be late or absent; takes charge of certain sectional rehearsals; and may conduct an occasional number at concerts. To be successful, such a person should be acknowledged by his fellow students as a superior musician and a natural leader.

(2) THE PERSONNEL MANAGER may assist in recruiting; collect passes and excuses; act as recorder for any point system or other evaluative device; notify players of special rehearsals; and check up on absentees, etc. These duties may be combined with those of the Student Conductor.

(3) THE EQUIPMENT MANAGER will set up chairs and racks; assist with moving and staging for concerts and trips; and help in the periodic inspections and locker checks. It is helpful if such a student is qualified to make simple repairs and adjustments on the instruments.

(4) THE LIBRARIAN distributes new selections and refiles them as directed; handles necessary transposition and duplication of parts; copies string bowings; distributes and collects folders for each rehearsal; and maintains the library in good order. These duties may be combined with those of the Equipment Manager. Being somewhat menial in nature, both of these tasks deserve financial reward if at all possible. Otherwise, the director may find himself spending too much of his time on these things.

Loyalty, dependability, and special skills are needed in these posts and it is thus imprudent to allow them to be filled on the basis of popularity. It is better to appoint new officers after consultation with the outgoing officers, or to call for volunteers, screen them, and have the players choose among the director's nominees.

Responsible Membership

Every director must achieve proper distribution of his efforts between organization and administration on the one hand, and teaching and conducting on the other. This balance cannot be secured without the cooperation of the players. Too often, this is taken for granted, or else becomes the subject of occasional harangues. Neither course is effective.

Responsible membership is achieved by making it more rewarding than lazy, selfish behavior. Part of the job can be done in terms of rules and marks, but the real result is achieved when the majority of the players come to realize that the director knows what he wants, has planned how to do it, and they will lose something valuable when they don't cooperate. Once achieved, this climate of opinion will be enforced by popular will upon any erring members. A general attitude of expectation is thus produced, one similar to that which usually develops with the appearance of a guest clinician and one which we hope can be maintained on a year-round basis.

Each director has his own threshold of frustration. A situation that to one is rather calm and pleasant, may seem perfect bedlam to another. What seems to be natural student deportment to one director may seem rank insolence and insubordination to his colleagues. So, one or more of these means must be used to define expected standards: (1) establishment of precedents through praise, criticism, and rulings occasioned by the specific action of students; (2) verbal promulgation of rules and periodic review of violations; (3) written rules and standards posted on the bulletin board or in music folders; (4) use of a formal merit-demerit system, translated into pins, letters, marks, or other rewards and penalties.

The main thing to remember is that *a rule is worse than useless if it is not enforced.* Another good maxim is that reward is more effective than punishment. So the director is wise to determine the level of conduct that is actually indispensable to him. By and large, we do not favor the idea of absolute military discipline in school bands and orchestras. An occasional laugh or buzz of excitement is a good sign, so long as the general attitude of attention is not destroyed. Similarly, an occasional burst of home practice on some passage where the player sees his weakness is often better than daily practice by the clock. Responsible membership should mean something like this.

(1) Once accepted as a regular member, the player recognizes his moral obligation to complete the season.

(2) The player will take exceptional care to see that his instrument is in good playing order, and will make immediate arrangements for repair in case of damage.

(3) The player who finds that he will be unavoidably late or absent from rehearsal will make sure his music folder is delivered to rehearsal and will attempt to bring or send written explanation in advance.

(4) The player should allow ten minutes to unpack and assemble his instrument, warm up, and tune up.

(5) The player does not attempt to settle his personal problems just before or during rehearsal. Any special arrangements with the director or other students should be made at the end of rehearsal.

(6) The player attempts to observe every word and gesture of the director, when he is on the podium.

(7) The player listens intently to his own playing in relation to the group, and attempts to anticipate the necessary corrections.

(8) Whenever the director stops conducting, the player is especially alert for all observations and directions.

(9) The player attempts to respond promptly and clearly to every question or direction addressed to him.

(10) The player marks the music as directed, and any other places where he may improve his chances of accurate performance.

(11) The student practices regularly, and attempts to clear up the more difficult passages in any programmed work as soon as possible.

(12) The player understands that absence or poor behavior at any public appearance is regarded as especially serious, and may cause the student to be dropped from the organization.

All directors have some such code in mind in dealing with their groups. Some apply it by directions to the players and also in determining marks, while others employ more formal means.

(1) A *point system* may be established to objectify the rules. A simple and workable version follows.

	POINTS
Reliability in performance during term	0 to 10
Rehearsal deportment during term	0 to 5
Each absence, tardiness, or early departure arranged in advance	−1
Each unexcused tardiness	−2
Each cut	−3

Basis of final mark: A = 10   B = 5   C = −5   D = −10

A broader system, used by many directors, awards points for solo appearances, participation in small ensembles, successful performance of duties as an officer or section leader, specific assignments completed, and similar types of activity which the director wishes to encourage.

(2) *Auditions* (rather than general impressions) may be used to determine improvement in playing at the end of the term.

(3) *Weekly practice blanks* may be used.

(4) *Wall charts or graphs* may be used to record progress of the students in terms of points.

(5) *Awards* such as letters, pins, or uniform stripes may be established for total performance or any special phase the director wishes to emphasize. Usually this kind of reward is best used for excellence over a two or three year span. For example, letters might be awarded for either A grades over two years, or as soon as one has reached a certain point total.

The director is cautioned that the above devices may look good on paper but are not easy to handle. The holding of individual auditions and the daily recording of points is so time consuming that the director often simplifies or abandons the process in later years. He may find that practice records tell him little of the *quality* of practice, and also, the veracity of some players will be open to question. So it is wise to remember these principles: first, a definite set of rules or expectations is needed, second, any objective plan for evaluation should be dignified, and simple enough to be sustained indefinitely, and third, nothing should obscure the real rewards—the individual's musical development and sense of a job well done.

Director's Attitude

Unless the director's approach is completely unrealistic, the players will tend to reflect his general attitude. Many directors are defeated merely by being defeatists, and aimlessness, tenseness, and distraction are also mirrored by the players.

What the director really wants is a chance to teach his players, and he needs their concentration and a spirit of whole hearted response. But he will not achieve this unless it is merited by his own competence. This competence, in turn, is a result of his general musicianship, specific preparation for the rehearsal, and practical ability to handle the rehearsal situation.

On the other hand, few directors are fully competent. There *are* gaps in their training, shortcomings in their knowledge of the scores, and lack of experience in rehearsal techniques. The director must not try to bluff, since this only leads to hypocrisy and an inferiority complex on his part, and results in his players becoming disillusioned. To put it plainly, the director must study and plan to the best of his ability, and then proceed in rehearsal in the most sensible manner possible.

The director's normal personality generally works out best on the podium. If he is ordinarily the genial type, he should not try to become severe; nor can the gregarious type long succeed in being impersonal.

But while he is being himself, the director must guard against carrying his temporary moods into rehearsal. His personal feeling of especial elation should not cause him to view everything through rose colored glasses, and a gloomy feeling should not cause him to storm at the players. *Their* work, alone, justifies such reactions.

Approach to the Players

The interest of the players is largely maintained by good music and intelligent pacing. The idea is to create an element of challenge and a sense of accomplishment. One does *not* employ the same procedure over and over. This ability to shift gears constantly is made possible by balancing the attention between the music and the players.

Whenever things do not work out as expected the director must first consider whether it is *his* fault, and if so, change his approach or defer the attack. Only when he is certain that it is not his fault, should he take deliberate action to reprimand his players, and then he must be decisive about it.

Great and famous conductors invariably illustrate this point. They have no magic formula in rehearsal. They simply have a superior conception of how the music should sound and some very effective techniques for conducting and explaining it. When results do not measure up, they exhaust every possible kind of approach to enforce their desires. Similarly, the school director may apply routine reproof, humor, mild derision, a plea for cooperation, sharp reprimand, or severe penalty (such as loss of points, loss of position in the section, or dismissal from rehearsal). But it is imperative to avoid all sarcasm and unenforced threats.

Most discipline problems will be avoided by keeping things moving so that the players are fully occupied. Full band or orchestra rehearsal is not the place for sectional rehearsal, steady technical drill, or long winded discussion.

The other secret of good discipline is simply *esprit de corps*. This is achieved by high standards and a feeling of successful endeavor. An improving and expanding group, well received public appearances, and good relations among director and players, create an enthusiastic membership which enforces suitable behavior upon all individuals. Needless to say, the director does all he can to achieve this result.

SUMMARY

Having developed a performing group and chosen the music, the director is faced with the process of teaching the players to play the selected music in a way that will produce sound educative results. The first step is personal familiarity with the score, including the problems of transposition and interpretation. This involves some marking of score and parts.

Much care is required in establishing the proper setting for rehearsal, including the physical environment, seating arrangements, announcements, planned rehearsal sequence, and the like.

The first steps in rehearsal are warm up and tuning. Many attempt special technical drills at this point. But the chief aspects of rehearsal are the reading of new material and corrective study of previously read material. There is no one pattern of procedure. Some works may be read at tempo and corrected by spot rehearsal, while others require many stops, and rehearsal by sections or at reduced tempos. One of the basic rules is to correct the larger faults first and go deeper and deeper in each succeeding rehearsal.

There is a point beyond which the players cannot go without injurious pressures. The idea is to procure the most expressive rendition possible, which delivers the chief educational value to the players.

Rehearsal techniques are supported by good organization of the players and well established rules of conduct. Point systems, awards, and marks may be of use. However, it is the director's attitude and basic competence which set the tone of the rehearsal and affect the morale and discipline of the players.

QUESTIONS FOR DISCUSSION

1. What types of musical scores are available, and what are the differences? Review the formulae for determining concert pitch from the transposed parts and *vice versa*.

2. How is interpretation of a work achieved? Practice determining tempos and estimating metronomic speeds.

3. What routines must be followed in setting up rehearsals?

4. How vital is the tuning and warm up period? How may this be handled?

5. What is the general procedure in reading new material? What measures are taken when the ensemble breaks down?

6. What are some good procedures to follow in polishing a number in rehearsal? How detailed should the director get?

7. How does one foster good attitude and deportment of the players? What characterizes an effective rehearsal approach by the director?

SELECTED REFERENCES

BOWLES, MICHAEL, *The Art of Conducting*. Garden City, N. Y.: Doubleday and Co., Inc., 1959.

DUVALL, W. CLYDE, *The High School Band Director's Handbook*. Englewood Cliffs, N. J.: Prentice-Hall, Inc., 1960.

GOLDMAN, EDWIN FRANCO, *Band Betterment*. New York: Carl Fischer, Inc., 1934.

KENDRIE, FRANK ESTES, *Handbook on Conducting and Orchestral Routine*. New York: H. W. Gray Co., 1930.

SCHERCHEN, HERMANN, *Handbook of Conducting*. New York: Oxford University Press, Inc., 1933.

VAN BODEGRAVEN, PAUL AND HARRY ROBERT WILSON, *The School Music Conductor*. Minneapolis: Schmitt, Hall and McCreary Company, 1942.

CHAPTER 6

Associated Activities

There is no doubt that the school instrumental music program revolves around the major concert groups. The band and orchestra are continuing organizations, which serve as the principal goal of the beginner and the basic units for instruction of the advanced player.

Once such groups are in operation, however, a number of other possibilities arise. A marching unit may be developed. Operas and musicals may be staged. Students may become engaged in supplemental individual study, solo work, sectional rehearsals, small ensembles, clinical groups, and so on. Such activities are extremely important, and in certain instances they may even secure more educative results than the principal organizations. However, they are not constant factors to each individual, but are regarded as seasonal, elective, or selective in nature. They supplement and extend the values of the concert groups. Because of this relationship, all of these activities will be treated in one chapter. They will be discussed one by one, however, since each has a specialized nature.

THE MARCHING BAND

The emphasis on marching varies widely. It may occupy none or most of a band's attention. Most directors deplore it, but some are enthusiastic devotees. All must agree that marching is a powerful factor in the school band movement. We can not ignore it in any treatment of the school instrumental music program.

Function of the Marching Band

The use of the band as a concert group for entertainment, and later as an educational medium arose only because it already existed as a military unit. The original function of the band was for parade and ceremonial. Consequently, it required little imagination to employ the emerging school bands for street parades and other outdoor functions. This activity has long been a regular part of the school band's role.

With the rise of interscholastic sports, it was thought fitting to bring the school band to the games as an expression of the all school nature of those events. It was as natural as having a choir in church. When attention was not on the athletes, the band played school songs and rousing marches, and it occasionally went on the field for a flag raising ceremony or a special presentation. Then, to fill out the intermission, a few groups concocted additional marching evolutions. The race was then on, for school pride dictated that what one school could do another could do as well. During the nineteen-thirties and -forties this pageantry developed into a highly specialized form. Colleges and universities, especially, have exploited the possibilities, and the high schools have emulated them.

The unfortunate part is that bands can no longer take it or leave it. Some people have become so accustomed to this form of entertainment that they demand it as a right. Just as they reserve the right to criticize the coach for the team's losses, they also feel free to express their opinions about the band's marching performance. So, many directors find themselves working to satisfy the demands of the public, rather than the musical needs of their students. When this point is reached, there is no doubt that marching pageantry has become dangerous to the goals of music education.

But marching in itself is *not* harmful. It is a mildly useful activity and a natural associate of an art form (the military march), just as dancing is identified with the waltz, the polka, and all the other dance forms. More important, it is a good means of strengthening the individual's sense of coordination and precision. Only those who have never marched in a good band can fail to realize the feeling for tempo and purposeful rhythm it gives.

Objectively, therefore, this is a legitimate, but not very critical part of the school band's role. The director who allows his band to spend half the year in marching and then basks in public adulation with a sense of a job well done is fooling himself. He is not in the music business at all.

While it is easy to deplore this exploitation of a musical unit dedicated to the education of youth, no one has yet explained how to throw off the shackles. Our position is that marching and pageantry should not be abandoned, but the process must become more streamlined and efficient. These are the principles that should be followed.

(1) The feeling of competition against other groups for crowd approval must be abandoned. The idea must be to do a respectable, workmanshiplike job and let the comments fall where they will.

(2) The band should not follow the team. Trips for marching should be severely limited.

(3) The time spent in marching rehearsal must be cut to the bone. No more than ten percent of a year's rehearsals should be outdoors.

(4) To do a good job in the time allotted, means long hours of planning by the director. The shows must be thoroughly worked out and charted before presention to the players.

(5) Turns, halts, flanks, and so on, should be taught systematically, and retained with little or no change from year to year.

(6) Where possible, a traditional entrance and exit routine should be established. This cuts the new material to be learned for each game to a minimum, and crowds seem to prefer it this way.

(7) Fanciful frills and gyrations which have appeared in the past two or three decades (the superfast cadence, the army of baton twirlers and flag wavers, the senseless format of unrelated tableaux which require an announcer to identify) all these must be renounced in favor of normal evolutions done to solidly played music.

Instrumentation

The school marching band may be identical with the concert group, except that the low reed and double reed players are used as extra drummers, twirlers, and supernumeraries. The group may also be augmented by extra brass players from the junior band.

The principle of stressing brass and percussion for marching may be carried to the extreme of forming a drum and bugle corps. The musical value of such a unit is so questionable, however, that it should be considered a device to employ volunteers and thus relieve the band of marching responsibilities in whole or in part. The marching procedures we will outline apply equally to this type of organization.

Parade Formation

For parades, the usual rule is that the band formation should be rectangular. Some directors place the tubas in the rear (for less obstruction to vision), along with the trumpets (so their sound carries through the band). Some very large groups split their instrumentation to favor flanking and frequent division of the organization. But the traditional plan is to have the big brass in front, drums, and trumpets in the center, and woodwinds at the rear. See Fig. 6-1.

The Basic Manual

Regular positions of *at ease* and *attention* should be defined. Carry position and playing position for each instrument must be prescribed and enforced.

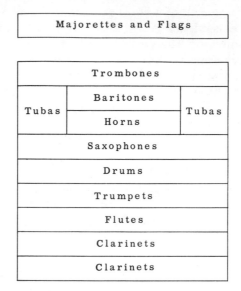

Fig. 6-1.

Facings should be chosen among the following types.

RIGHT FACE
   Flank type: (1) take step with left foot, (2) pivot on right heel, (3) bring left foot up to a halt.
   Kick type: (1) kick left foot and pivot on right toe, (2) bring left foot up to a halt.
   Military: (1) pivot on right heel and left toe, (2) bring left foot up to a halt.

ABOUT FACE
   To the Rear type: (1) Take step with left foot and pivot on the toe 180 degrees to the right, (2) replace the right foot in the new direction, (3) bring left foot up to a halt.
   Military: (1) place right toe a few inches to rear and left of left heel, (2) pivot 180 degrees on left heel and right toe, ending with heels together.

   The step off must be well coordinated to produce a precise effect, and a ragged gathering of momentum must be avoided. Some bands are trained to take a full pace after the signal, while others mark time on the first count and proceed at full pace at the second count. Still others kick immediately upon the command and lower the foot slowly to count one.
   Pace depends somewhat upon tempo, age, and sex of the marchers.

The Army pace of 30 inches was designed for full grown men marching at a cadence of 116 to 128 (steps per minute), but many bands have found the 22½ inch pace very effective, particularly as on the gridiron this produces eight steps between yardlines. This fact practically solves the problems of alignment and has obvious possibilities in coordinating music and formations.

Marching posture is of great importance. The natural stride is a springing step so the weight is brought forward to the ball of the foot, and the move from heel to ball of foot may be conceived as a flam. The high step, however, becomes more natural with a faster cadence and shorter pace, thus, dictating that the toe strikes the ground first. Arms not holding an instrument should swing, but the amount and direction are defined differently in various bands. A swaying or rolling gait needs to be avoided, although some groups deliberately exaggerate the natural swing of shoulders and instruments.

The flank pivot may be executed in traditional or cross over style. Both must be used (to maintain exact intervals) whenever the band is split into units that march and turn in different directions (see Fig. 6-2).

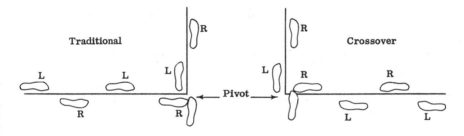

Fig. 6-2.

In learning flanks (the basis of good turns), the band members may be lined up in single file and tested one by one as they pivot around a point (see Fig. 6-3).

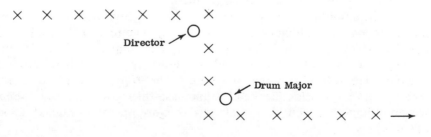

Fig. 6-3.

The regulation military halt should be enforced from the beginning. This apparently simple matter takes much drill, because the players are concentrating on other things and tend to add a pace or two.

Block Style Maneuvers

The traditional block style formation is usually best for parades or sustained periods of marching because of the solidity of the group and beauty of the vertical, horizontal, and diagonal lines. It is based on an interval of two and a half yards between all adjacent ranks and files. Assuming a 22½ inch pace, the odd numbered ranks will all reach the yardlines at the same instant and the even numbered ranks, four paces later (either on the eighth count or the first count, depending on the style of step off). (See Fig. 6-4.)

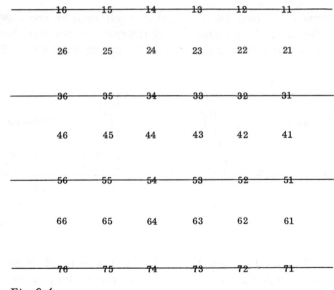

Fig. 6-4.

There are three commonly-used turns.

(1) The military turn is accomplished by a flank pivot executed by the inside man, two obliques by the remaining members of the rank, and then half steps by all until the outside man has completed the turn and arrives in line. It is the quickest and simplest way to get a band around a corner. The difficulty is that the number of steps to be taken is not definite, and the outside files tend to increase their pace and make their second oblique too soon, thus, making the entire operation ragged. (See Fig. 6-5.)

(2) The wheel turn is a modification of the military turn. It is slower

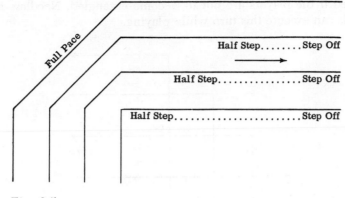

Fig. 6-5.

and can look either very fine or poor, depending on the care in alignment. The corner man again executes a flank and half step, while each file executes an arc at a different pace to maintain the alignment. (See Fig. 6-6.)

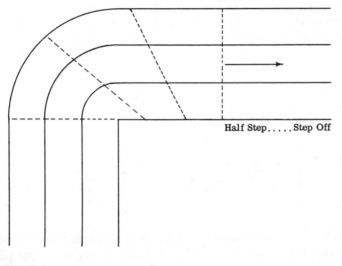

Fig. 6-6.

(3) The most beautiful and effective corner is the "minstrel turn" (Fig. 6-7) where the members of each rank pivot in succession (at every fourth pace) commencing with the man at the *outside* of the corner, and thus move across and through the oncoming ranks. Because some distance is lost in pivoting, those who have turned must pass just behind those who have not. Paces must be counted, and the length must be very carefully

maintained if the players are not to become entangled. Needless to say, few bands can execute this turn while playing.

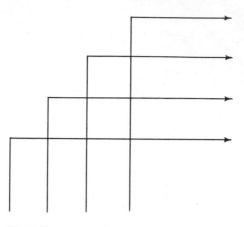

Fig. 6-7.

There are two standard countermarches (see Fig. 6-8). The box turn, pictured at right, may also be used as a form of countermarch, if the players proceed around two sides of the box. Some bands simply use *To the Rear* or two consecutive flanks to reverse direction.

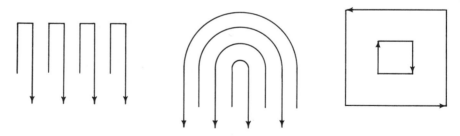

Fig. 6-8.

The oblique is one of the most difficult movements to execute properly but it produces a striking effect. The difficulty arises when the players at the rear and side tend to swing forward and out. The remedy is to rivet their attention on their own steady pace and direction. This can be done by first practicing *brief* obliques of two, three, and four paces. (See Fig. 6-9.)

Small Unit Maneuvers

The small unit formation is a comparatively recent development which is well adapted to flexibility in maneuvering. The distance between

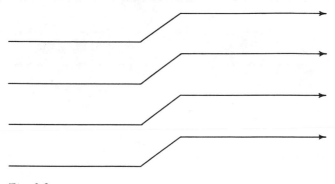

Fig. 6-9.

ranks is increased to five yards while the ranks or half ranks are likewise five yards in length. Thus each unit may maneuver freely within this space. (See Fig. 6-10.)

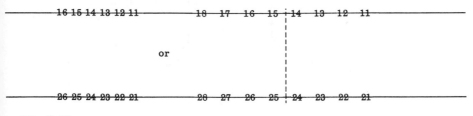

Fig. 6-10.

Marching forward with the 22½ inch pace, all ranks arrive at yardlines at the same instant and all ranks can wheel in eight counts (with modified pace) to a company front. (See Fig. 6-11a.)

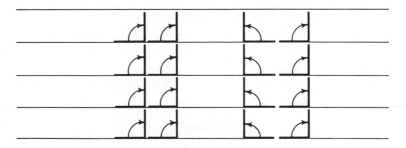

Fig. 6-11a.

It is also possible to march one rank forward while the neighboring rank wheels as shown in Fig. 6-11b. Such movements can be developed into drills of the type shown in Fig. 6-12.

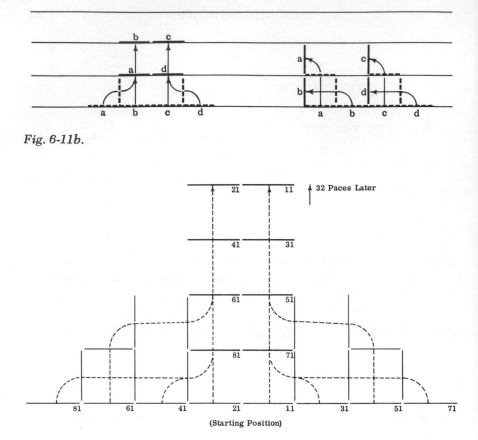

Fig. 6-11b.

Fig. 6-12.

Endless possibilities are thus created in which the problems of turns and countermarches are inherently solved, and the difficulties in alignment are greatly reduced. The main problem is in figuring out the formations and training the players to remember them.

The continued evolution of such techniques has led to an advanced form of precision drill which features special arm movements, "drags," "freezes," phalanx drill, progressively expanding and contracting patterns, and the like. Figs. 6-13a and b illustrate this fast moving type of drill.[1]

Pageantry

MUSIC AND TEMPO. There is no point in worrying too much about the quality of music to be used on the field. But it should always make the

[1] From A. R. Casavant, *Precision Drill Line Movements* (San Antonio, Texas: Southern Music Co., 1958), p. 283. Other books by Casavant include *Precision Drill, Block Formation Drill, Street Parade Drills, Phalanx Drill Movements, Field Entrances, Staggered Block Drill Movements, Precision Flash, Precision Drill Team, Manual of Drill, The Fast Break, Six to Five, Rhythmic Arm Movements for Marching,* and *Progression Drill Line Movements.* All are available from Southern Music Co.

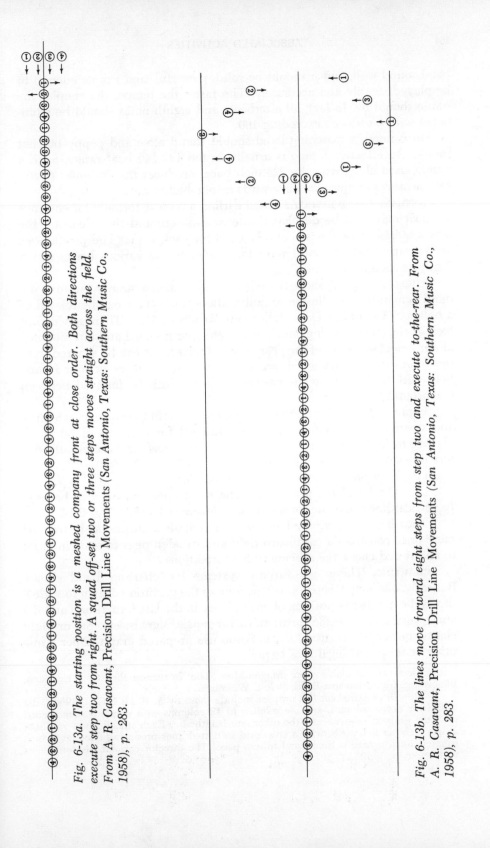

Fig. 6-13a. The starting position is a meshed company front at close order. Both directions execute step two from right. A squad off-set two or three steps moves straight across the field. From A. R. Casavant, Precision Drill Line Movements (San Antonio, Texas: Southern Music Co., 1958), p. 283.

Fig. 6-13b. The lines move forward eight steps from step two and execute to-the-rear. From A. R. Casavant, Precision Drill Line Movements (San Antonio, Texas: Southern Music Co., 1958), p. 283.

band sound well, and it should be solid, powerful, and simple enough to be played cleanly and accurately. The faster the tempo, the simpler the music should be. In fact, all afterbeats and eighth notes should be eliminated with a cadence exceeding 160.

In general, a marching band should sound alive and peppy but not frantic. An effective tempo is usually in the 132-140 beat range. Such a tempo, used along with the 22½ inch pace, produces this formula: thirty-two measures of music = forty yards = one-half minute.

ENTRANCES AND EXITS. As stated earlier, a regular formula for entrance and exit may well be developed into a tradition, and thus decrease the new material to be devised and learned for each game. The possibilities are so varied that we must refer the reader to the various books which illustrate such formations.

THEMES. A good show is built around a theme simply because the mind demands some illusion of unity. Many times these can be related to a holiday (Columbus Day, Halloween, Armistice Day, Thanksgiving), a local event (homecoming, anniversary, etc.), or national and international affairs (election, "man of the year," etc.). Other ideas can be secured from the commercial shows which are available. Usually three or four formations outline the idea, while various evolutions can be inserted between and around these.

Figures suitable for a 150 piece university outfit performing in a large and steeply sloped stadium are not practical for a group of 50 or 60 playing to low bleachers. Those that are used need to be carefully distorted to give the proper illusion.

(1) Horizontal lines require close spacing.

(2) The lower the grandstand, the more open spacing can be used in vertical lines, and the longer these lines must be. See Fig. 6-14.

The director is advised either to purchase a magnetic board and men[2] or to construct a cardboard field and wooden pegs to scale in order to adjust and check the spacing of his formations.

CHARTING. There are various systems for charting band shows. Basically, one simply represents a portion of the gridiron (drawn to scale), shows the numbered position of each player in the last formation (and the next), and gives specific instructions for music, signals, etc. Six or eight charts thus cover the usual show. Some use prepared graph paper while others cut special legal size stencils.[3]

---

[2] These are available from Magno-Men, The Instrumentalist Co., Evanston, Illinois and from Maneuva-Band, Beloit, Wisconsin.

[3] Stencils prepared for this purpose include those by A. B. Dick Co.: #960F, die #26918 in seven columns, and die #26919 in 13 columns with numbers. One stencil plots the gridiron sidewise and the other one lengthwise. Each stencil gives yardlines at one inch per five yards, with a cross grid in dotted lines producing one-eighth inch squares. Each square is thus equal to one pace. The director can cut his formations with stylus.

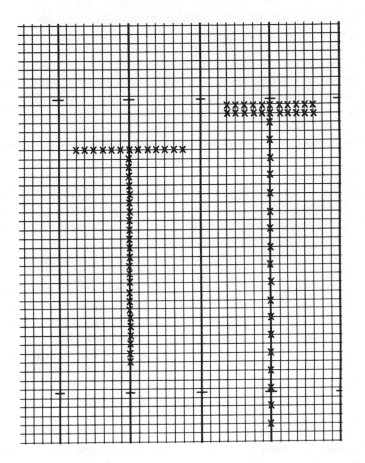

Fig. 6-14.

In charting any show, one must count on having every position filled. It is thus wise not to employ every band member and risk having incomplete ranks, but rather to have three or four reserve players who can fill in, when players are unavoidably absent from rehearsals or performances.

FORMATION BREAKS. There are three methods for entering and leaving special formations.

(1) The individual players move quickly to their positions by the shortest route and without music.

(2) The ranks and files are kept intact and march in cadence to their positions. This is slow and tedious to plan, but saves headaches in re-assembling marching formation.

(3) The players are moved simultaneously and in cadence in small units of three or four. The units proceed in straight lines and simple

wheels, continuing motion for a specified number of counts and arriving simultaneously in the new formation.

Soft music is usually employed for these formation breaks (wood-winds, lyre, whistling, singing, drums on the rim, etc.). Ideally, the PA announcement of a formation should be made just as it is assuming form.

SPECIAL EFFECTS. To avoid complete dependence upon precision marching or upon figures which may be rather obscure, the following ideas are suggested.

(1) Arrange for a mass band formation with the visiting band(s).

(2) Present a short composition from standing formation conducted from the sidelines.

(3) Establish the band in suitable formation, turn off the field lights, throw on a large spotlight, and use a cooperating group for a short square dance or pantomime. For example, a piccolo player, drummer, and flag bearer, moving diagonally across the field under a moving spotlight, with *Yankee Doodle* played by the motionless, unseen band is rather effective pageantry.

(4) For night games, do part of the show without field lights. Use cap lights or secure uniform material which glows under infra-red light.

(5) The band can go into some appropriate formation (flag, ship, cannon, etc.) the lights go out, the band plays, and rockets may be fired from a prepared position beyond the end zone. Firing equipment may be secured from a manufacturer, and permission must be secured from the local fire department.

(6) Use smoke effect for moving vehicles, etc.

Teaching Procedures

Band drill on the gridiron often conflicts with practice sessions of the team. In such a case, another practice field may be scheduled and this must be lined and supplied with sideline markers. The director should have a portable speaker or megaphone for marching rehearsal.

In teaching the fundamentals, the big thing is demonstration, individual practice, and closely supervised trial. It does little good to trot alongside the band and exhort the players to get in line. Instead, they should be divided into squads for intensive practice under the eye of the best marchers. Practicing by the numbers is also effective. That is, each movement is done to a separate count, with time between for checking the execution. In the early stages, it is also useful to have the group count paces aloud, between yardlines and in changing formation.

In learning the show formation, it is usually most efficient to give the band members a general idea of the formation, then teach the music, and have a "skull session" with the charts. Then the band should go to the field and practice a few times with charts and no music, then several times without charts, but carrying instruments, and finally with music.

After the first couple of trials, the best place for the director is in the stands or at sidelines where he can see and hear the total effect and call attention to the more glaring weaknesses.

COOPERATIVE ENTERPRISES

Many instrumental organizations consist of students from more than one school or city, or of mixed student and adult membership. Such groups include all-city bands and orchestras, district or state clinic bands and orchestras, civic symphonies and bands, and the like. Some of these are organized on a temporary basis, while others are of permanent or semi-permanent nature.

Since these specially formed groups are generally composed of nominated or auditioned members, they tend to be of higher caliber and often possess a more complete instrumentation than the individual school organizations. That is one reason for their existence. A select group can more nearly approximate professional quality, and do literature of a more advanced grade. One of the sponsoring directors, or a guest conductor of some reputation, is usually secured for such an organization. All these arrangements are calculated to heighten the effect of the experience upon each player. If all goes well, the students secure a clearer picture of music and their future in it, and thus strengthen their resolve to participate in college and adult life either as amateurs or professionals.

Results depend greatly upon the participation and attitude of the school director. If the enterprise is worthy, he should make every effort to enlist his own students who may be qualified, assist them as needed, and support the organization in whatever capacity he can.

Civic Symphonies

Community orchestras range from fully professional organizations to strictly amateur groups, which are often little more than school orchestras with a few sympathetic adults who volunteer to play the concerts. Between these extremes, lie a number of semi-professional groups involving a considerable degree of cooperation between town and gown. These groups usually occur in middle sized communities where some of the high school players will be invited to supplement the nucleus of adult and college age players. Under certain circumstances the school director may play in the group or be called upon to conduct it.

There is a tremendous opportunity here to provide valuable orchestra training for qualified students, while serving the interests of more and better music within the community. Nevertheless, since local pride and individual prestige are so heavily involved, it is well to recognize that the best interests of the school music program may be gradually sacrificed to the needs of the civic group, and especially when that cause is supported by well-meaning individuals in the name of culture. The school director must never allow such a situation to develop.

(1) Control of the civic orchestra should be vested with those forces which make it possible. That is, if the personnel is largely nonschool, and the finances are provided by receipts and public subscription, then a board should be elected from the community. If, however, the conductor, library, instruments, and players are substantially provided by the school, then the school must have the determining voice.

(2) Knowing the needs and qualifications of his own students, the director should have candidates to suggest when openings occur in the community group. All new members should have his especial help in meeting the new technical and musical problems to be faced.

(3) In any case, students who are not members in good standing of their school groups should never be accepted for membership. The school director's consent is needed before any student is invited to play.

(4) If the group is to be considered an independent organization, steps should be taken to establish a separate library and basic equipment. School instruments should be loaned only to students already using them in the school groups.

(5) Any substantial participation by school students demands careful coordination of the calendars of performances and rehearsals, and the works to be programmed.

(6) The school director's interest and loyalty to such a group, especially if he happens to be the conductor, must be carefully weighed against his school responsibilities. One of the dangers is that a conductor who is in the position to influence the selection of music teachers in the schools may tend to count the ability to fill an important orchestra post for more than teaching competency. Unless this policy is avoided, the school program in instrumental music is clearly jeopardized.

Municipal Bands

Municipal bands are not as common as they once were. But there are still some highly professional groups and many that are loosely organized for a few summer park concerts. The school director should be guided by the same principles as for the community orchestras.

All City School Bands and Junior Symphonies

Large city school systems often develop picked groups from the various schools to rehearse and perform on a more or less regular basis. Normally, the instrumental supervisor is in charge, or delegates this responsibility to a committee of the school directors. These may conduct on a joint basis, select one of their number as a regular conductor, or secure a local professional conductor.

Such groups ordinarily rehearse after school hours at a central location. Auditions for membership and seating must be carefully handled to be fair to each school. The various directors should cooperate in holding sectional rehearsals, promotion, and other operational problems.

Clinic and Festival Groups

Temporary organizations are often formed by cooperating schools in a city, district, or state to rehearse and perform on a schedule of one or more days. Such units are usually sponsored by local colleges or universities, or by associations of music educators. Some very careful management is involved, for every minute of rehearsal is precious. Directors should ascertain if the event is likely to be educationally worthwhile, and if so, should participate as vigorously as possible.

A committee of directors is ordinarily elected or appointed to make the arrangements. These include:

(1) selection and reservation of date or dates and establishment of rehearsal schedule,

(2) selection and procurement of conductor,

(3) selection of numbers to be played and provision to secure the necessary scores and parts,

(4) dissemination of information and invitation to participating schools,

(5) financial arrangements (from sponsoring organization, school budgets, concert receipts, or player assessment),

(6) needed provision for housing, meals, equipment, and publicity,

(7) selection and seating of players (usually it is wise to secure all possible nominees listed by age, instrument, and relative proficiency, and then choose the best players to complete a predetermined instrumentation with adjustments as necessary to provide fair representation from each school),

(8) management at rehearsal, including seating, tuning, announcements, etc.

Participating directors need to be prompt and efficient in returning information asked by the clinic manager, in securing the parts, and in coaching their entrants. Unless it is a sight reading clinic, much of the success depends upon the players' prior ability to play the notes, so that the conductor may deal mostly with the finer points of performance.

Choral-Instrumental Works

The possibility of performing choral works with orchestra or band accompaniment should not be overlooked, especially upon the occasion of a joint concert. The number of usable works in this category is small, but the experience can be very stimulating to both performers and audience.

The conductor may be the chorus, band, or orchestra director, depending largely upon the relative importance of the vocal and instrumental parts, who selected the work, and who proposed the idea.

During the early stages of preparation, it is usually advisable to handle the cooperating groups in separate rehearsals, and principally under the baton of the one who will conduct the performance. For example, if the choir and orchestra are preparing to do sections of the *Messiah,* the conductor would rehearse the chorus and orchestra separately, and the assisting director might give added attention to the more difficult sections with his own group. As soon as all the parts are reasonably secure, joint rehearsals are arranged for chorus and orchestra, soloists and orchestra, and finally, a dress rehearsal with the entire ensemble.

As Michael Bowles so aptly puts it, "the basis of good choral singing lies simply in having all the singers know all the notes."[4] Then the conductor is free to concentrate upon style and diction, and the other expressive qualities of the music.

In programming such joint presentations, it is best to avoid establishing the tradition of an annual performance of any specific work. Several good works should be found, so that repetition is not necessary for at least four or five years. Singers and players should always be exposed to the widest possible repertoire.

Musico-Dramatic Productions

Operas, operettas, and musicals suitable for school use are becoming available in greater quantity. Only a few years ago, the task of finding something of musical value (in English, and with enough brevity and simplicity to be practical) was indeed a formidable job. But such works can now be found and they are of great educative value. There are several unique problems to be faced, and the director should consider these suggestions.

(1) The works selected should not be all of the same type. One should consider alternating musicals or operettas with something more substantial, such as one of the works of Menotti or Kurt Weill, or one of the lighter standard operas in English translation.

(2) The overriding criterion in selecting specific works is the availability of qualified singers for the lead roles. Other factors include quality and difficulty of the music, the instrumentation, length, suitability of staging requirements, royalties, etc.

(3) Three teachers are ordinarily needed to assume major responsibility: the *musical director* (usually the vocal teacher) who determines the general interpretation of the work and prepares the singers; the

---

[4] *The Art of Conducting* (Garden City, N. Y.: Doubleday and Company, Inc., 1959), p. 191.

stage director (usually a speech teacher) who advises and coaches on stage action, preparation of scenery and lighting; and the *conductor* (usually the orchestra director) who prepares the orchestra and conducts at the dress rehearsals and performances.

(4) Because amateur voices are notoriously weak, it is better to have an orchestra too small than too large. A good pit orchestra for school productions consists of 12 to 40 players. The normal seating is shown in Fig. 6-15.

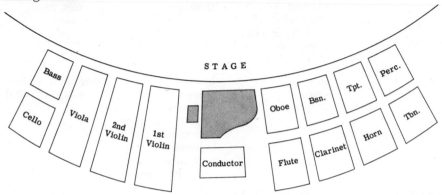

Fig. 6-15.

(5) Insofar as possible, any players not involved in the production should rehearse at the regular class period, as a unit or in sections, on sight reading material or on numbers scheduled for an ensuing concert.

(6) The orchestra conductor should make every effort to minimize the pressures on his players. After all, they do not have a starring role in the production and should not be forced to rehearse endlessly with the singers. A pianist should be relied upon for much of this work. Unless the chosen work is too long or difficult, it is best to rent the parts for only a month's rehearsal, and to schedule only a couple of special evening rehearsals. Regardless of receipts, a two night stand is ample from an educative standpoint.

(7) The conductor should study his score exhaustively, and attend early rehearsals of the cast, in order to gain the familiarity that will save time when the orchestra and singers are combined.

(8) Any profits or losses from the venture should be shared equitably among the organizations involved, in proportion to their contribution to the production.

CHAMBER MUSIC

One of the most effective steps a director can take is to organize a series of small ensembles. These groups offer tremendous educational dividends with a minimum of investment. The classic combinations include the string trio, the string quartet, and the woodwind quintet. But good literature can be found for all of these standard groupings.

Duos	flute	horn	piano
	clarinet	trumpet	violin
	saxophone	trombone	cello
Trios	flute	trumpet	string (violin,
	clarinet	trombone	cello, and
	woodwind (flute,		piano)
	oboe or clari-		
	net, and		
	bassoon)		
Quartets	flute	horn	string (2 violins,
	clarinet	trumpet	viola, and cello)
	saxophone	trombone	
		brass (2 trumpets,	
		trombone or	
		horn, and	
		trombone or	
		euphonium)	
Quintets	woodwind (flute,		string (string
	oboe, clarinet,		quartet and
	bassoon, and		additional viola
	horn)		or bass)
			piano (string
			quartet and
			piano)
Sextets	saxophone	brass (2 trumpets,	
		horn, trombone,	
		euphonium, and	
		tuba)	
Choirs	woodwind	brass percussion string	
Mixed ensembles	stage band	pep band	

Composers have also written for more unusual combinations such as flute and string quartet, violin-viola, flute-clarinet, and so on. In such a case, an ensemble may be created to play the specific work, and retained by making necessary transpositions of other suitable literature.

All small ensembles tend to highlight individual responsibility and teamwork. The player cannot easily escape the need to play his part with authority and skillful coordination. Indeed, ensemble work is the natural outlet for the really gifted players, who may not be fully extended in the school band or orchestra, and it is also one of the best devices for strengthening those who are not such strong players. Such groups are in great demand for performances before various community organizations and the players may thus achieve much ease and finesse in public appearance.

The beauty of it is that no great effort is required of the director. He chooses players, provides music, helps schedule rehearsals, and then coaches the groups from time to time. Sustained responsibility to rehearse and perfect the ensemble, however, is left to the players. This procedure tends to create qualities of leadership and initiative on the part of the players and enhances the possibility that they will continue to participate in such groups after graduation.

It is very important that the members selected be well matched in ability and motivation. Any ensemble is no better than its weakest member, and a very weak one will cause frustration. This suggests that the members of a group will often need to vary considerably in age, and that it is sometimes advisable to substitute instruments. For example, a good trombonist who can transpose would be preferable to a weak horn player who might hold back an otherwise excellent woodwind quintet.

Members of a small ensemble must also be personally compatible. Feuding among the players is not unknown, and since they will not always be under the director's supervision, it is best to reshuffle the group if this tendency is noted.

In setting up the ensembles the following procedures are recommended.

(1) Acquire a basic library for all the common groupings that are likely to be formed over a period of years. This should include at least a couple of numbers or collections of graded difficulty for each type of group. Whenever a new ensemble is formed, it will thus have something suitable to rehearse until additional music can be secured.

(2) Go over the list of band or orchestra members to determine those who are serious enough to profit from ensemble work. This needs to be done each fall, since the number of eligible players and types of instruments may vary considerably from year to year.

(3) Establish provisional groupings which include all of these players. For example, if there is only one eligible trombonist, he could be assigned to a brass quartet or sextet, and if there happens to be a surplus of trombonists, they could be used in a trombone trio or quartet. But players of the same general level of ability should be grouped together. Naturally, any successful ensemble from the previous year should be kept intact.

(4) Consult each player about his assignment to a particular group. Observe all reactions and suggestions carefully for any hints which could lead to a more practical grouping of individuals in the ensembles.

(5) As each group is organized, call a meeting and choose a regular rehearsal time.

(6) Meet the first rehearsals of each ensemble and launch it on

a number or two. Designate a leader to manage each group on a sustaining basis and give him the necessary instructions.

(7) Order additional music as necessary.

(8) Attend enough rehearsals and provide sufficient coaching to keep each group progressing, and to spot any unfortunate choices of personnel or music. Make any necessary changes as tactfully as possible.

(9) Arrange public appearances when a group is ready. Attend and manage any first appearances, and then allow the groups to appear, unsupervised, as soon as they seem to be capable.

(10) Spread the public appearances among the groups as much as possible. Avoid any tendency to overuse the groups (beyond the needs of adequate educational experience) by carefully screening requests for appearances. Depending on the extent that these public appearances are permitted, one might consider calling upon the hosts to provide meals, transportation, or a modest contribution to the music library fund. Appearances might also be tactfully limited to one per year per civic group. Needless to say, any such regulations need to be thoroughly considered and very carefully applied.

The larger groups usually require the most attention from the director, since student leadership cannot always cope with the complexity of the parts and the disciplinary problems. Indeed, many directors schedule stage band, pep band, and woodwind, brass, or string choirs as regular activities under their own direction. The strings, for example, may rehearse as a unit during three or four of the weekly orchestra rehearsal periods. Likewise, band directors sometimes schedule the woodwinds one period per week, the brass another, and meet the full band on the remaining days. Strictly speaking, separation of the strings, woodwinds, and brasses, for rehearsals of the orchestra and band parts is simply a broad form of sectional rehearsal, whereas true string, woodwind, and brass choirs are specially picked and balanced groups that rehearse literature specifically written for those combinations. Both approaches should be employed from time to time.

The pep band is a small and versatile group, usually consisting of volunteers from the concert band, which plays for pep rallies and indoor athletic events. Some directors choose two pep bands to alternate the public appearances. For best results, the instrumentation should be weighted in favor of the brasses:

flute	0 - 2	trombone	2 - 3
clarinet	2 - 4	euphonium	1 - 2
saxophone	2 - 4	tuba	1 - 2
trumpet	2 - 4	percussion	2 - 3
horn	0 - 2		

Appropriate literature for pep band includes street marches, school songs, and popular arrangements. These may be taken at a comparatively rapid tempo, since marching is not involved. However, any tendency to overblowing and sloppy execution must be curbed. Good style and precision should be stressed as usual, but a bit of modest improvisation need not be discouraged.

In some schools, pep bands are called upon to participate in the halftime pageantry at basketball games. This practice is not entirely mis-educational but can become quite burdensome. Some schools have found an answer by coordinating the pep band with a girls' drill team or dance group.

(1) The pep band rehearses and tape records a good, popular arrangement.

(2) The leader of the dance group constructs an appropriate routine and the girls rehearse it to the tape recording.

(3) The band and dance group perform jointly as scheduled, while taking care to maintain the original tempo.

A school sponsored stage band (dance band) is frowned upon in some circles but can offer valuable educative experiences. It should be remembered that popular music is well established as a social phenomenon and first hand familiarity with the style is an appropriate function of music education. Well over seven thousand of such groups now exist in the schools.[5]

However, this activity can easily become troublesome unless the following rules are observed.

(1) The big band of ten to twenty players is usually more suitable than the small combo of four or five, because the popular classics are avaliable for this instrumentation and more players are given experience.

(2) Search hard for the better arrangements of easy enough grade.[6]

(3) Do not allow bland, pseudo jazz style, but teach authentic style. Don't just run through the numbers, but rehearse them.

(4) Attempt to teach the art of improvisation.

(5) Arrange for special appearances when the group is ready, but do not allow the school group as such to accept paid engagements.

SECTIONAL REHEARSALS

Sectional rehearsal is a rather obvious supplement to the development of school bands and orchestras. In essence, it is a continuation of the homogeneous class method of instruction. Sectionals may be scheduled simultaneously during the regular rehearsal periods, by splitting the orchestra or band into six or eight manageable units, with each re-

[5] American Music Conference, "Report of Amateur Music in the U. S. A.," *Music Journal*, October, 1963, p. 62.

[6] The Art Dedrick arrangements have proved quite practical for starting stage bands.

hearsing under its section leader in a different room. Such a plan is usually invoked periodically, just after a new number has been introduced or during final polishing for public performance. Or, instead, each section may be scheduled regularly (perhaps every second week) in addition to the usual rehearsals of the full group. This plan enables the director to conduct all the rehearsals personally.

The principle of the sectional rehearsal is efficiency. It allows concentration upon problems peculiar to one section, without occupying the time of the other band and orchestra members. Thus, a judicious mixture of full and sectional rehearsals, under competent direction, should produce greater results than the same amount of time spent entirely in full rehearsals.

The sectional rehearsal is a logical place to conduct any intensive drill. For example, a certain rapid clarinet passage may be hampering the band's perfection of a number and the players are not clearing it up by individual practice; working as a section, ten or fifteen minutes may well be devoted to establishing the correct fingering and articulation, while trying it slowly and then gradually faster and faster, until the entire section develops the necessary facility.

In addition to rehearsal of the music at hand, the sectional may be used to introduce certain exercises and procedures that are aimed at better tone production and articulation. The practice of scales and arpeggios, lip slurs, and rhythmic figures attains maximum effect here, because the fingerings are identical for each player (allowing easy demonstration and correction), and tempo and key may be adjusted to the requirements of the particular instrument. Likewise, special trill fingerings, clefs, transpositions, muting techniques, and other such matters can be handled here very efficiently. This is also a good chance to hold tryouts, to check the condition and adjustment of instruments, and to tend to other matters which are of unique importance to any one section.

Sectional rehearsals need to be carefully planned for maximum results. Too often, the leader starts at the beginning of a piece and simply runs through it. This could be done at full rehearsal. The director must have either a written or mental record of certain points to be made and certain matters to be accomplished. This is especially true if the rehearsal is to be entrusted to an assistant conductor or to the section leader. In many instances, it is wise to assign such rehearsals to the principal of the section, for he may sense the difficulties of the part and the players' needs even better than the director—particularly if the director is not an expert player of that instrument. But such a student must be mature and have potential teaching skill, if he is to be successful, and he must be thoroughly coached by the director, and have full authority to deal with the players.

INDIVIDUAL STUDY

Individual Coaching Sessions

A special form of sectional rehearsal arises when players are coached on an individual basis. Obviously, this occurs when a section has only one player, such as a lone bassoonist, or when certain players seem to require special help. Some directors prefer to arrange all of their coaching on an individual, rather than a sectional basis. The feature that distinguishes these coaching sessions from regular individual instruction is their sporadic nature, and the fact that the main emphasis is on the literature being used in band or orchestra. True individual instruction, on the other hand, consists of a series of regularly scheduled lessons, devoted to the utmost development of the player's skill and artistry on his instrument. The emphasis, here, is usually upon technical material and solo literature.

Our previous discussion of sectional rehearsals has covered the essential philosophy and procedure affecting individual coaching sessions. We make this distinction in order to clarify the following discussion of individual study in its more classic sense.

Individual Lessons

Previously, we have stated the belief that group instruction for beginners is generally more successful than individual instruction, unless both can be accomplished. Once the players have been installed in one of the school performing groups, the value of supplemental instruction by means of individual lessons becomes more apparent.

We have also pointed out that individual study is often the most natural and efficient means of learning a second or third instrument, or converting from one to another. Since such a student is not really a beginner, he simply needs expert guidance in transferring his musicianship and adapting his muscular responses to a new medium.

Yet, continuing individual study should never become the basic form of instruction in the schools if the true role of school music is to be accomplished. Inherently, it is the method of specialization, and is best reserved for those who exhibit extra talent and motivation. Hence, much time and energy is wasted by directors, who assume the burden of universal individual instruction in their schools, because they believe that it is the ideal plan. Many of their pupils merely mark time and wonder why anyone should take the trouble to work with them so intensively.

These directors, having been dedicated early to the profession of music, were properly subjected to the regimen of private instruction and therefore assume that it is the fitting process for everyone. It is also easy for a director to imagine that he can teach any instrument adequately, as long as he has any advantage of experience over his pupils. However, it is presumptuous to consider one's self qualified for such an intimate process unless he has actually achieved considerable finesse on that specific instrument. Few are really qualified on more than three or four. Note how often the expert musician hesitates to entrust his own son or daughter to anyone but the most specialized instructor.

Nonetheless, in any flourishing program a number of students will advance to the point where individual instruction is indicated. These pupils are identified by their speed of advancement coupled with an attitude of curiosity and serious intention. In other words, these are the students in whom the director sees extra promise and potential. A number of plans have been used to meet this need.

(1) No definitive policy is established. Students arrange for private lessons, whenever and wherever they so choose.

(2) Students are referred to any qualified instructors who are available either locally or in nearby centers. The students pay the required fee. (In order to make such referrals, it is necessary to ascertain the competence of the various teachers and their availability for additional students.)

(3) The director attempts to handle the entire load to the best of his ability. He may do this on school time or after school hours, and charge a fee or not, depending on the school policy.

(4) The director is permitted by the school authorities to organize an informal conservatory, with the cooperation of local specialists, to operate outside school hours. A standard fee is charged.

(5) The director assumes the task in his own field and other local instructors are secured by the school, on a part time basis, to handle the rest.

(6) The school staff includes enough full time instructors, who are qualified on the various instruments, to handle the job.

The latter two plans are obviously superior. The question is not really whether a fee is charged, or even whether the school undertakes direct responsibility, since this matter is not wholly within its realm. The point is that talent which the school has fostered should not be abandoned at the critical point. Some responsibility remains to see that qualified players have some opportunity to secure adequate individual instruction.

The inherent goal of individual instruction is nothing less than thorough professional competence. That is, every student is to be originally regarded as one who may make a career on that instrument as a performer or teacher. To be sure, this is not often the case, but the teacher remains concerned that it will lead to a strong avocation for the student. This conviction is in the conservatory tradition, and it results in a strongly systematic form of instruction, which is right and proper.

By the same token, the teacher has every right to refuse unpromising students, and to drop those who do not apply themselves. After all, the teacher is not really working strictly within the province of public education, and he will not often support himself on the fees. His motive is largely altruistic, and so his time is best employed with only those who respond to his efforts.

The teacher is interested in these goals.

(1) Good playing habits (position, tone production, technical development) that will lead to natural mastery of the instrument.

(2) Regular, sufficient, and efficient practice.

(3) General musicianship (aural skill, theoretical understanding, and historical knowledge) and the application of it through authentic style and interpretation in his performance.

(4) An expanding repertoire.

(5) The desire and ability to prepare numbers for public performance and to perform them freely and capably.

(6) The desire to continue study and improvement on his instrument.

In Chapter 3 we discussed certain technical matters and recommended a few materials for the beginning level of instruction. But, we will not presume to recommend specific procedures and materials suitable for each instrument at the more advanced levels, since we have stated the belief that anyone who offers individual lessons, on a sustained basis, must already be considerably advanced on the instrument. Of necessity, he is familiar with the special problems to be faced and either knows what literature he can use, or where he can find it. If he is not, he must undergo further individual study himself.

But performing skill and experience in themselves do not guarantee good teaching. Teaching has to do with *application* of knowledge, through wielding one's personality, understanding of the student, and good learning principles, toward legitimate goals. Many understand and accept this fact in relation to classroom and rehearsal situations but fail to recognize the application in the private studio. That is to say, some accomplished classroom teachers are very ineffective as individual instructors because they apparently assume that one simply tells the student what he should do, and he does it. So, we will have something to say about the general approach to individual instruction.

(1) The general procedure with a new pupil is to check his instrument and tuning, ask him about his playing experience, and hear him play a little to assess his strengths and weaknesses and to discover his relative advancement. The teacher may then point out certain basic flaws in the pupil's approach and demonstrate appropriate corrective drills. But it is usually unwise to be extensive in this preliminary analysis, for the pupil has many preconceptions and attitudes which will need to be

modified. It is better to concentrate on a few points at a time. For example, one might begin the attempt to improve the young violinist's bowing stroke and to readjust the position of his left elbow; or, seeing the young trumpeter employing his tongue wrongly, between the teeth, it is wise to stress the proper technique for tonguing. But a complete overhaul of playing position or embouchure is not wise at first. Indeed, it is not always possible at any time.

The teacher must try to inspire the pupil at the very beginning with a greater sense of the possibilities of the instrument, the teacher's capability, and his own (the pupil's) prospects of achievement through careful attention and practice. It is neither wise to suggest that the pupil had poor instruction before, nor is it helpful to brag or show off. But, it is good practice to demonstrate a matter or two quite casually and thus provide a good model for the pupil.

(2) New material must be assigned which is of the proper type and difficulty to be useful in advancing the pupil's musical skill and understanding. It is necessary to check the exercises or pieces to be practiced with the next lesson date and hour, or, this information should be written on a separate piece of paper, together with special directions about the matters to be corrected. The usual assignment includes some useful technical material (scales, bowings, lip slurs, etc.) and/or an étude, and appropriate short pieces, or a section of a larger number.

(3) The first lesson should close with any necessary directions about practice rooms, lockers, securing new music, fee payment, etc.

(4) The normal procedure in ensuing lessons is, first, to hear the previous assignment, second, to make corrections by demonstration, verbal explanation, or notation on the music, and third, to reassign the material as necessary, or assign new material that is deliberately calculated to advance the student's insight and skill. Several further observations are necessary.

(a) In hearing the assigned material, let the student play a bit. Don't stop him on every measure, and don't dwell on the same two or three things.

(b) Tell the student clearly wherein he failed or succeeded.

(c) If the student can learn more from his previous assignment, it should be repeated. If he has done rather well, or if he has not, but is obviously tired of the struggle, give him something new.

(d) Demonstrate, or have him try enough of any new assignment to show what is wanted. Make notations as necessary. Do not stress technical matters at the expense of style and interpretation. The glory of music is expression, which can be especially well taught in the private studio.

(e) In making new assignments, don't always take the next page in the book. Many times something more appropriate is found a page or two earlier or later, or in another book.

(f) Indeed, all students should not have the same material assigned sequentially. A strict course of study should not be followed. The possibility of special assignments is one of the primary values of individual instruction.

(g) Be careful not to move too fast, especially if the pupil is not mastering the assigned material. Many young pupils are harmed by shallow coverage of major works long before they are ready.

(h) Younger students need more concrete explanations, and less theoretical discussion, than their elders. Don't explain your entire theory of embouchure or bow movement to a youngster, but simply show him how to set the lips or move the arm.

(5) Never beg a pupil to practice or threaten him about his practicing. A pointed observation about his need for concentrated, thoughtful practice is enough. Over the long run, insufficient practice is simply a reflection of conflicting interests or of the teacher's inability to provide stimulating lessons and assignments. Unless there is hope of a change it is best to dismiss the student as quietly and easily as possible.

(6) It is important to schedule the student for an occasional recital appearance. This is not designed to prove anything except the teacher's confidence in the pupil. It should be an incentive, if the number is chosen to push the student ahead without jeopardy. Memorization is usually wise. The entire operation should result in a consolidation of the progress made over several months.

(7) The teacher should communicate his general satisfaction in the student's recital performance to the student and his parents. But he should avoid any manifestation of pride in the student's accomplishment. This can be terribly damaging to the pupil, as well as to the teacher's relationship with his professional colleagues.

(8) The teacher should take care to establish a clear policy regarding missed lessons and fees (when not covered by the school contract). Any student who misses lessons frequently should obviously be dismissed.

(9) No advantage should be taken of any relationship with dealers, in order to profit from the student's purchase of instruments or music. But the teacher can expect certain preferences in the purchase of his own music and supplies.

(10) The teacher should be naturally interested in his students as persons. Occasionally some time can be spent before or after lessons in general conversation. On the other hand, these personal relationships should not be allowed to become too close.

SUMMER PROGRAMS

Summer activity offers possibilities for supplementing and extending the basic aspects of the school's instrumental program. This does not mean that additional activities should be organized, over and above the ones we have discussed, but any and all of them can be employed in a special setting.

One of the most stimulating forms of summer activity is available to those who attend any one of the hundreds of excellent summer music camps that are established in this country. Over fifty thousand attended in 1963.[7] These offer competent private instruction, experience in large and small ensembles, recreation, and social activity. In short, the student participates in a very stimulating form of cooperative endeavor. It gives him an excellent opportunity to evaluate his competence and return home with stronger motivation. The only drawbacks are expense and a certain tendency to set unrealistic goals.

The other possibility is to set up a local summer session (of five or six weeks' duration) designed for the needs of the local students. In some localities, this is directly subsidized by the school or by the city, while others allow the use of the school facilities. The teacher usually charges individual fees to cover his expenses.

The possibilities include: (1) beginning classes for new volunteers and older players wishing to learn a second instrument; (2) individual instruction; (3) small ensembles of all types; (4) a summer band and/or orchestra consisting of those regular members who are in attendance, plus those becoming eligible for the group next fall; (5) a class on marching fundamentals for next year's new band members; (6) community band and/or orchestra, usually organized of school age players and former graduates (such groups can be scheduled for regular "pops" concerts); and (7) special classes in basic harmony, arranging, conducting, baton twirling and drum majoring. These activities, not usually considered integral parts of the instrumental music program, are an excellent supplement to the summer program.

The inherent advantages of such an operation are several. Chief among these is the lack of interference with and distraction from other school activities. Scheduling is a joy and the concentrated practice achieved by the players is often amazing. It also offers many electives that the student cannot manage in his regular schedule. Finally, it can sustain the program so that work begins again next fall, not at the bottom, but somewhere nearer the point that was achieved in the spring.

The teacher should avoid regarding such a program as an operation to provide him with extra income. He must offer something fresh that is not available during the school year. Planning and announcements must be made early. A preliminary questionnaire is advisable. The most practical period for the session is usually during late June and July, in order to allow some needed rest after school closes and yet avoid August vacations.

[7] American Music Conference, *op. cit.*, p. 62.

If the size of the regular school program does not promise success in such an undertaking, it is sometimes feasible to combine with one or two nearby schools and their directors, to offer a really well balanced summer course. Another possibility is to arrange to bring the entire band or orchestra to a nearby college campus for a week's work with a staff of specialists.

SUMMARY

One of the principal activities associated with school instrumental groups is the marching band. It is not the marching itself, but the outside pressures which often cause an overemphasis in this field. The remedy is to avoid the elaborate panoramas and curtail rehearsal time. A pace geared to the yardlines, military evolutions, and careful charting are definitely recommended. More concentrated efforts are also possible when entrances and exits are repeated, and when certain special effects can be used that do not involve marching evolutions.

The possibility of special combinations of school band and orchestra personnel should not be overlooked. These include civic symphonies and bands, all city bands and orchestras, and clinic groups. Personnel are also usefully employed in choral-instrumental works and staged productions. Enthusiastic participation in such ventures is important, so long as they are well organized and do not unduly interrupt regular activities.

A flourishing chamber music program is one mark of a good director. The effort required is not great and the rewards are many. Dozens of combinations are considered standard, from duos to stage bands and large choirs of like instruments. Good literature is available in most instances. Such groups become a prime outlet for the musically gifted and help establish student initiative. But it is important to acquire a library of suitable literature and to form well matched groups of players.

Sectional rehearsals are an indispensable adjunct of the full band and orchestra rehearsal. They should be concentrated upon the unique problems of the instrument and the literature being studied.

Individual instruction becomes important when players have advanced to the performing groups and have developed serious intentions. The inherent goal is professional competence. Few teachers are qualified to teach all the instruments on such a basis. Instead, specialists should be engaged by the school or director, or students should be referred to qualified instructors. A stimulating approach to each pupil is absolutely essential.

A summer camp or school is a natural extension of the regular instrumental program. It provides an excellent opportunity to improve the band and orchestra, to start new beginners, to organize chamber groups, and to offer special elective subjects.

QUESTIONS FOR DISCUSSION

1. How legitimate is the marching band? How may its chief dangers be avoided?

2. Review the basic marching evolutions. How are these best explained and taught?

3. Chart at least one formation with the accompanying music and announcements.

4. Describe the various types of cooperative musical ventures. How are these organized? What is the director's role?

5. What are the chief types of chamber groups? How are the members selected and assigned? How are rehearsals arranged and conducted? What are the advantages and disadvantages of public appearances by these ensembles?

6. When and how are sectional rehearsals scheduled? What are the principal objectives?

7. Who merits individual instruction? How may qualified teachers be supplied? What are the principal objectives and procedures?

8. Describe the organization of an effective summer instrumental music program.

SELECTED REFERENCES

HJELMERVICK, KENNETH AND RICHARD BERG, *Marching Bands: How to Organize and Develop Them.* New York: The Ronald Press Company, 1953.

LEE, JACK, *Modern Marching Band Techniques.* Winona, Minnesota: Hal Leonard Music, Inc., 1955.

LOKEN, NEWT AND OTIS DYPWICK, *Cheerleading and Marching Bands.* New York: The Ronald Press Company, 1956.

LONG, A. H., *Marching to the Yard Lines.* Ponca City, Oklahoma: Luther Music Co., 1952.

MARCOUILLER, DON, *Marching for Marching Bands.* Dubuque, Iowa: Wm. C. Brown Company, 1958.

NIMAC SELECTION COMMITTEE, *Selective Music Lists for Instrumental and Vocal Solos, Instrumental and Vocal Ensembles.* Washington, D. C.: Music Educators National Conference, 1963.

TOTGENHORST, TED C. AND DONALD L. WOLF, *Precision Marching with Band.* New York: Bourne, Inc., 1954.

WALN, GEORGE (ED.) AND COMMITTEE, *Materials for Miscellaneous Instrumental Ensembles.* Washington, D. C.: Music Educators National Conference, 1960.

WRIGHT, AL G., *The Show Band.* Evanston, Illinois: The Instrumentalist Co.

CHAPTER 7

Facilities and Equipment

Elaborate facilities and equipment do not insure a good instrumental music program. Some of the finest educational results are being produced in old, dingy surroundings with over age instruments, poor storage facilities, and lack of space. In such a case, however, the old instruments are kept in top condition, and the old buildings can be quite solid and acoustically responsive. Mere newness often conceals flimsy, unsuitable construction.

Physical surroundings are only one factor in good musical instruction, but it is a very important factor and is more critical than in most educational fields. It requires a good deal of attention from any instrumental music teacher. Though he should not be expected to serve as an architect, draftsman, electronic engineer, and instrument repairman, as well as musician, teacher, counselor, and public relations expert, he must have a basic understanding of these concrete matters, so that he may at least discern what is wrong with what he has and work toward better solutions.

This chapter does not present a detailed sketch of an ideal music plant and its equiment, but rather outlines these needs as they relate to instrumental instruction. It covers space needs and the related matters of sound, air, light, and furnishings. It deals with the storage, maintenance, and control of the equipment connected with instruction.

MUSIC ROOMS

The Auditorium

An auditorium is an enclosure with staging facilities for the performers and seating for the audience which listens and watches. There are many sizes and designs. Many a hall is simply a large room with level floor, no proscenium arch, and no provision for scenery. Under these circumstances, chairs may be arranged for the audience to face an open space at one end of the room, which serves as a stage for the performers. The situation is improved with temporary risers or platforms, and some form of demountable shell or set of reflectors to direct the sound toward the audience. Another type of hall has a built-in shell and elevated stage, but no arrangement for scenery.

Properly, a stage has a regular proscenium arch, and the stagehouse must be more than double the height of the arch in order to accommodate changes of theatrical scenery. Such a stage should be fitted with a removable shell or acoustical ceiling for concert work to help avoid loss and distortion of sound. Acoustical ceilings can be built in sections and hung from the battens (long pipes), allowing flow of light between sections and adjustment of the angles of sound reflectance.

Near the top of the stagehouse will be a grid and pulley arrangement for the battens to which are attached lights, curtains, legs, teasers, canopy, etc. Spacious enough dressing rooms and storage areas for scenery, pianos, and other equipment are needed offstage. Lighting controls are backstage and/or at the rear of the hall.

Stage dimensions vary greatly, depending upon the size of the hall and the original uses for which it was planned. Eighteen square feet should be figured for each player in the band or orchestra. The practical extremes are about fifteen feet by thirty feet, and forty feet by sixty feet. An organ loft may be located over the stage or to the sides of it. The loft and organ console must be placed so that the player can hear his production clearly.

In front of the curtain there should be an apron of at least six feet to accommodate a piano, speaker, or small group when the curtain is closed.

Before and below the elevated stage is the orchestra pit which is used for orchestral accompaniment of staged works. This is often merely a space of ten or twelve feet between the stage and front row of seats, but it is highly desirable to have a sunken pit and railing. The pit should be low enough so that the seated players and their lights do not obstruct the view of the audience; this usually means a pit floor of from ten to twenty feet in width about five feet below stage level, which can be recessed about three feet underneath the apron. A pit floor fifteen feet by forty-five feet will accommodate about forty-five players. See Fig. 7-1.

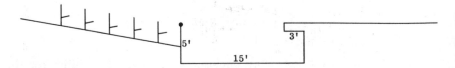

Fig. 7-1.

In many cases it is convenient to have a removable floor over the pit so the area may serve as a corridor. In more elaborate arrangements, the pit floor is an elevator that is adjustable to any height between stage level and the floor below. This is a great help in transporting heavy equipment and in extending the stage for mass performances.

Sufficient electric outlets are needed so that rack lights will not require the frequent use of hazardous extension lines.

The audience is seated bleacher style or on fixed or movable seats on a flat or raked (sloping) floor. The finest type of auditorium, of course, has theatre seats and steeply raked seating, which provides excellent vision and minimum loss of direct sound. There may be balconies and boxes to increase the seating capacity. Necessary provision for the comfort of the audience includes ventilation and air conditioning (cleaning, heating, or cooling), sufficient lighting with dimmer control, and adjacent lobbies, lounges, and washrooms.

The matter most critical for instrumental music is that of proper acoustics. This depends not only upon the size of the hall and the types of music to be presented, but also upon specific shapes, surfaces, and materials built into the hall. There are so many variables that much detail is left to chance. The acoustical problems that appeared prior to and after the 1962 opening of Philharmonic Hall in the Lincoln Center for the Performing Arts demonstrate that the most careful engineering may lead to puzzling results.[1] This highlights the fact that halls need to be planned with more capacity for experimentation and adjustment.

Musical sounds received in an open field are basically pure, or direct, except for extraneous noises and wind distortion. Indoors the effect may be approximated by reducing reverberation with highly absorptive materials (including the audience which is highly absorptive). But listeners are conditioned to a more reverberant sound produced by reflections from surfaces within the room. The sound waves reach the listener by various routes, at different times and in different strengths and frequencies, which causes the music to take on characteristic qualities. The final result depends upon the control of certain acoustical phenomena which we will discuss briefly in order to clarify some of the problems of concert halls and other types of music rooms.

Intimacy is a function of the "initial time-delay gap," which is defined as the difference in times of arrival at a listener's position between the direct sound and the first reflected sound. A short time gap provides a focus to the sound and a long gap makes the room sound hollow. This is obviously no problem in smaller and medium size rooms, because the walls and ceilings reflect the sound quickly, but becomes a major problem in larger halls. It is corrected by control of shapes and angles of wall surfaces

[1] See Leo J. Baranek, *Music, Acoustics, and Architecture* (New York: John Wiley and Sons, Inc., 1962), pp. 511-540.

and may involve the use of side balconies or suspended sound reflecting panels. See Fig. 7-2.

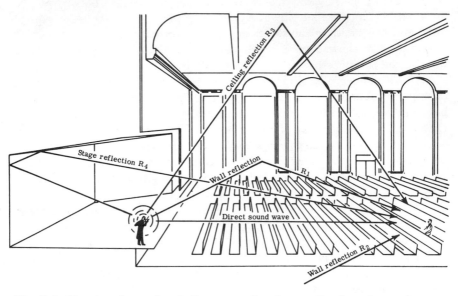

Fig. 7-2. *Showing the paths of direct sound and several reflected sound waves in a concert hall. Reflections also occur from balcony faces, rear walls, niches, and any other reflecting surfaces. From Leo J. Baranek,* Music, Acoustics, and Architecture *(New York: John Wiley and Sons, Inc., 1962), pp. 511-540.*

Liveness is a function of "reverberation time," or persistence of sound after the tone-source has stopped. "Reverberation increases the fullness of tone; it enhances the bass; it contributes to the blending of the instruments; it increases the range of crescendo and diminuendo; and it diffuses the sound so that it seems to be distributed throughout the room rather than emanating from one direction only."[2]

The optimum reverberation time varies with the size of room and the type of music to be performed. Fig. 7-3 gives an approximation:[3]

Thus the ideal reverberation time may vary from about half a second for the small practice room to over two seconds for the large auditorium. The actual reverberation time will depend upon the cubic volume versus the absorptive values within the room. That is to say, sound waves will naturally be reflected back and forth in a room and will gradually decay unless they are more quickly absorbed by various materials.[4] Heavy and

[2] *Ibid.*, p. 425.
[3] Committee on Music Rooms and Equipment, *Music Rooms, Buildings, and Equipment* (Washington, D. C.: Music Educators National Conference, 1955), p. 33.
[4] Tables of absorptive values may be found in Committee on Music Rooms and Equipment, *op. cit.*, p. 41, and in various architectural treatises.

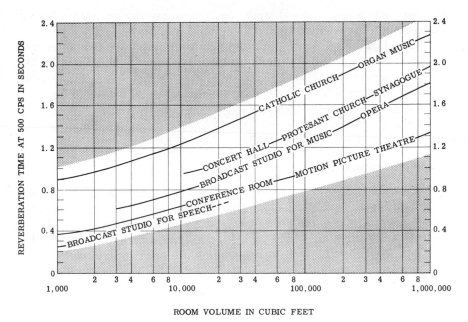

Fig. 7-3. Optimum reverberation time for rooms of various sizes. From Chapter VII, "Acoustics," by Richard Bolt in Music Rooms, Buildings, and Equipment *(Washington, D.C.: Music Educators National Conference, 1955) p. 33. Used by permission of the publishers.*

porous materials are generally more absorptive than thin, hard materials. Good concert halls generally feature high ceilings and conventional surfaces of smooth plaster or thick wood paneling to assist reverberation. Patches or strips of acoustical tile are commonly employed in smaller rooms to reduce reverberation.

Warmth is a quality which derives from a strong bass, and is related to the reverberation time of the lower frequencies. Baranek attributes weak bass principally to the modern use of thin wood paneling with air space behind it, since this arrangement absorbs an unusual proportion of the lower frequencies.[5]

Loudness of the direct sound is naturally related to the power of the performers and the sound projecting values of the shell, to the distance of the listeners, and to the presence or absence of intervening obstructions (such as heads). Raked seating and good shell design will improve the strength of the sound but a sound amplification system is needed in very large or poorly designed halls.

Sound diffusion is produced by irregularities in wall and ceiling surfaces and in the placement of specially absorptive materials. Such

[5] Baranek, *op. cit.,* pp. 436-438.

irregular surfaces, or splayed walls, are a common device used to avoid echo and other distortions in any size music room.

Though there are numerous other matters to consider, this discussion provides a summary of the problems in auditorium construction and a basis for further technical study. It is plain that many inadequate solutions are attributable to preoccupation with costs and appearances. The instrumental director should be able to contribute to the discussions with school officials and architects in planning the construction and remodeling of concert halls and other phases of his plant.

Combination Auditoriums

To conserve costs several functions are often combined. Thus we have the ballroom with stage, the gymnasium with stage, and the cafetorium. Such combinations are more prevalent in the smaller high schools and elementary schools (see Fig. 7-4). The difficulty lies in the usually

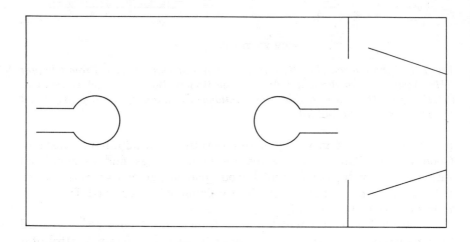

Fig. 7-4. Ballroom, gymnasium, or cafeteria with stage.

inadequate stagehouse and shell, lack of raked seating, and acoustically unfortunate shapes, materials, and surfaces. Unplanned addition of acoustical wall tile is a likely but probably inadequate solution. Recommendations from acoustical engineers are advisable.

Even more severe problems are presented when bleacher seats are built at one side of the gymnasium and the center part of the basketball court is also the stage floor. Since the stage must often be installed or dismantled within minutes, the usual solution is to have curtains which can be lowered on three sides (opening toward the audience) to define the performing area. See Fig. 7-5. Faced with such awkward building dimensions and so primitive a stage enclosure, it is imperative to secure the advice of a competent acoustical engineer, who can recommend certain types of plywood or fiberglass panels to serve as sound reflectors, both above and to the rear of the stage.

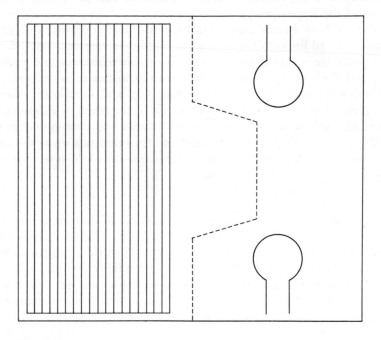

Fig. 7-5.

Rehearsal Rooms

Band and orchestra rehearsals are best accomplished in rooms built specifically for that purpose. Eighteen square feet per player is the minimum, but extra space is needed for aisles, storage, and acoustics. Ceiling height should be at least twelve feet for good sound. Pillars are a great nuisance and can be avoided in one story structures. Since a large volume of sound is contained within a relatively small space, moderate use of acoustical tile or other absorptive material is usually required.

Some directors like a flat floor (for better flexibility in use) and others prefer risers. The trend seems to be toward permanent risers, six or eight inches high and four feet wide. This aids in eye and ear contact between director and players.

Adequate storage spaces are needed at the sides and rear of the room, or in adjoining areas. The director's office and practice rooms should be nearby.

In elementary schools and in smaller high schools having one music teacher, it is common to provide an all-purpose music room for instrumental and choral rehearsals and other types of musical activity. Some difficulties may arise because of the different seating and acoustical requirements of the various activities, but these are necessarily resolved in favor of the larger groups.

Many school bands and orchestras use the auditorium stage for rehearsals. In addition to the savings in building space and costs, there is some advantage in avoiding the move for dress rehearsals and performances, and the consequent readjustment to acoustics of a different hall. But there are obvious problems in scheduling and equipment management, particularly if the stage is part of the gymnasium or cafeteria, and there is also the likelihood of unwanted visitors and consequent distraction. The practicability of this arrangement thus depends upon the ability of the music department to keep its rehearsal schedule intact over the demands of other school activities.

Practice Rooms

The need for practice rooms varies according to the size of the instrumental music program and school policy about practicing at school or at home. Any extensive program of ensembles and individual instruction will require several such rooms. These may vary from individual rooms as small as 40 square feet to larger ensemble rooms of 120 square feet or more.

The acoustical properties of these small rooms require nonparallel walls and heavy sound absorption. But since such rooms are most often arranged in series, and near classrooms and rehearsal rooms, the biggest problem is often the *isolation* of sound. This problem is discussed later in this chapter.

Office-Studio Space

Offices for the instrumental instructors are multipurpose rooms for study and office work, individual lessons, and conferences. They will usually contain a desk and cabinet or shelves for books, music, and equipment. Most important, they should have the necessary privacy but should be located where all departmental activity can be supervised.

Music Libraries

Legal-size steel filing cabinets are becoming more and more the favorite method of storing band and orchestra music, ensemble literature, and solo material, and small march size files can also be obtained. This procedure has the advantage of compactness and easy filing, fire resistance, and ready expansion. The files may be kept in the rehearsal room, the director's office, or in a separate library room. A large table or sorting rack is a great convenience.

As bandsmen know, most concert music is ordered in "small," "full," or "symphonic" sets—each containing a fixed number of parts. Marches come in standard sets and often two sets are needed. An orchestral number, however, is usually ordered in terms of a score, a set of parts, and extra strings as required. In ordering music, it is well to be liberal in the estimation of the number of parts needed for future growth, since emergency ordering of extra parts is very inconvenient and copying or photocopying music is laborious and illegal. All parts should be individually stamped with the school name before using or filing.

Envelopes of concert size, octavo size, and march size can be purchased, and as a number is filed, the composer, title, character, and parts list should be listed on that envelope. Performance dates and loss of parts are noted as they may occur. The numbers may be filed and indexed alphabetically by composer or title. Some keep a card file and others prefer the simple and compact running list.

Listening and Recording Facilities

One or more of the following procedures is recommended for music listening and recording.

(1) The necessary portable record players and tape recorders may be checked out from the director's office or other central point.

(2) A listening room may be provided, fitted with record cabinet, table(s) and multiple headphone outfits, or side booths with fixed turntables.

(3) Stereophonic speakers and record console may be installed in classroom(s) and/or rehearsal room for mass listening.

(4) A windowed, soundproof control booth may be built at the rear of the auditorium or rehearsal hall, complete with professional recording equipment, overhead adjustable microphones, etc.

Repair Facilities

Some convenient point should be fitted for instrument repairs, which may be a portion of the director's office, the music library, instrument locker room, or a separate room near one of those locations. The essentials include running water, electrical outlets, workbench, and cabinet space. A list of necessary tools and supplies is included at the end of this chapter.

Instrument Storage

Some rehearsal rooms contain open bins or shelves for the smaller instruments, leaving the string basses, cellos, and tubas either on rollaway racks or chair stands and the percussion in place. This system works fairly well if the director is in the immediate vicinity throughout the school day and the room is always locked in his absence.

Others have small side rooms for the piano, the percussion, the larger instruments on their racks and stands, and for the smaller instruments in bins. These doors may be locked, except at rehearsal times.

Some schools provide no storage space at all for the smaller instruments, but allow the students to carry them to and from school as if they were personally owned instruments. During summer vacations, these instruments are stored in one of the music rooms.

Individual lockers provide the safest and most convenient plan of storage. This keeps the instruments secure yet available for practice at any time and pinpoints responsibility. These lockers can be installed along either a hall or a side room. Standard size steel lockers will accommodate most instruments and special sized ones can be purchased or built for awkward sized instruments. But the specially built bank of plywood lockers helps avoid damage through squeezing and dropping, is less noisy, give a good appearance, and is amazingly compact, inexpensive, and durable.

Each type of instrument is of a different length, width, and height. Different models of cases add to this complexity. If sufficient wall space is available, a bank of lockers fifteen inches deep (and of proper lengths and heights) will accommodate all but the largest instruments. But that format requires an inordinate amount of wall space and such a variety of locker sizes that the standard thirty-six inch depth is considered much more practical under ordinary circumstances. All instruments can be stored within five or six basic locker sizes built to the specifications shown in Fig. 7-6.

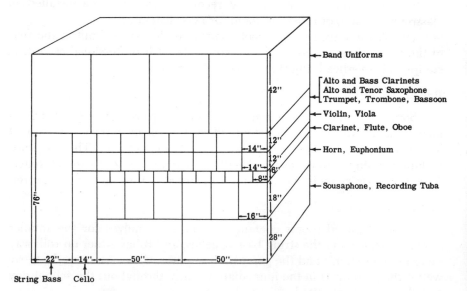

Fig. 7-6.

Each locker can be fitted with hasps and a combination lock. Some prefer grills in the locker doors for air circulation, but their chief benefit is for easier locker checks.

Location of Music Rooms

In many respects, the placement of music rooms is the most critical factor in the music plant and does much to determine all of its internal arrangements. Good location depends not only upon logical grouping of facilities and good traffic control, but also upon sound control since sound is the most basic property of instrumental music. A room must be protected both from sound coming in and also from too much sound going out. A noisy room can make instruction in adjacent areas almost impossible. Such isolation is not easy to obtain. It is not done simply by adding extra amounts of absorptive materials within a room (which can ruin its internal acoustics). The chief means are *distance and insulation.*

Insulation is achieved by (1) tight seal of doors and windows, (2) thickness and density of materials used between rooms, (3) disconnection of sound conducting units (walls, ceilings, beams, pipes, floors, and doors) by means of jointed supports and double-slab construction, and (4) special absorptive treatment of any open ducts such as ventilating circuits. This kind of construction needs to be avoided as much as possible because it is quite expensive and only *reduces* sound transmission.

The easiest method of sound isolation is *distance.* Instrumental music facilities should be located in a separate building or wing of a building. The music area itself should be constructed so that the rehearsal rooms, offices, and practice areas are well separated by corridors, washrooms, and various storage areas.

For example, the arrangement shown in Fig. 7-7 maintains easy access to the stage, yet assists sound attenuation by the placement of offices, etc. This does not remove the need for special construction to further insulate these rooms, especially the practice rooms, but does allow effective results at a minimum cost.

This only illustrates the principle. There is tremendous variety in the size and types of plant and the consequent possibilities of arrangement. Music educators who become involved in a building program are wise to visit other schools and to check model blueprints. Several excellent plans are illustrated by the Committee on Music Rooms and Equipment.[6]

Air Conditioning

Air conditioning involves the circulation of a sufficient volume of fresh clean air of the proper temperature and humidity. Rehearsals of instrumental groups require an increased rate of ventilation, coupled with reduction of sound transmission via the air ducts. Additionally, any undue

[6] *Ibid.*

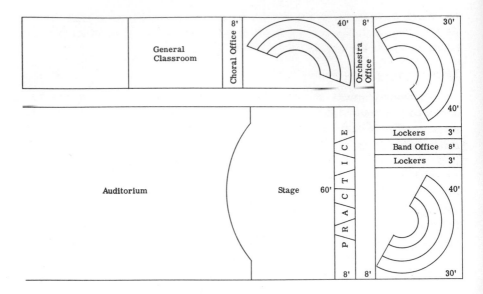

Fig. 7-7.

variation in temperature and humidity causes expansion and contraction of the musical instruments, with consequent intonation problems in rehearsal, broken drumheads, and possible cracks in woodwind and string instruments.

The following arrangements are important.

(1) Assuming forced air ventilation (rather than window and gravity ventilation), ventilating ducts should be constructed of or lined with asbestos or similar fireproof acoustical material and should have numerous bends and baffles. The gratings should not be so fine as to produce a noticeable hum or whisper. Radiant heat produces less drafts and drying effect on the air, but may result in noisy, rattling pipes.

(2) Any hot-air heating system should have humidity control or an independent humidifying-dehumidifying system should be installed. This is especially needed in areas with pianos and instrument storage.

(3) Temperature should be controlled by a thermostat. In warm climates, a cooling system is desirable for good working conditions. Temperatures must not be allowed to go unchecked over weekends and vacations.

Illumination and Color

The nature of music activities requires careful attention to lighting. A light intensity of at least fifty footcandles is needed at the racks in rehearsal rooms, stages, and practice rooms. The color and reflectance of the room surfaces should be contrived to reduce glare and to produce a good psychological effect. Reflectance should likewise be controlled in room hardware and equipment, such as chalkboards and music racks.

Planning Music Facilities

A former director of ours was getting no action on his request for acoustical treatment of his very live rehearsal room. With school permission he tacked burlap bags loosely over the entire ceiling and walls and thus greatly reduced the reverberation. Soon after this demonstration, the funds were found for the needed remodeling.

The instrumental music teacher should realize that he is not condemned to suffer unrelieved until a new building is planned and constructed. Much can be done by way of remodeling and upgrading present facilities. Such alterations can be accomplished for a fraction of the cost of new construction and that solution is better than waiting fifteen or twenty years for the ideal facilities.

The director should consider these questions.

(1) Are instructional activities suffering from lack of space? If so, is expansion into adjacent areas feasible? What are the possibilities of constructing an addition to the present facilities, or transferring instruction to more spacious quarters? In particular, which rooms are too small? Can room assignments be revised, or can partitions be removed to employ the space more effectively?

(2) Is there wasted space? Could this be converted to practice rooms, listening rooms, repair or storage rooms? Is there a need for additional instrument lockers or uniform cabinets, and where could these be constructed?

(3) Are there areas where noise from other rooms is a particular problem? If so, can doors be sealed more tightly? Can the ventilating ducts be improved? Can added partitions be installed to reduce sound transmission?

(4) How is the quality of sound in the auditorium, the rehearsal room, and the practice rooms? If it is too dead, can anything be done to remove absorptive materials and to arrange more effective reflection? Where the room is too live, can heavy curtains and acoustical tile be added on some of the surfaces?

(5) Are heating and humidity control satisfactory and if not can special controls be established? Is lighting unusually dim or glaring in any area so that remedial steps should be taken? Are the ceilings tight and safe? Are there areas that need repainting and new floor tiling?

The problem of planning a new music facility consists in anticipation of needs and active participation in the development of specifications. Such a study is wisely supported by a practical understanding of the potentialities of music activities and some technical background in the problems of construction, such as we have outlined.

The director must think ahead ten or fifteen years. In view of enrollment trends and natural growth, what will be the size of his groups? Does he foresee need for additional teachers and added equipment? Has his experience made him aware of special problems in coordination with vocal, dramatic, and athletic programs? These conclusions should be summarized in terms of activities, number of rooms and their appropriate sizes, and locations, and these conclusions should be submitted to the building committee.

Once preliminary sketches have been drawn, it is important to review them with an eye to any basic flaws in design (such as insufficient space, undue proximity of music and academic classes, poor stage access, flat auditorium floor, low ceilings). At this stage, there is yet hope that favorable revisions can be made, especially if the recommendations are supported by sketches and the reasons are submitted in writing. Helpful ideas can be obtained by the study of drawings and by visits to other schools having up-to-date music facilities.

The areas assigned to instrumental music should be carefully analyzed. What is the most natural arrangement of the rooms? Is any space too small or possibly more than ample? Is there a better way to separate performing areas from nonperforming areas? Both at this stage and later it is usually found that one can not get all he wants, so the decision must be made whether to cut down on the size, or the number, of rooms. In general, the latter course is preferable because later expansion is more easily arranged.

As these plans begin to crystallize, it is crucial to indicate the special treatment which would seem necessary in terms of dual walls and ceilings, ventilating ducts, room acoustics, heat and humidity control, lighting, and so on. If these ideas seem to be taken lightly, it is well to point out the noise factor to other classes and to suggest consultations with an acoustical engineer.

It is usually wise to plan as much built-in equipment as possible. This helps to make the use of the rooms explicit, but if it is cut out of the original construction, it can perhaps be added later. Thus one becomes as particular as possible in measuring and diagramming risers, lockers, cabinets and shelves, desks and tables, electrical outlets, thermostats and humidistats, telephone jacks, sinks, etc. All this should be much more carefully done than charting any football show.

There will be several revisions of the blueprints. The director needs to check each of these carefully and do his part both to refine and to correct any oversights. A similar process is undergone when the contract is finally bid and accepted and work is in progress. Construction errors are often made which can be corrected en route but not later.

EQUIPMENT

Standard Furnishings

Standard furnishings are usually purchased by the school with general usage in mind, and not out of special concern for the instrumental director. However, certain specifications should be kept in mind.

Rehearsal chairs should be sturdy, comfortable, and conducive to good playing posture. The aluminum or steel frame variety, moderately padded and plastic covered, is an excellent chair for this purpose but it is comparatively expensive. The wooden or steel frame straight chair with flat wooden seat and curved back piece is more commonly used. One should be sure that when this chair is purchased, it is not too low, but that it has the eighteen-inch seat height for high-school age. Folding chairs should be avoided because they are generally too low, poorly shaped for posture, and tip easily.

Any available type chair will serve for the audience where seating is on open floors, and chairs are to be set up and removed, but the more comfortable the better. For an auditorium, the preferred type is the fixed theatre type seat, upholstered, and with cushioned folding seat.

Eight or ten stools, either adjustable swivel type or fixed thirty inch height, are needed in the rehearsal room for string bass players, drummers, and conductor.

Standard type office desks and swivel chairs should be available for offices plus reception chairs with arm rests. Regular tables or folding banquet tables may be required in certain classrooms and offices.

The typewriter with elite type and wide carriage is probably the most suitable for the director's work. In addition to the regular ditto or mimeograph machine, one of the newer photo-copy machines will enable quick and legible duplication of special arrangements, etc. For musical use, one should have the extra-wide model with overhead exposure rather than the letter-size, feed-through type.

Audio-Visual Equipment

As mentioned earlier in this chapter, the methods for using recordings range from the simple portable phonograph to elaborate stereophonic equipment installed in special listening rooms, with side booths or multiple headphone sets. A great deal depends upon the monitor. If the director himself, or a special assistant, is to play the recordings, then the highest type equipment should be purchased and placed in a locked room or console. If machines are to be left open or checked out by students, then sturdy, practical construction is indicated. It is impossible to recommend models and specifications in view of the various types and sizes of rooms, and the continuous experimentation and rapid development of equipment in this field.

The same remarks apply to tape recorders. For fine work thousands of dollars may be invested in recording equipment, which is installed in a special control booth. A bit less elaborate and more flexible solution is provided by a good quality semiportable machine (usually in two cases) which may be kept and transported on a small two level table on rollers. The microphone may be attached to an adjustable boom.

Several lighter and cheaper one-piece models of good quality are now available. They have the advantage of greater compactness and easier operation, although the fidelity is not as fine. The 7½ inch speed, single track model, is preferable for common use.

Other audio-visual aids include:

> radio—AM and FM
> television—regular or closed circuit
> public address systems
> portable amplifier—battery operated
> film projector
> slide projector
> opaque projector

Special Equipment

About two-thirds as many music racks as players are required for any band or orchestra room, as well as those needed in practice rooms and studios. The most satisfactory model now has no screw adjustment at all, but is raised, lowered, and tipped to the proper angle by moderate hand pressure. If the available music racks are of more than one model or color, the director may easily make them more uniform with a spray can of black paint, and the school name or initials may be stencilled on the bottom shelf. Music racks need to be assembled, counted, and readjusted before school opens each fall.

The use of risers depends upon local circumstances and the director's preference. Some schools use none, having a general purpose rehearsal room and an auditorium with well-raked seating. Others use built-in risers in rehearsal room or portable risers which can be moved to the stage. Risers help a group produce a balanced, authentic sound, but are even more important to communication between director and players, and to expose all players to the view of the audience. (See Fig. 7-8.) If risers are to be used in the rehearsal room the permanent ones are best. Fully curved risers are highly desirable, but practical considerations often dictate angular construction. Portable risers in wedge-shaped sections are also avilable from several manufacturers. (See Fig. 7-9.)

The use of risers reduces the need for a podium and thus contributes to the conductor's freedom of movement and makes him less of a focal

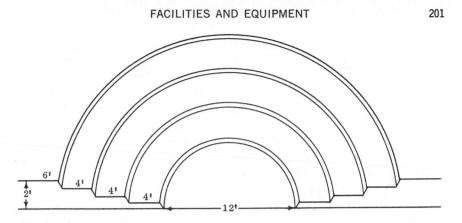

Fig. 7-8.

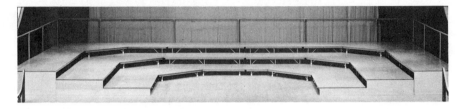

Fig. 7-9. Used by permission from Mitchell Manufacturing Company, Milwaukee.

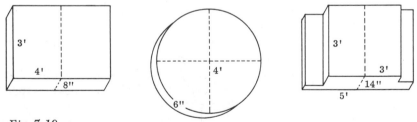

Fig. 7-10.

point to the audience. If a podium is desired, it can be easily built of three-quarter inch plywood, and it should be low and wide for stability. (See Fig. 7-10.)

Stroboconns or Strobotuners are owned by some schools as a means of accurate tuning. However, many schools have purchased electric tuners which sound a steady A or B flat (with knob controls). Some directors still prefer to have the oboist sound the pitch, because he may be heard more easily, but the electric tuner will never vary in pitch and it can be turned on to sound as the players begin to arrive.

Band Uniforms

The evolution of band uniforms from white duck trousers and capes to some of today's splendid creations has been remarkable. It is hardly useful to recommend particular styles because of rapid changes in taste and design. Besides, every band director and future director has some pretty definite ideas on this subject. It is useful, however, to discuss certain principles and trends involved in uniform selection, fitting, and care. One of the basic decisions has to do with the band's function. The more colorful attire desired for marching seems undignified in concert.

Since they make perhaps six or eight outdoor and six or eight indoor appearances per season, most bands today are equipped with uniforms which represent a compromise between marching and concert styles. One popular style of uniform has a broad lapel which for concert can be closed and for marching buttoned back to expose a vivid, contrasting color. A different plan is to purchase a conservative style suitable for concert use, but convertible to outdoor use by the addition of colorful accessories, such as spats or leggings, crossbelts, gloves, citation cords, ties, and button-on panels for front or back.

Another basic choice is between the suit coat style and the military style which has a high-collared tunic. It is thought that the high collar is uncomfortable and creates fitting problems, but this has been largely overcome with modern design. This style *does* solve the problem of shirts and ties. A cross between the military and suit type is provided by the Eisenhower jacket, which has lapels and a fitted waist. This gives the high-waisted effect and an illusion of height, but creates fitting problems.

In earlier days, boys wore trousers while the girls wore skirts, but recently the trend has been to outfit the girls in slacks, since the effect in marching is so much more uniform. Some bands provide the girls with slacks for marching and skirts for concert. Short overcoats are sometimes provided in severe climates, but shoes and socks (of a prescribed color) are normally the responsibility of the individual.

There are three popular hat styles—the high, round, plumed shako, the Pershing cap or modified soft Air Force type (with or without plume), and the folding overseas cap. Many other varieties are also in use, including the campaign hat (U. S. Ranger style), tin helmet, and soft beret.

Majorettes costumes exhibit great variety and are often designed by the individual; the typical outfit is tights and lined flaring skirts or shorts, and vests or bolero tops. The drum major's suit is traditionally of modified full dress cut, with the bearskin hat of the Grenadier Guards. The director may be uniformed similarly to his band but many prefer a plain white or blue serge suit with Pershing cap.

The life of a uniform is about ten years. Since a complete set of uniforms may cost from 2500 dollars to 15,000 dollars, the original purchase usually requires financing outside of the school budget. Bands are often forced to put on fund raising campaigns (sometimes over a period of several years) to secure the money. It is therefore important to stretch the life of the uniforms as long as possible. This is done by not only securing good quality, good style, and well-fitting uniforms, but also by using appropriate measures to avoid their damage and loss.

The policy of maintaining the stock indefinitely, that is by adding eight or ten new outfits each year, has been tried, but has not been too successful because the manufacturer cannot duplicate the cut and dye, and after a time, a new style is wanted anyway. Therefore, the original order must include extra uniforms to provide for any expected increase in the number of bandsmen, as well as to insure a good fit for the yearly change in personnel. The sizes of these extra uniforms must be carefully selected, even though the remaining outfits may be tailored to the present band members. It has been our invariable experience that the shortage eventually shows up in the medium and the large sizes (thirty-six inch, thirty-eight inch, and forty inch chest), so that most of the extra stock sizes should be ordered in this range.

Indeed, the sizes of the current band members are not always a good guide. Some uniform companies will supply a stock selection that from their experience provides fewer fitting problems, over the years. Sometimes a local clothing store will handle the purchase, without profit, and give simple alterations free, anticipating that the people coming into their store will make enough purchases to offset the cost of the service.

It is best to limit alterations to the adjustment of cuffs and hems (unless given special permission). This insures that the marked sizes can always be trusted and simplifies the fitting process. The yearly fitting process can be very unorganized. Often the first students pick over everything and succeed in fitting themselves perfectly and leave the last dozen uniforms hopelessly ill-matched and requiring major alterations. This procedure is also time-wasting. There is a very logical system which will usually get seventy-five reasonable fits out of eighty uniforms.

(1) Students do not select uniforms or supply their sizes, but at the end of first rehearsal, two girls and two boys act as measurers and recorders. All the girls and boys line up separately and their chest, waist, and head sizes are quickly taken with tape measure, and height is taken against a wall. One assistant takes the measure while the other marks the uniform card. (See Fig. 7-11.) This can be done in fifteen or twenty minutes.

(2) The coats are already indelibly numbered from small to large, and coats of the same chest size are numbered from short to long. The trousers are numbered according to waist size and inseam length.

(3) After school, the director and one or two assistants arrange the cards in sequence for coat size, lay out the matching coats in suit boxes, and mark the students' names on the boxes and their coat numbers on the cards. The process is repeated for trousers and hats. Then, the accessories are put in each box and checked off on the cards. This will take from two to three hours.

(4) At the next rehearsal, each student receives his card and **uniform**

```
┌─────────────────────────────────────────────────────────────┐
│                                                               │
│    UNIFORM  CARD        Chest _____      Height _____     │
│         for                                                   │
│                         Waist _____      Cap _____        │
│                                                               │
│    ─────────────────────────────────────────────────         │
│                 Name                                          │
│                                                               │
│    Coat # _____      Plume _____         │
│                                                               │
│    Trousers # _____       Spats _____         │
│                                                               │
│    Skirt # _____       Gloves _____         │
│                                                               │
│    Cap # _____       Belt _____          │
│                                                               │
│                                                               │
└─────────────────────────────────────────────────────────────┘
```

Fig. 7-11.

box, and the girls and boys go to separate large rooms to try them on. A few exchanges are allowed, and then the students sign and return the cards. This process takes thirty or forty minutes. The uniforms are taken home where cuff lengths are easily adjusted.

Uniforms should be stored in mothproof bags or cedar lined cabinets. They should be cleaned and mothproofed each summer. Any cleaning required during the year is the responsibility of the student. A uniform deposit is a good idea to discourage loss of plumes and other accessories which are often kept as souvenirs.

Instruments

The various rhythm, melody, and keyboard instruments associated with classroom music instruction were discussed in Chapter 2. Responsibility for such equipment is usually assumed by the music supervisor or principal, but the director is wise to see that an adequate supply of these instruments is on hand and kept in good condition, even if the costs must be charged against his regular budget.

Pianos (and organs) for the stage, rehearsal room, and practice rooms are more likely to be either a specific responsibility of the instrumental director or shared with the choral director. There are several good brands of upright pianos available at a school price of five or six hundred dollars. Grand pianos for the stage and rehearsal rooms can be purchased for around $2500 and up. However, excellent used, or rebuilt grands, can sometimes be secured in the community for a fraction of this cost.

All pianos should be placed on rolling frames for easy maneuvering and if they are to be kept in good condition, they must be tuned twice a year, and often more frequently. This tuning, along with certain minor adjustments and repairs, is most efficiently accomplished by yearly contract with a competent local tuner.

A good pipe organ in the auditorium is of course a dream of every music teacher but it is usually considered too costly. Larger schools with well rounded music departments can and should possess a good electric organ for about the price of a grand piano. The console can be specially mounted on rollers for moving.

The orchestral instruments are of course the special province of the band and orchestra director(s). It is recognized that the proficiency of the players and their quality of tone can rise no higher than their instruments allow. So the director must be especially careful to secure the most complete stock of good quality instruments that he can, and, to the best of his ability, see that they are adjusted and maintained. This task is considered here in some detail.

There is no table of instruments that can fit every situation, and certainly no models or brands that could be agreed upon by all. In any case, the stock is seldom acquired all at once, but is built up over a period of years as the groups expand, and new instruments replace the worn out or obsolescent ones.

There are two basic categories of instruments to be considered: the popular instruments (flute, clarinet, alto saxophone, trumpet, trombone, and violin) that are needed for loan on a short-term basis until the students secure their own; and all the other instruments which are seldom purchased by students, but are needed for full band and orchestra instrumentation or for training purposes. For example, parents are usually uninterested in purchasing half and three-quarter size string instruments and if the school does not have them to loan, their children will never start.

A growing instrumental program demands steady acquisition of instruments in both the basic categories, and each year there is an attempt to anticipate needs for the new crop of beginners, and also for the expansion of instrumentation in the large groups. So long as this growth continues, the administration tends to view increased budget requests favorably and the director's concept of essentials likewise expands. He may once have worked for a 60 piece band and thought four good sousaphones would be perfect, but when the group approaches 80 he needs another pair, and really hopes for a set of recording tubas for concert work. He begins to think of a contrabass clarinet, a harp, flügelhorns, and a celeste— which luxuries he never seriously contemplated before.

Such a process continues until the program levels off or diminishes. Then instrument acquisition tends to cease and deterioration sets in until some new strength in the program revitalizes the policy of instrument acquisition and replacement.

The director needs to have in mind some long term goals as well as some very specific notions of immediate needs. *He must set up priorities* based on a thorough acquaintance with the current condition of his establishment. The process of instrument acquisition is actually self-sustaining so long as wise decisions are made concerning which instrument should be bought now, which deserves overhauling, and which should be traded in. *The fact that every instrument is playable, and in use, constitutes the most powerful argument for new acquisitions.*

But it should be noted that each addition to the inventory of instruments eventually results in increased upkeep and replacement costs until, at some point, no funds are available for expansion without further budget increases. To reduce costs, it is imperative that the director select the most durable instruments he can find. He must also work for *consistency* in his selections, fixing on brands and models that he will not regret in five or ten years' time. This means some investigation and discussion with other instrumental directors and specialists. While they probably will not be in total agreement, they can give valuable tips on what brands and models to avoid.

One finds that there are two or three top brands of each instrument which are favored by the professionals, and two or three other brands which are considered reliable. Then, there are numerous student models of varying dependability, including the plastic and metal clarinets, plywood basses and cellos, etc. None of these should be discounted, since, it depends upon the type of instrument needed in each instance. For example, a pair of top quality oboes is a necessity for the solo players in the band and orchestra, but the third instrument could be a cheaper, less delicate model, for training purposes. Again, good plastic clarinets may be the most practical choice for beginners, whereas the advanced players are encouraged to purchase reliable wood instruments.

Some like open hole flutes and oboes while others prefer the "plateau" system. Many choose lacquered rather than silver-plated brasses. Most directors definitely prefer cornets over trumpets, and even desire that all of the brasses be of large bore. Such choices are a matter of opinion, but it is important that the opinion be definite and consistently applied. Some standard instrument specifications follow.

All wind instruments tuned to standard pitch (A-440).
All brasses and saxophones with brass or gold lacquer, or silver plated, as desired.
Flutes and piccolos—metal, in C, Boehm system, closed G sharp key, open hole or plateau system.
Oboes and English horns—grenadilla wood, Conservatory system, open hole or plateau system.
Clarinets—Boehm system, wood, composition, plastic, or metal as required, low E flat key preferred, medium lay mouthpiece.
Bassoons—Heckel system.
Saxophones—Boehm system.

Cornets and trumpets—in B flat, medium or large bore, first and third valve
triggers preferred.

French horns—in F, B flat, or double horn in F and B flat.

Trombones—medium or large bore.

Baritones and euphoniums—medium or large bore, 4 valve model preferred.

Sousaphones—all BB flat, or BB flat and E flat in a three to one ratio.

Recording tubas—BB flat, 4 valve model preferred.

Tympani—25 inch and 28 inch, plus 23 inch and 32 inch if possible, pedal
model.

Snare drum—6½ inch by 14 inch, double tension.

Parade drum—12 inch by 15 inch, double tension.

Bass drum—14 inch by 30 inch, to 16 inch by 36 inch, double tension.

Cymbals—16 inch to 18 inch, medium weight, with leather thongs.

String instruments—back and sides of maple, belly of spruce, ebony fingerboard
and fittings, bows of pernambuco wood.

The young director would do well to prepare a simple chart, listing
the kinds of instruments that he intends to buy and that he will urge his
players to buy. (See Fig. 7-12.) He may later discard the chart and his
opinions will change with experience and the development of newer
models, but the process of making the choice is educational and practical.

		Brand	Model and Type	Finish	Retail
Piccolo, C	Reliable				
	Professional				
Flute	Reliable				
	Professional				
Oboe	Reliable				
	Professional				
B♭ Clarinet	Student				
	Reliable				
	Professional				

Fig. 7-12.

One should also consider whether there is any advantage in purchasing reconditioned instruments. Often, if he is a good appraiser, one can
secure more value for the money in this way. But, unless the director keeps
strictly to his predetermined standards, the result is usually a motley
collection of instruments. Also, it should not be forgotten that the list price
of new instruments can often be reduced a third by the process of bidding.

The director is very unwise to consult only one local dealer and purchase whatever he has on hand. In purchasing any instrument, the brand and model should be specified and at least three firms should be invited to bid. Loyalty to a dealer is only appropriate in terms of incidental supplies, music, repair work, and the chance to bid on new equipment.

INSTRUMENT MAINTENANCE

Once instruments are acquired, the struggle to keep them in good playing condition and extend their life begins. As the mechanism of most of the instruments is quite delicate, they will be in the repair shop frequently. It must be remembered that maintenance has two sides—prevention and cure. Many repairs and replacements can be avoided by careful *management* of the instruments.

Instrument Loans

A number of cards similar to the one shown in Fig. 7-13 may be printed or mimeographed.

Instrument	Locker Number
Description	Combination
Accessories	Date Checked Out

THE BORROWER AGREES:

1) When not in use, the instrument will be kept in its locker.

2) The instrument or locker combination will not be loaned to others.

3) To accept responsibility for any damage or loss through carelessness.

Borrower's Signature	Address	Phone

Fig. 7-13.

Each instrument's description and locker combination is entered on a card before school opens in the fall. Tentative instrument assignments are made in advance of the first rehearsal, insofar as possible. Each player copies his locker combination from the card, opens the locker to check the playing condition of the instrument, signs and returns the card. A reasonable deposit may also be collected to help cover small repairs, and any balance can be refunded when the instrument is returned and checked. This system tends to produce better care of the instruments.

The arrangement works best when there is one instrument and one player to each locker. However, as additional instruments are acquired, two must often be kept in each locker. Also, occasionally an instrument supplied with extra mouthpieces will be released to two or three players—perhaps one in the band, another in the orchestra, and another in the beginning class. In these cases, it becomes difficult to assign the blame in the event of accidental damage or loss and when a doubt exists, the school must assume the costs.

Insurance

Group instrument insurance may be secured at an annual rate of about one dollar per hundred dollars valuation. Students may also include personally owned instruments under the plan. The main value of the insurance is not in the recovery of ordinary yearly losses, but in the protection against fire or other major catastrophe.

Inventory

A most important device in instrument maintenance is an up-to-date inventory. (See Fig. 7-14.) This enables the director to correct any mix-up in assignment, substantiate any losses, anticipate needs for overhaul, and to plan for replacements.

Instrument	Description	Serial No.	Accessories	Locker No.	Date Acquired	Est. Value

Fig. 7-14.

Instrument Check

Regular inspections should be held, and at the end of the school year the instruments should be checked against the inventory, the value re-estimated, simple repairs and adjustments made, the necessary new strings or parts ordered, and instruments selected for overhaul or refinishing. If there is a good local repairman who will do the work, he can be called upon to assist in this check, and give advice and estimates on the spot.

Instrument Repair

As we have just indicated, the main responsibility of the director is to see that the instruments are checked regularly and kept in good playing condition. He must also instruct his students in the rudiments of proper care and repair. Although he does not have to do the work himself, he should be able to *diagnose* mechanical problems and to make emergency repairs and adjustments. This involves considerable technical experience. The director can nearly always handle instruments of the kind he has learned to play as well as others of the same family. However, he should be alert to pick up similar skills with the other types of instruments by attending special instrumental repair courses or by experimentation, using the repair manual. This intricate topic can only be summarized here, in the hope that the reader will acquire a better idea of the gaps in his knowledge.

WOODWINDS. Assembling a woodwind instrument is delicate because the instrument must be properly grasped to avoid bending keys while joining the sections; this process is complicated by the presence of bridge keys which overlap the joints. In general, the fingers must avoid the rods and side keys and grasp only bare wood or those keys that are depressed in playing. Pressure is then exerted to twist and push together the two sections, avoiding any rocking motion, and taking care that overlapping bridge keys do not meet until they are properly situated one beneath the other. Needless to say, the joints should be properly fitted and greased in advance. Special care must be taken in adding the bassoon bocal (mouth-pipe), which must be grasped at the thick end, near the cork, to avoid bending or cracking. All sections of an instrument must be properly aligned, and the coverage of the octave and whisper keys must be checked. Reeds and mouthpieces must also be carefully adjusted. On clarinets and saxophones, the ligature is slipped over the mouthpiece, the reed is inserted and aligned, and the ligature tightened at the mark.

The same care must be used in disassembling the instrument and replacing it in the case. To avoid jamming the keys, the parts *must* face properly in the case.

Care and cleaning of the woodwinds is largely a matter of moisture control and lubrication. Swabs are provided with bassoons, and flutes are equipped with tuning rods with eyelets for the insertion of a cleaning rag. For the other instruments, swabs are made of chamois or silk cloth, with attached string, and weight. The mouthpieces are cleaned with a brush.

Moisture on the pads can be removed either with a blotter or by blowing. Sticky pads may be cleaned with a light application of alcohol or cleaning fluid, which must be removed immediately.

Oboe and bassoon reeds need a periodic flushing with warm water. Reeds should be kept in a reed case or tube, which is ventilated for proper drying. (Needless to say, lipstick will quickly ruin a reed, and must be removed from the mouth, before playing.)

Octave and register key holes and tubes, bocals, and all such small apertures need special care, because they so easily fill with dust and grime. This cleaning is done with pipe cleaner or pin.

All moving parts should be oiled periodically with key oil applied with a toothpick, but no excess oil should be left since it will pick up dust. The bore of wooden clarinets, oboes, and English horns should be oiled occasionally. Blotting paper is inserted between pads and holes, a little bore oil is poured into the instrument, and the swab is used to spread the oil.

Only saxophones are polished (with high-grade lacquer or silver polish). The other woodwinds are kept clean and bright with a soft cloth to remove moisture.

Reed selection and trimming is a high art. Good reeds are generally well tapered, evenly grained, and rather golden in color. However, each player must find the type and strength best suited to him, by trial and error. Amateurs have a tendency to select reeds that are too soft. Such reeds blow easily after a slight moistening, but close up as they absorb more water. Reeds should not be judged without thorough soaking and testing, in both top and bottom registers. In general, trouble on low notes means too much thickness at the base of the lay, while thinness at the tip causes difficulty with the high notes and closure of the reed. For single reeds, a clipper or a sharp knife is used to trim a frayed reed or to shorten it for added stiffness. A razor blade and sandpaper can be used judiciously to thin and reduce stiffness.

Oboe and bassoon reeds should be subjected to the following procedure. (1) Place the reed loosely in the mouth and blow through it. It should produce a low-pitched "crowing" sound. If not, (2) check the reed opening. It should be about 1/16 inch wide (or a bit more for bassoon and less for oboe). Using pliers, one may adjust the opening by carefully squeezing the wire at the side to widen the aperture, and squeezing it top and bottom to narrow it. Finally, (3) hold the reed up to a shaded lamp. A shadow should come to within 3/32 of an inch of the reed tip (¼ inch for bassoon). If it does not reach that far, one may trim and reshape the tip, but, if the shadow is too close, each blade is scraped near the tip. The back of the lay may be scraped if stiffness persists.

If a leaky pad is suspected, it may be checked by closing all openings and then blowing smoke into the joint; for saxophones, a small light can be lowered into the bore. When a new pad is needed, the old pad is removed by heating the back of the pad cup to soften the cement and lifting the pad with a pin or prick punch. The pad cup is cleaned out, the new pad is pricked at the side (to allow moisture to escape), pad cement

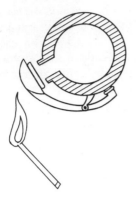

Fig. 7-15.

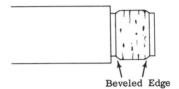

Knife blade   Press Here

Fig. 7-16.

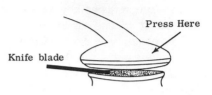

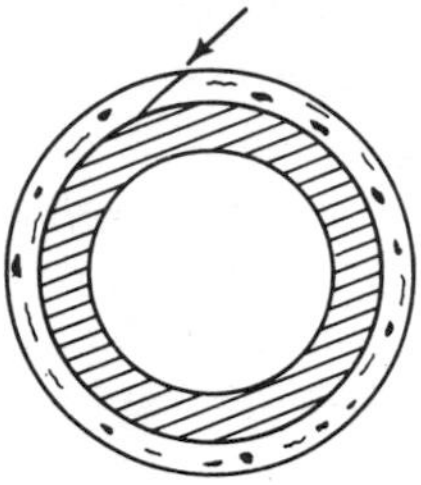

Beveled Edge

Fig. 7-18.

Beveled Joint

Fig. 7-17.

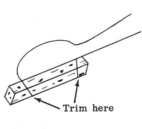

Trim here

Fig. 7-19.

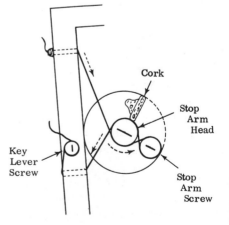

Cork

Stop
Arm
Head

Key
Lever
Screw

Stop
Arm
Screw

Fig. 7-20.

Adapted from Clayton Tiede, The Practical Band Instrument Repair Manual *(Dubuque, Iowa: William C. Brown Company, 1962). Used by permission.*

is smeared on the back of the pad, the pad cup is reheated, the new pad is placed in position, and the key pressed firmly against the tone hole. (See Fig. 7-15.)

Many times a pad is in good shape but leaks or falls out due to poor cementing. In this case, the back of the cup is heated and the pad is left in place, being pressed against the tone hole until the cement hardens again. The key may be tied down for a time to seat the pad.

If leaks persist, the key may be bent, in which case, a knife blade is placed under the pad, *opposite* the leak, and the leaking side is pressed or tapped down. (See Fig. 7-16.)

Recorking joints and keys is another operation requiring only ordinary skill. The old surface is scraped clean, a new cork is cut to size, shellac is placed on the wood or metal surface, and the cork is applied. Where two cork edges adjoin, they must be beveled, overlapped, and sanded to size. Loose cork joints can be temporarily improved by heating the well-greased cork over a flame, which swells and softens the cork and produces a good fit. (See Figs. 7-17, 7-18, and 7-19.)

BRASSES. Care and cleaning of the brasses is largely a matter of avoiding dents, keeping the mechanism well oiled, and protecting the finish. The instrument should be cleaned, polished, and oiled two or three times a year. The valves and slides are removed and the instrument is flushed inside with warm water and flexible brush, and then dried. The finish is cleaned with a good lacquer or silver polish. Valve tarnish can be removed by soaking the pistons several hours in vinegar. The tuning slides and valve caps are greased, oil is applied to the valves (or trombone hand slide), and the instrument is reassembled.

The French horn valve mechanism, however, should be disassembled only by the repairman unless the director has the experience, and the time to teach the job to his horn students. If a French horn is not to be used for a few days, it is wise to put oil on the valves *before* putting it away. The valve slides are removed and several drops of valve oil are placed in the slide tubing so that the oil runs down into the valves as the keys are being worked, or the bottom valve cap is unscrewed and the oil applied directly to the valve shaft.

The student should be taught to restring a valve using the following steps.

(1) Loosen Stop Arm Screw and Key Lever Screw.

(2) Feed line through hole in key lever and knot on back side.

(3) Bring line around Stop Arm Head and twist a loop around and under the Stop Arm Screw (thus returning the string under itself).

(4) Press the Stop Arm against the cork and tighten the string to produce a level valve key, then, tighten the Stop Arm Screw.

(5) Continue the string around the Stop Arm Head, through the end

hole in the key lever, and loop it around the Key Lever Screw, and tighten this screw.

Certain other difficulties with the brasses are treated in the following ways.

(1) A series of firm jerks with a looped handkerchief will often free stuck slides, but penetrating oil should be tried on more stubborn cases.

(2) A few taps against the side of the mouthpiece receiver pipe (while twisting the mouthpiece) will often loosen the stuck mouthpiece; otherwise, the use of a mouthpiece puller is recommended.

(3) Leaking water keys are corrected by wedging in a new cork and/or tightening the spring.

(4) Dents in valves or tubing require that the instrument be taken to a qualified repairman.

(5) When the lacquer is worn or flaked, or the silver plating is worn through (especially on the mouthpiece rim), the instrument should be sent for refinishing.

PERCUSSION. New heads should be ordered already mounted. The art of tucking is becoming unnecessary. When it must be done, the head is first soaked in water and then tucked around and under the flesh hoop with a tucking tool or similar instrument (crossing from one side to the other as in tuning the head).

Tension of snare and bass drum heads is only adjusted to suit the changing humidity. When a head is tightened in damp weather, it must be loosened when put away or it may split when the humidity drops.

Loss of moisture eventually narrows the range of the tympani. The counterhoop is then removed from the kettle and the head is thoroughly dampened (keeping moisture away from the flesh hoop), until it is quite soft and flabby. The counterhoop is then replaced and the head is pulled down a half inch and covered with newspaper or a damp cloth to retard drying. Tympani heads are best kept near their top pitch between rehearsals and the cardboard covers should be placed on them. Care must be exercised in moving the tympani, as the pedal mechanism is quite delicate. Most damage should be referred to the repairman, but extra tension screws may be kept for replacement.

STRINGS. General care of string instruments involves wiping the instruments to remove resin and moisture after use, loosening the bow hair, careful insertion of instruments into their cases, and cautious transportation to avoid bumps. Changes in temperature and humidity should be avoided.

String instruments are quite vulnerable to damage when left in precarious positions. Cellos, for example, should always be leaned in a corner or placed on their sides with end pins retracted or removed.

Frozen tuning pegs are tapped out from the far side with a blunt punch. Graphite or soap may be applied to keep them free, and chalk dust applied to help them hold. Commercial peg dope can be secured to combine both actions.

The sound post transmits vibrations from the bridge to the back of the instrument. The closer it is to the bridge, the stronger and harder the tone, and the farther away from the bridge, the weaker and mellower the tone. Balance between the treble and bass strings can also be partially adjusted by moving the soundpost slightly to either side. Resetting a post is not easy but is worth the trouble, since a hundred dollar instrument with well-adjusted soundpost may sound better than a five hundred dollar one which is poorly set. Since many repairmen do not take the time for trial and readjustment, the director who learns the technique himself shows intelligent foresight.

A curved rod with sharpened point is used to insert the post through the F hole and is then reversed to push or pull the post, while it is held upright with a sort of pliers. The job can also be done with twine or a hooked wire. The post is set perpendicularly just below the top string foot of the bridge—about ¼ inch below for the violin, ⅜ inch for the cello, and ¾ inch for the bass. But further readjustment is required if the tone is not satisfactory.

A casual inspection in most school orchestra rooms will reveal a number of bridges in need of adjustment. In general, the strings should be as low as possible without rattling or buzzing. However, a bridge naturally lowers as the instrument shrinks in dry, heated air. An instrument should thus have a summer bridge and a winter bridge or, for school purposes, the bridge may be adjusted once, for proper height, in late fall.

The normal distance from the top edge of the fingerboard to the bottom of the strings should be approximately the following.

Violin	steel E	3 mm.	wound gut G	4½ mm.
Viola	steel A	4½ mm.	steel C	6 mm.
			wound gut C	6¼ mm.
Cello	steel A	4½ mm.	steel C	6½ mm.
	gut A	6¼ mm.	wound gut C	7 mm.
Bass	steel G	8½ mm.	steel E	11 mm.
	gut G	11 mm.	wound gut E	16 mm.

The middle strings naturally conform to the arch of the fingerboard so the bow will clear neighboring strings when playing fortissimo.

To lower a bridge, the grooves are simply deepened as necessary and the top and sides are sanded until the proper height and taper are reestablished. A new bridge must be fitted whenever a bridge is too low, since adding height is impractical.

New bridges are first thinned by sanding, and the feet are roughly shaped down by grindstone or rasp. Sandpaper is then placed face up on the belly where the feet will be, the bridge is set in place (between the

F hole notches), and the feet are ground down to conform exactly to the curve of the instrument. (The bridge is tilted very slightly toward the tail-piece and the grinding stroke is made in that direction.) The bridge is then carefully measured, cut down, notched, and further thinned as necessary.

Broken tail gut is repaired in the following fashion. If the broken gut is too short, a new length is secured. The ends are run through the holes in the tailpiece and tightly wound with strong waxed thread. The tips are slightly spread apart with a knife and then heated over a flame (which swells and hardens the gut).

Openings between belly and sides are due to climatic variation and the resulting swelling and shrinking of the instrument. Indeed, the glue is deliberately weak here, so the cracks will not occur elsewhere. House-hold glue is applied to the openings with a toothpick, and the necessary pressure is arranged with clamps or rubber bands. A loose fingerboard may be repaired in the same fashion.

Cracks in the sides, belly, or back, broken necks, refinishing, and bow rehairing are more formidable operations requiring the services of a skilled repairman.

A warped bridge can be straightened by soaking it in water and dry-ing it under a weight.

Buzzes are usually due to loosened string wrapping, loose tuner screws, cracks or openings, or looseness in the tail gut and tailpin assembly. The remedy will be obvious, once the buzz is located.

Bow screw threads are sometimes stripped and the screw must be replaced. Lack of bow tension is sometimes caused by excess humidity and can be remedied by carefully drying the hair. If this is not the cause, the hair has slipped and rehairing is required.

Tools and Supplies

The operations that we have described, on care and repair of instru-ments, can be mastered by the director and his more serious-minded stu-dents. Repair manuals, tools, and supplies should be kept at hand. Supplies needed for the above operations include:

small pliers	mouthpiece puller
small screwdriver	household glue
single-edged razor blades	pad cement
cleaning rods and brushes	stick shellac
needles or prick punch	assortment of pads
reed clippers	sheet cork
knife	pipe cleaners
key oil	sandpaper
bore oil	cork grease

penetrating oil
valve oil; slide oil
spool of thread
wood clamps
sound post setters

lacquer cleaner
silver polish
fishing line, for horn valves
peg dope
assorted sizes of tailgut

SUMMARY

Although proper facilities and equipment do not guarantee good instruction, the lack of them seriously hampers the instrumental program. Much can be done in planning or altering physical surroundings and in selecting and maintaining equipment to provide a better learning environment.

The auditorium where performances are to occur is one of the principal items to consider. Besides staging facilities and audience space, the primary factor is the acoustics, and special care must be taken to ensure adequate direct sound and good reflectance. Other important facilities are the rehearsal hall, practice rooms, offices, music library, listening and recording rooms, repair and storage arrangements. Much care and expense is involved in securing the needed sound isolation in these areas. Ventilation and humidity control are also major factors. The director must take an active part in promoting needed remodeling, and in planning whatever new buildings are authorized.

General furnishings and equipment are also within the director's province. Chairs and racks, risers, filing cabinets, record players, etc., must all meet certain specifications. Band uniforms must be chosen with the function of the band well in mind, and good fit is indispensable. The acquisition of instruments is a critical problem. A budget allocation must be established, priorities, brands, and models determined. Skillful planning is required to maintain pace with the needs of growing organizations.

Good instrument maintenance is one of the chief preoccupations of instrumental directors. This requires good storage provisions, a check-out system, regular inventories and reconditioning, and careful instruction of students in the assembly, care and adjustment of their own instruments. The woodwinds are particularly delicate, and some of the standard operations for them include cleaning and oiling, reed trimming, pad replacement and re-corking. The brasses must be kept clean and moving parts well-greased or oiled. Stringed and percussion instruments need special care to avoid breakage. Adjustment of sound posts and bridge heights, regluing joints, and replacing tailgut are some of the standard operations required with stringed instruments. A kit of basic tools and supplies should be kept for all these operations.

QUESTIONS FOR DISCUSSION

1. How much space per player is needed on stage? What staging equipment should be available?

2. What is "raked seating?" What is the advantage?

3. What is the importance of "reverberation time?" Of "initial time-delay gap?" How are these controlled?

4. What are the inherent weaknesses of the combination auditorium? How may these be minimized?

5. Describe the sizes and appointments of the various types of music rooms.

How is sound transmission reduced? How can the director work to improve facilities?

6. What items of general equipment are appropriate? What types and models are preferred in each instance?

7. Describe the basic types of band uniform and their suitability. How are proper sizes secured and fitted?

8. Develop a list of models, types, and costs of instruments that would serve as a guide in future purchases. What is the general priority in which these would need to be acquired?

9. Describe various means of instrument storage and loan policy. What measures are appropriate to avoid loss and damage?

10. Practice assembling and disassembling the various instruments. Test the ability to accomplish some of the simpler repairs and adjustments to be made on the various instruments.

SELECTED REFERENCES

BARANEK, LEO J., *Music, Acoustics and Architecture*. New York: John Wiley and Sons, Inc., 1962.

BRAND, ERIC D., *Selmer Band Instrument Repairing Manual*. Boston: E. C. Schirmer Music Co., 1946.

COMMITTEE ON MUSIC ROOMS AND EQUIPMENT, *Music Buildings, Rooms, and Equipment*. Washington, D. C.: Music Educators National Conference, 1955.

DEPARTMENT OF AUDIO-VISUAL INSTRUCTION, *Planning Schools for Use of Audio-Visual Materials*. Washington, D. C.: National Education Association, 1953.

HILL, FRANK AND SUB-COMMITTEE, *The Selection and Care of a String Instrument*. Washington, D. C.: Music Educators National Conference, 1957.

HODGSON, DICK AND H. JAY BULLEN, *How to Use a Tape Recorder*. New York: Hastings House Publishers, Inc., 1957.

How to Buy Band Uniforms. New York: National Association of Uniform Manufacturers, 1959.

MUSIC INDUSTRY COUNCIL, *Business Handbook of Music Education*. Washington, D. C.: Music Educators National Conference, 1959.

NILLES, RAYMOND J., *Basic Repair Handbook for Musical Instruments*. Fullerton, California: F. E. Olds and Son, 1959.

OLSON, HARRY F., *Musical Engineering*. New York: McGraw-Hill Book Company, 1952.

SHEPARD, JOHN AND SUBCOMMITTEE, *String Teachers and Music Dealer Relations and Problems*. Washington, D. C.: Music Educators National Conference, 1957.

TIEDE, CLAYTON H., *Practical Band Instrument Repair Manual*. Dubuque, Iowa: William C. Brown Company, 1962.

You Fix Them. Cleveland, Ohio: Scherl and Roth Incorporated, n.d.

CHAPTER 8

Program Coordination

Now that the principal elements of the instrumental music program have been outlined, it is time to admit that things do not always work out ideally. The director may have the best intentions in the world but may find himself frustrated for lack of backing from school and community. What any good teacher wants is simply a number of interested students and the means to work with them. In instrumental music this does not just happen.

The director should not be too quick to blame others for his difficulties. Perhaps he needs to explore the local situation more in detail. Why don't the students sign up to play and why doesn't the public come to hear them? How can the teaching schedule be improved? Where can the necessary money be found and used most effectively? The answers to such questions lie partially beyond the realm of instruction and within the fields of administration, supervision, and public relations.

In this chapter, we are concerned with the operational problems associated with all instrumental instruction such as financing, scheduling, programming and staging, evaluation, promotion and publicity, school and community relationships. While these topics are in themselves widely different in quality and scope, they all relate to the building of a successful program. Lack of understanding produces a crippled program.

FINANCIAL OPERATION

Any instrumental director could readily name several items needed for better instruction, such as instruments, trips, new music, and so on. With careful consideration he could expand the list almost indefinitely. The combined needs of the nation's instrumental music teachers must be astronomical.

Some directors are very conservative, merely accepting their assigned budgets and taking care of their most pressing needs. Others refuse to accept the limitation and embark on special fund raising campaigns. However, if undertaken too readily, these drives may preclude further budget raises and become more and more imperative to the support of the program.

Many budgets could be used with more foresight, which would develop more momentum in the music program and strong justification for additional funds. The director must know what he really needs, get it at the lowest prices, use it wisely, and be alert for any extras he can pick up or promote.

Determining Needs

Needs are either immediate or long term. The immediate ones are easy to recognize. However, it is a mistake to go from day to day on the basis of immediate needs, because the plant and services will steadily deteriorate until strenuous efforts are required to re-establish smooth operations. The director must: (1) periodically survey the activities he is sponsoring and their objectives; (2) determine what expenditures would be most serviceable in meeting those goals; (3) consider any other activities he could and should be instituting and what expenditures would be most needed to launch them; and (4) establish priorities.

During actual operations emergencies will arise and conditions will change so that the list of needs and priorities will be subject to revision. Nevertheless, a practical plan is necessary if the program is not to languish, for otherwise it is entirely possible to allot too much money to a particular need—a trip, new uniforms, or the instruments needed to complete the instrumentation—at the expense of equally needed instrument overhauls, music, new recordings, or books.

There are minimum needs that must be met in order to maintain current operations at the same level of efficiency despite any marked change in enrollments. These needs are priority items, and lower priority goes to those items which would expand or upgrade the program. A list of needs, arranged according to priority, is a good basis for budget requests. Following is an example of such a list.

PRIORITY	ITEM	BASIS OF NEED	ESTIMATED COST
1.	Recurring and fixed charges: office supplies; piano tuning; instrument repair; insurance; printing and mailing; telephone; uniform cleaning; etc.	currently running at	$850

PRIORITY	ITEM	BASIS OF NEED	ESTIMATED COST
2.	Music for beginning groups, band, ensembles	training material	400
3.	Overhaul sousaphone and bass clarinet	dented, out of adjustment	300
4.	Legal size filing cabinet	overflow of music library	50
5.	Dozen music racks	larger groups	90
6.	New recordings	serious gaps in library	100
7.	Books (music education)	reference	25
8.	Two B flat clarinets (with trade-in)	15 years old, bad condition	400
9.	Director's expenses to state music educators meeting	professional responsibility	75
10.	Band to district and possibly state contest	experience, motivation	150-450
11.	Four 30 inch stools	for percussion players	25
12.	Baritone saxophone	to improve instrumentation	400
13.	Acoustical treatment of rehearsal room	room too "live"	400-600
14.	Two double French horns	new players being started	800

Securing Funds

Funds for the instrumental program may come from several sources, each demanding a different approach from the director.

SCHOOL FUNDS. Taxes provide the major share of funds for the public schools. Ideally, this should be the only source of funds for a school subject which is being taught in the interests of society at large.

The apportionment of public moneys within a school are controlled administratively on a year by year basis. The pattern varies considerably from school to school.

The school budget is established through consultation with representative individuals. Salaries and general maintenance and building costs are estimated and then operating expenses are divided into certain categories and subjects. The instrumental director is finally authorized to spend within certain limits for his needs. In effect, he has an account for that sum.

But what is part of the music budget in one school may be covered by a different budget in another. Printing costs may be assumed by the principal's office. The library may buy all books or they may be charged to the various departments. Trips with the team may come out of the band fund or the athletic fund, or the individual students may be expected to bear these costs. The music budget itself may not be very clearly divided into portions for the various musical activities, and thus be subject to some negotiation among the music teachers.

In many schools, a large share of the money is kept in a rather indefinite status directly under administrative control. The nominal budget for instrumental music is really treated as a flexible guide to regular expenditures, and the director is expected to secure administrative authorization for all large items. Using this arrangement, the aggressive director will often have more funds at his disposal than with a fixed and comprehensive budget.

Expedience has dictated the establishment of patterns unique to each school which work well for those who are familiar with them. Any personnel changes, however, are likely to cause temporary confusion. Budget figures, given in job interviews, mean very little without an understanding of current conditions and administrative intentions.

However, there are two rather general principles in budget authorizations: (1) Since school budgets are seldom very severely cut, one may expect about the same amount as he spent the year before; (2) if there is any general increase in funds, the larger percentages will go to those who have shown the most expansion and development in their programs, and can thus point to the most pressing needs.

This is the bureaucratic system; expansion breeds expansion. But the fact is that practically every instrumental music program has room to expand.

RECEIPTS AND FEES. Most public schools today depend to an extent upon hidden fees and gate receipts. This is due to increasing educative costs and heavy tax burdens. In music, such sources include: (1) concert receipts (or free will contributions); (2) a portion of athletic receipts; (3) instrument rentals or deposits; (4) uniform rentals or deposits; (5) individual or class lesson fees.

These charges really constitute double taxation and should be minimized as much as possible. Nevertheless, the sale of tickets is a form of advertising and helps stimulate concert attendance, and deposits on instruments and uniforms help protect them against careless use. The music program is also morally entitled to a sufficient share of receipts from athletic events to cover the costs incurred by the band's participation.

Collection and use of such funds, however, will tend to replace regularly budgeted funds unless care is taken to earmark the money. For example, a yearly percentage of gross athletic receipts could be assigned and held for purchasing uniforms, while concert receipts could be held for subsidizing trips. In this way, the public is directly contributing to the extras for these groups and not for basic instructional costs.

Fund Raising Activities

School instrumental groups sometimes become involved in special activities of the following variety: (1) campaigns for special donations—tag day, etc.; (2) benefit concerts, shows, parties, or dances; (3) sales campaigns—game concessions, candy, reflectorized house numbers, bake sales, rummage sales, etc.

The director obviously wishes to avoid this sort of thing whenever he can, because it is inconvenient and noneducational, and it also puts him under special obligation to the public or to certain groups and individuals. As much as possible, such drives should be sponsored by units like the Band Parents' Club and should be linked to a particular need which cannot be met by ordinary means.

Budgeting

Whatever funds are to be made available to the instrumental program should be budgeted, either formally or informally. A budget is simply a reasoned forecast of expected receipts and expenditures so that the needed funds are reserved for each particular item or kind of expenditure. Without some sort of budget, it is possible to exhaust the funds before certain critical items are cared for. For example, piano tuning may be overlooked until several successive tunings are required to restore the instruments to usable condition.

If an adequate list of needs and priorities has been kept, the chief problem in budgeting has been accomplished. Only now limits have been set, and a certain sum of money is to be available for the year. The budget is thus figured in terms of categories and detailed as much as need be.

ESTIMATED EXPENDITURE		ESTIMATED RECEIPTS
Music		
for band	$ 300	
for beginning classes	50	
for ensembles and soloists	50	
Maintenance		
overhaul sousaphone	250	
overhaul bass clarinet	50	
incidental repairs, supplies	250	
piano tuning	100	
instrument insurance	200	
uniform cleaning	100	
New Equipment		
filing cabinet	60	
12 music racks	90	
2 B flat clarinets (with trade-in)	400	
4 stools	25	
to uniform fund	500	

ESTIMATED EXPENDITURE			ESTIMATED RECEIPTS	
Travel				
director to state convention	75			
band to district contest	150		music fund	$2,000
Miscellaneous			from concert receipts	300
office supplies	50		instrument deposits	200
telephone	50		from athletic receipts	500
printing and mailing	50			
recordings	100			
miscellaneous	100			
Total	$3,000		*Total*	$3,000

Once established, the budget should not be regarded as sacred. Actual costs and receipts will be either over or under the estimates, and certain emergencies and unexpected expenses will occur. In such a case, certain items may have to be deferred or additional money solicited either from the school's miscellaneous fund or by special contribution. The budget should be flexibly operated.

The director should not overlook those items which he needs but, fortunately, are charged to other budgets. We have mentioned that plant maintenance, salaries for current and new teaching positions, general furnishings, books, office supplies, etc., usually come from general funds. The need for any such items should already have been noted, and the director must make his requests in due form.

Purchasing

Wise purchasing is a matter of careful selectivity and timing. Most purchases are usually made near the beginning of the fiscal year when instruments are sent for overhauling, new equipment is ordered, and much of next year's music is selected. It is always wise to think ahead, have time for unhurried choice, and then be able to regard the frequent delays in shipment with equanimity.

The director should not limit his choice to whatever happens to be in stock locally, but should have in mind exactly what he wants. The music he orders should have been heard or the scores examined, the instruments to be serviced should be taken to the best repairman, and new instruments should be specifically requisitioned on bid. Hundreds and thousands of dollars will be saved over the years by following this process.

Enough of a balance should be retained in the budget to give some flexibility. This balance is gradually reduced toward the end of the fiscal year when all money must be spent. If all budgeted items are cared for, then one can purchase some extra recordings or music, which were planned for the following year.

It is also important to be alert to any unexpended balances in general funds. The administration always tries to hold back some money for emergencies and, if these do not occur, this money will be available to those who ask for it and have demonstrated their need. Successful requests are for tangibles (a new piccolo, a tape recorder) and *not* for extra recordings, books, music, or repair costs.

The mode of purchase varies somewhat with the particular school and the class of equipment or service, and is a matter of office procedure and bookkeeping. Larger items are usually formally requisitioned. This may be true of incidental items also, but a director may be authorized to negotiate directly with music stores on repairs, new music, strings, and reeds, and merely picks up the articles and clears the bills for payment.

SCHEDULING

There is little need to emphasize the tremendous effect of scheduling on the instrumental music program. Indeed, some directors attribute most of their success or failure to a particular type of schedule. "Shop talk" among music teachers about their work and prospects frequently comes to the point where one individual says, "It won't work with my schedule"— and thus closes the discussion. It is true that any important program changes or expansion demand basic schedule changes.

Many schools and directors have become so accustomed to a particular schedule that they are unable to conceive of any other pattern. This is understandable, but it is unfortunate, for it puts the program into a straitjacket.

The difficulty in scheduling is that other people's interests are involved. Whenever the schedule is altered to increase the offerings or the time assigned to any course, it necessarily reduces the time assigned to another course, or the number of students enrolling in it. The instrumental groups are particularly vulnerable to such pressures, because a certain table of organization must be approximated. The problem is compounded by the fact that musical subjects are normally elective in the senior high school.

Today's increased pressures for academic emphasis are no help. The teacher must recognize that instrumental music is regarded as a co-curricular subject. Curriculum requirements have increased until there is little time for electives. This also has the effect of increasing home work which puts study hall time at a premium (a period which was formerly often dropped by individuals in favor of electives). The seven period day is one response to this situation which seems to offer more flexibility but little relief from the basic academic pressures.

School consolidation is another factor which is not an unmixed blessing to the music program. Many activities which formerly were held after school (small ensembles, lessons, marching drill) are difficult to arrange because of the great number of students who travel by bus.

So, while music is by no means losing its status in the curriculum, it is increasingly hampered by scheduling restrictions and competing pressures. Students have less time for practice and trips, and today, few can conveniently elect two musical subjects at a time. Chapter 4 treats of some of these problems in connection with band and orchestra scheduling.

Weekly Schedules

The director would like to arrange his weekly schedule to apportion his time to his various responsibilities and to translate this time into those school periods which would allow as many students as possible to elect the music courses they desire, without upsetting their scheduling of other courses. The actual pattern that evolves depends upon (1) the number of instrumental teachers and their qualifications and objectives; (2) the consequent pattern of activities which is conceived; and (3) the school administration's basic scheduling system. There is an infinite variety of possible schedule patterns, each built on a few general principles as outlined in the following discussion.

OFFERINGS. Like everything relating to instruction, changes in schedule patterns should be geared to an evaluation of the current program within the school. Any basic schedule change should be designed to improve the learning situation of the students.

Often, it is taken for granted that the program automatically consists of certain specific activities, that these groups should meet a certain number of periods per week, and that the training program should begin in a particular grade. Enlightened music educators recognize no such conventions. The weaknesses in the current program must be discovered and related to an overall picture of the purposes and possibilities of instrumental instruction. Thus an immature junior high school string group may reflect either recruitment difficulties, relatively unpromising students, a delayed beginning program, poor equipment and rehearsal facilities, lack of parental interest and support, lack of rehearsal time, lack of opportunity for supplementary individual instruction and small ensemble work, or simply uninspiring and ineffective teaching (or some combination of these).

What must be done? Basic decisions must be made concerning the essential course offerings and the capacity of the instructional staff to handle them. A properly staffed department has the teachers to handle every aspect of instrumental music in depth, but when there is a shortage of teachers, instructional time must be stretched—by larger classes, by more reliance upon student leadership of small ensembles, and so on. In fact, it may be wiser to curtail or temporarily postpone certain offerings rather than to maintain them on a marginal basis.

TIME. The amount of time which should be allotted each week to any particular offering depends not so much on its importance (they are all important) but upon the time required to accomplish the results that have been planned. Fortunately, the time factor can be estimated with rough accuracy. For example, most would agree that a beginning student needs an assignment and a few hours of practice each week to make any appreciable advancement. About the same results are achieved by (1) three hours in a large class, (2) two hours in a small class, or (3) a twenty-minute individual lesson and three or four hours of practice at home. Similarly, a particular group of band numbers might be prepared equally well in these ways: (1) thirty hours of full rehearsal, with no member practicing his part at home; (2) twenty hours of full rehearsal, plus four hours of supervised sectional rehearsal (each section); (3) fifteen hours of full rehearsal, plus home practice by each member as required to play his part. In other words, if part of the rehearsal is accomplished elsewhere, fewer full rehearsals need to be scheduled or else more concerts can be given.

This Marxian analysis, of course, is not intended to give any rule of thumb (few would agree with the figures), but to illustrate the principle that there *is* a choice of means, and that schedule time should be weighed carefully in terms of what is to be accomplished.

SEQUENCE. Although school music activities are seldom labeled in terms of prerequisites, there is a very definite sequence in that the student progresses to more difficult music and more demanding performance responsibilities, and the activities become more specialized. In fact, at some point, many drop out because they do not wish to further specialize in this field. The schedule should reflect this. Elementary rhythm, keyboard, and listening work is brought *to* the students in the classroom. Beginning instrumental classes are organized at those hours in which the most volunteers can be accommodated. At the junior high school level, there is a need for breadth, i.e., a chance to try other instruments or to sing and certainly to take General Music. The senior high school performing groups naturally require more rehearsal time as well as adequate opportunity for solo and ensemble experience.

SCHEDULE PATTERNS. Within the school day there are only four basic methods of scheduling music instruction.

1) *Regular periods.* Each class is assigned specific periods during the week—usually MWF, TTH, or every day. (See Fig. 8-1). This system is usually associated with scheduling and is normally used for the large groups. However, there is the ever present problem of conflicts, since students must choose between these courses and other subjects offered during the same periods. Classes meeting TTH or MWF must also be coordinated with the offerings meeting on the alternate days (sometimes Physical Education, Art, Industrial Arts, or study hall).

	M	T	W	Th	F
First Period	Band	Band	Band	Band	Band
Second Period	Jr. Band	Bgn. Cornet Class	Jr. Band	Bgn. Cornet Class	Jr. Band

Fig. 8-1.

2) *Rotating periods.* Certain offerings can *superimpose* the regular schedule so that each student will miss only a small portion of any one of his subjects. This plan is especially practical for small groups that meet only two or three times a week. A clarinet class, for example, could meet

Period	M	T	W	Th	F	M	T	W	Th	F	M	T	W	Th	F
I		X													
II				X											
III							X								
IV									X						
V												X			
VI														X	

Fig. 8-2.

as shown in Fig. 8-2. These clarinetists would thus miss any one subject only once in three weeks. The difficulty of course, is in working out the complicated schedule patterns and keeping the students on them.

A variation of this idea is the "floating" period, by which each day a different period is designated the "floater" and used for rehearsals of band and similar all-school groups. On certain days the floater may be used for a different type of activity, such as clubs and small ensembles.

3) *Appointed periods.* Small groups and individual lessons may be scheduled by appointment. A survey of students' schedules will usually reveal a suitable pattern for these meetings.

4) *Flexible periods.* A flexible pattern is usually used in the elementary classroom, where the music period occurs at a convenient point in the daily sequence of activity, or is adjusted to the schedule of the traveling special music teacher.

The only other means of scheduling instruction is outside school hours—before or after school, or on Saturdays. This practice is not so prevalent as it once was, because of changing patterns of American life, and not through professional choice. The number of students commuting by school bus or car pool, holding part time jobs, or participating in various organized recreational activities has become so large that few are available for instruction just before or after school. Yet those who are available can often be scheduled for lessons and ensembles, thus making the school day more flexible.

SCHEDULE ARRANGEMENT. The problem in arranging schedules is to achieve good coordination and to minimize conflicts. Each instrumental teacher in a school must adjust his own pattern to make the best combination with the other offerings in instrumental music, the entire music program, and the total curriculum. This requires much consultation with administrative and academic colleagues.

It is practical to start with the large groups. These are elective offerings, and it is necessary to avoid periods occupied by either single-section required courses or a popular elective. It is impractical to readjust for every shift in the over-all schedule, but any serious encroachment demands a further analysis. If the conflicts seem insurmountable, it may be necessary to consider the floating schedule previously described.

If there is a string program, thought should be given to the possibility of overlapping band and orchestra periods in the interests of both organizations (discussed in Chapter 4).

In seventh and eighth grades, particularly, care should be taken to coordinate performing groups, General Music, and instrumental classes for late beginners so that the students do not have to make a final choice so soon. As illustrated in Fig. 8-3, all students in each grade enroll in Music at the same period. However, within this period, there is a wide latitude.

Once the larger groups and classes are organized, a good deal of ingenuity is required in scheduling individual sessions, small ensembles, sectional rehearsals, and the like. As we have mentioned, these offerings must usually be scheduled in and around the regular academic offerings. The students' schedule cards are examined, the most logical times are selected, and clearance is arranged through regular channels. Some students will have to rearrange their schedules in order to meet with specific groups. As far as possible, these arrangements should be foreseen before the students' individual schedules are created. Then, by pre-registration, the members of each group can be assigned to a common study period (which is used for periodic rehearsals of the group).

Calendar

Arranging the calendar of instrumental music events for the year is an aspect of scheduling that is often done haphazardly. In some cases

	Teacher	M	T	W	Th	F
Period X 7th Graders	Smith	Band	Bgn. WW	Band	Bgn. WW	Band
	Jones	Orch.	Bgn. Strgs.	Orch.	Bgn. Strgs.	Orch.
	Brown	Gen. Mu.[1]	Gen. Mu.[3]	Chorus[1]	Gen. Mu.[3]	Gen. Mu.[1]
	Wills	Gen. Mu.[2]	Gen. Mu.[4]	Chorus[2]	Gen. Mu.[4]	Gen. Mu.[2]
Period Y 8th Graders	Smith	Band	Bgn. Brass	Band	Bgn. Brass	Band
	Jones	Orch.	Gen. Mu.[2]	Orch.	Gen. Mu.[2]	Orch.
	Brown	Choir	Gen. Mu.[3]	Choir	Gen. Mu.[3]	Choir
	Wills	Gen. Mu.[1]	Gen. Mu.[4]	Chorus	Gen. Mu.[4]	Gen. Mu.[1]

Fig. 8-3.

directors prefer to plan one event at a time, but after a few experiences with conflicts and postponements, they are usually ready to be more systematic in their scheduling.

The yearly spacing of events assumes a rhythmic character of its own, based upon the seasons, school events and vacations, and the repertoire development of the players. There are also certain days of the week that are favored or avoided because of community events and habits.

These patterns affect *all* the activities of a school and of neighboring schools, in parallel fashion. Football season, Christmas orchestra and choral program, basketball season, midwinter band concert, tournaments, operetta, contests, and spring concerts march inevitably across each year's calendar. One must stay in step, yet not *exactly* in line with everyone else.

With experience, the director learns what events he wishes to sponsor, how they should be spaced for good motivation and preparation, and what periods and days are most favorable for attendance. Then he consults others who have similar responsibilities (the other instrumental teachers, vocal teachers, athletic coaches, theatre department, chamber of commerce) to ascertain what dates they may have already established. It is helpful if either the principal's or superintendent's office or some other agency becomes recognized as the clearing house for this information. With this data, the director adjusts his own calendar as necessary.

A well-planned calendar allows considerable space between major events that affect the same group of performers or audience. For instance, an orchestra concert and a musical would not be scheduled a week apart, since several performers will be involved in both and need time to catch their breaths, to do some studying, and to prepare for the next event. Publicity is also difficult with two major events competing for favor. Events should be well distributed throughout the year. The tendency in music is to concentrate performances toward the end of the school year, because the players are arriving at their peak of proficiency. On the other hand, programs scheduled in normally slack periods, such as November and January, tend to attract listeners.

If the particular evening the music director wants is already reserved, it is wise to consider alternative days rather than a two or three week postponement. Many have found that Sunday afternoons and Friday evenings work as well for some types of program as the more favored Tuesdays and Thursdays.

When one's choices have been made, it is imperative to establish claim to the dates and times by placing them on the school calendar or in the hands of any others who sponsor major events. Thereafter, an occasional calendar check is wise.

PUBLIC APPEARANCES

Although public appearances are not the goal of instruction but rather another form of educative activity, it is undeniable that special planning and arrangements are required. Proper handling of concerts and contests, solo and ensemble appearances, and outdoor events is critical to the morale and effect upon players and public alike. The staging of any public performance needs to be done with the greatest finesse.

Concerts

For purposes of discussion, concerts include not only the major evening programs of the band and orchestra in the school auditorium, but also any special programs before school assemblies, civic groups, neighboring schools, or programs of the outdoor park type. Concerts do not have the connotation of *incidental* or *occasional* music, such as is used in church services, games, rallies, dances, teas, and ceremonies.

People come to a concert to hear the group play music and to evaluate, consciously or unconsciously, the work of the performers, although this is not a contest (which is deliberately evaluative and competitive). The idea is to give the listener something of musical worth, that is, to give him a taste of the values which the players have already absorbed. In a sense, then, the performance is *educational* for the listeners, and it may also be *interesting* simply because of the melodious music and the obvious efforts of the players to do the best possible job.

To the player, the concert is a summation of his work and a test of his ability to perform as rehearsed. Rightly or wrongly, he is influenced by the size of the audience and its reactions. Consequently, the director must guard against any fiascos. This means suitable music, thorough preparation, adequate publicity, and competent staging.

PROGRAMMING. The first step in preparing a concert is to select the music. Repertoire is discussed in Chapter 4, but programming is choosing particular numbers and evaluating their relationship as a series of works to be performed at a concert.

When either selecting music for purchase or choosing the numbers to be placed in the folders and rehearsed, the director is naturally conscious of their possible program value. He is usually certain of a few works and considers the others optional. As rehearsals continue, the picture becomes clearer, i.e., this number will be very effective, that one must be discarded, and this other one is not pretentious but may serve as a change of pace. He may then add other works to rehearsal which will fill out the program.

One should be concerned with the musical quality of the selections, their congruity, the ability of the group to learn and present them effectively, and the over-all time required for their presentation.

If a number is being seriously considered for a concert, a director must know its performance time, and if this is not indicated he must time it in rehearsal (or by humming through the score). All of the numbers combined must approximate the allotted time. For example, allowing for tuning, introductions, and applause, the timing for a twenty-five minute assembly program would need to be twenty minutes or a bit more. Full evening concerts in this country are expected to be about seventy to a hundred minutes in length, including any intermissions, and one governs his selections accordingly. This rule is, of course, relaxed in the case of single work programs such as operas, or oratorios, but even then (by judicious cuts), the program can be held to a reasonable length.

Because listeners (and players) have widely different musical understanding and taste, it is important to choose numbers of different "weight." The untutored listener will suffer through a rather taxing work, if he is rewarded with something light and catchy. Conversely, the most sensitive individual will bear with the more obvious numbers, if they are followed by something more aesthetically challenging. This is educationally sound practice.

It is also important to present several idioms. It is difficult to secure the desired variety, if the choice is limited to works of one composer or of one era. Such concentration on one style is even more unsupportable in rehearsal.

The principle of contrast is also the basis for sequential arrangement of the works. There are several theories on this, all resolving to the exercise of instinct. Some follow the chronological arrangement of composers, some believe in the *heavy to light* principle, and others like to build to a climax.

However, in any list of numbers there are a variety of ways to arrange the sequence.

The director should make certain that numbers of the same general type are separated at a concert. This principle even extends to the keys, because the listener unconsciously tires of the repetitious tonality. Another universal rule is that the opening numbers should be safe and solid (so the players and listeners may calm their apprehensions), and the conclusion should have an element of excitement and drive. This is why band concerts so often begin and end with marches, include something heavy or traditional just after the opener, and proceed with solos, suites, and specialty numbers placed according to their essential character. Sequence is different when there is to be an intermission for, in a sense, there are two short programs.

PREPARATION. In Chapter 5, the matter of rehearsal (including the conductor's preparation and teaching procedures) was treated. Numbers selected for public performance are merely subjected to more detailed and intensive preparation. Care is taken to work out every passage and to develop an easy familiarity with each number. However, this process must not be extended so far that the rendition becomes rigid and mechanical. At the performance, the conductor must be able to adjust the dynamics and tempo to the hall, as well as to his heightened perception of expression, and the players must still be able to feel a sense of inspiration.

The depth of preparation thus depends upon the maturity of the group. Years of experience cannot be compressed into a few weeks. One tries to take a step in the right direction by concentrating upon the more obvious weaknesses of the group. But there is a certain deliberateness about concert preparation. Once a preliminary idea of the numbers is achieved, sectional rehearsals are instituted and individual practice is enforced. Some directors select and bracket two or three critical passages in each part which the player is expected to prepare for tryouts or auditions. This is remarkably effective with immature groups or for contest selections.

As the numbers begin to take shape, it is a good idea to tape a rehearsal or two. This is done not only to check the rendition, but also to ensure good rehearsal attention, and to impress the players with the need for security in their playing.

Careful pacing of effort is a key factor. Many a group is allowed to dawdle peacefully until two or three weeks before the event, when the director becomes frantically aware that things are not shaping up, and he may call several exhausting special rehearsals. Such a group is invariably tense during a performance. Naturally, one can demand more as the time of performance nears (this is the real purpose of the concert) but a little early pressure saves wear and tear at the end.

The final preparation for the concert is the dress rehearsal on stage, which is mostly devoted to acoustical and staging problems. A little pep talk or expression of confidence is in order.

PUBLICITY. Unless a program is presented to a captive audience, a publicity campaign is a necessity. A large number of the parents may be expected to attend because of family loyalty and the need to deliver and return their children. But publicity is necessary if additional listeners are to appear.

The director actually cares little about the size of the audience (if it includes those whose loyalty and opinion he especially values), but he *is* concerned with the effect upon the players. It is not the actual attendance which is so important but the number relative to the last concert, or to other school programs. If the school play and the choral concert draw full houses, then the band or orchestra members feel let down with a half-filled auditorium. Such a result is often due more to publicity than to the relative merits of the performances.

Many times, a director views news coverage as a form of advertisement. It *is*, to him, but the news media are interested in news, and they are reluctant to advertise in their news columns. When the tickets are already on sale, it is a poor time to release the announcement of the concert. The real news value may be weeks in advance of the program, when the engagement of a guest soloist or the decision to program a student-composed number may be announced. This creates the anticipation, and the final releases are mere squibs announcing time and place, but even these should have something original to feature—the trumpet trio is composed of graduating seniors or the new contrabass clarinet is to be employed for the first time. As everyone knows, the best read stories are accompanied by pictures. If possible, no news release for a concert should be submitted without a picture.

Saturation, high pressure tactics, and superlatives should be avoided, for eventually they are ignored. What is needed is legitimate items of news value. These should be released to all news media simultaneously, i.e., local newspapers, school paper, radio, and TV. Of course, the school paper would or should be interested in more copy. Certain types of news may be suitable for release to metropolitan and national publications.

Unless the school has a policy of clearing news releases through a central office, the director should hand all releases directly to any reporters he knows (and he should get to know some). These contact persons are important, for when they think the organization is good and the program is special, this tone will be set in the coverage.

In fact, what really induces people to attend events in large numbers is the conviction that this one is unusual and that everyone will be there. This phenomenon accounts for much of the drawing power of visiting artists.

Instrumental directors seldom write good news stories. Lengthy program notes are not news, and reporters prefer to write their own stories in their own style. Often, therefore, it is wise to submit the story in outline form.

Event:
Organization:
Conductor:
Date, time, and place:
Tickets available at:
Featured works and soloist(s):
Other special features:

This information should be keyed to the pictures and whatever emphasis is desired.

Among other forms of publicity are:

1) ticket sales by the players;
2) brief "teaser" programs for school assembly, radio, or TV;
3) public address announcement at games (or by cruiser car);
4) personal announcement to P.T.A. and other community groups;
5) paid newspaper, radio, and TV ads;
6) post cards to a selected mailing list;
7) window cards and placards;
8) window and automobile stickers;
9) circulars or doorknob rings;
10) paper arm bands or badges for the players;
11) announcement in printed programs of Coming Events.

Another form of publicity often overlooked is the review *after* the program. Serious reviews probably affect a different kind of reader and, over a period, may build the prestige of the group. These are useless if they are consistently flowery and promotional. Charitable but honest words are required. (Some professed critics have never said an unkind word in their lives!)

STAGING. The format for staged concerts varies from the serious symphonic type to the variety show type. Most school programs can bear a little freedom and flexibility simply to relax the players and audience. We have seen programs in which the organization was seated in diagonal rows rather than in semicircles. Stage bands have been used to play the intermission, while some concerts take the form of skits with cooperating dance groups and pantomimes. Special lighting effects are used, and trumpet and trombone players have been known to come forward to the footlights for the final strain of the *Stars and Stripes Forever*. All this comes under the heading of showmanship. If used as an occasional change, and if done with taste and precision, there is value in such device. Traditional concert format, of course, wears better over the years.

Whatever format is to be used, proper staging is critical to a concert's reception. Many do a haphazard job, although nothing is required but foresight. What is wanted is simply a smooth operation without hitches which would distract the players or audience. To do the job right, the following steps should be observed.

(1) The stage is reserved for final rehearsal(s) and concert; this is done when the dates are reserved on the calendar.

(2) Program and ticket copy are prepared and sent to the printer in plenty of time; arrangements are made for proof reading and delivery.

(3) A list is made of the equipment that will have to be moved— piano, harp, string basses, drums and traps, risers, podium, racks, drum stools, box of music, tuner, etc.

(4) A seating diagram is prepared.

(5) Whoever moves and sets up the equipment (custodians, student assistant, or committee of players) is given the list of equipment and seating diagram, and arrangements are made for the work to be done at a specified time.

(6) If the program is to be taped, the operator is notified and arrangements are made to set up the recording equipment.

(7) Ushers and box office personnel (if used) are selected and notified.

(8) Tickets and programs are picked up, and tickets are distributed as necessary; complimentary tickets are sent if this has been planned.

(9) When the time arrives for the equipment move, the director supervises and assists as necessary; but in any case he must check and make adjustments on stage unless he has a very reliable assistant.

(10) The stage manager or custodian is consulted about the lighting control and given instructions, or someone is delegated to handle the lighting changes. Curtain control is also determined (although an open curtain allows the audience to observe the entrance of the players and their warm up activities, and thus contributes to a relaxed and authentic atmosphere).

(11) The final rehearsal is conducted (including any special coordination with cooperating groups), with special attention to acoustical adjustment and the psychological preparation of the players.

(12) A few hours before the concert, the programs are delivered to the hall or given personally to the ushers; any possibility of poor ventilation or heating is noted and checked with the custodians; and the stage arrangement is readjusted as needed.

(13) The director arrives with the players and assists in tuning unless he either has capable section leaders or an assistant to do the job.

(14) As the lights go down, the director enters, bows, and begins the concert. Some directors like to say a few words to the audience between numbers; this is chiefly to produce informality, if that is wanted. The director should have instructed the players to stand together on signal and to remain on stage at the intermission and conclusion until the applause ceases.

(15) After the program, the director remains to receive the congratulations of the audience and makes a point of commending his students. He leaves any equipment packing or moving to the players and assistants, at least until the hall is cleared.

This procedure may seem formidable to the future director but it is normally followed in staging any performance.

Ensemble and Solo Performances

Appearances of small groups and soloists require the same general pattern of preparation as does the band and orchestra concert but, obviously, the entire operation is less complex.

The director usually arranges or accepts these engagements for his players, and then he contacts them for their consent. At that time, he must be sure the players know what the event is, when and where, how transportation is arranged, who is accompanying, and whom to contact upon arrival (unless the director is to be there). The director must either determine or help to decide what numbers are to be played. If it is necessary to hear and coach this material again, he must make the necessary appointment.

The publicity and staging arrangements are usually left to the sponsoring group, but the names of the players must be supplied and the condition of the piano will have to be checked.

Contests

Instrumental directors must avoid a closed mind, either pro or con, on the subject of contests. Contests are simply a means of motivation and evaluation and can be overstressed. The scholar who wants a high mark more than knowledge is just like many players and their directors.

A contest does tend to raise the level of performance within its geographic area. The danger arises when it is regarded as the main musical event of the school year and the rating is taken as the measure of success or failure. Pressures can become so great that a director's job is endangered, not because the superintendent really believes him a failure, but because the public demands a winning team.

Unfortunately local attitudes are often aroused by the competitive approach of the other participating schools. A calm, sane group *can* become infected by thoughtless appraisals expressed by their fellow musicians. In such a case, the director has no choice but to withdraw his groups for a time. Indeed, most of the educational values can be gained when groups are entered in alternate years.

Another good means of de-emphasis is to avoid protracted rehearsal on the contest selections by withholding them until six or eight weeks before the event. This is difficult to do if the other schools are making sustained and strenuous efforts. The sight reading contests held in several areas may help to produce the proper psychology.

There are inherent values in contests or else they would have passed from the scene long ago. Indeed, the many abuses of the system, and the consequent attacks upon it, have only resulted in modifications, without significantly decreasing participation. Hence, most directors will become involved at some point, and when this occurs, the individual director must realize that his self-control is the key to useful contests. It is he who must avoid unreasonable pressures on his players and set an example of good sportsmanship. His approach must always remain calm, efficient, and sensible. The following suggestions are offered.

(1) The director takes care to comply fully with all regulations on eligibility, fees, musical selections, and application dates; contest managers and judges are often plagued with late and incorrect entries.

(2) If music is not prescribed but chosen from a list, any unfamiliar scores are checked and numbers are chosen which best display the talents of the players. Although the numbers should challenge the players to develop new powers, it is unwise to depend upon a trumpet player to quickly extend his range, or to expect a brassy sounding band to suddenly achieve a smooth, symphonic style.

(3) As soon as received, the numbers are read to double check their suitability and then put away until the proper time. Of course, the director studies the score and marks the parts as usual. Soloists and ensembles are given their parts and coached as necessary. Before the contest, the measures should be numbered consecutively in scores to be supplied to the judge (for more efficient adjudication).

(4) The band or orchestra entries are subjected to regular concert preparation, and a trial run at a concert is a good idea. Soloists and ensembles are also given an opportunity to perform their selections for an audience.

(5) During this process, the director's attitude is no different from usual. The numbers are prepared to the best of the players' ability, and without undue stress or strain. The possibility of achieving one rating or another is discussed coolly, with no reference to the comparative chances of the other entries.

(6) Arrangements are made for the trip (if required) as will be discussed later in this chapter.

(7) Contest procedures and the trip schedule are discussed with the

players, and the players are given the necessary warnings and instructions.

(8) At the contest center, every effort is made to keep the students in a good physical and mental state and to maintain their equipment in good order. Also, students are encouraged or required to listen to as many entries from the other schools as possible (thus making their own evaluations).

(9) As the contest is run off and results come in, the director is restrained in his expressions on the ratings, and comment sheets are held, if possible, until the following rehearsal.

(10) At the next rehearsal, the comment sheets are read and explained *objectively*. The director's attitude toward a I, II, or III rating should be, "That is about what we deserved; we can do better next time."

Such procedure may seem insensitive, but it is almost guaranteed to produce the best possible performance, as well as an objective attitude from students and parents, and the most benefit from the judges' evaluation.

Outdoor Events

Parades, games, and outdoor rallies are in a somewhat different category from concerts. The orchestra is not involved, and the band itself occupies a different role.

Outdoor events are difficult chiefly because of weather, noise and confusion, and acoustical problems. Marching itself involves special problems, which were treated in Chapter 6. Too often, a band that is well-disciplined indoors, loses its cohesion outdoors.

Much of this effect can be overcome by good preliminary arrangements. For rehearsals on the gridiron, the director should be sure that the yardlines and markers are properly fixed, and he should have a portable amplifier to project his announcements and observations. Before the game, he must be sure that the band section in the grandstand (or chairs on the track) is reserved. Sometimes, seats painted white are more effective than railing or ropes in marking off this section. Any preparations with lights or PA system need to be made.

Then the director must give the necessary instructions for the occasion. Because of the noise, excitement, and the public's proximity, it is well to have simple signals that are clearly defined, for use in the stands. For example, some directors have a complete set of hand signals, e.g., ten pieces are marked with arabic numerals for the first half and ten more with Roman numerals for the second half, and after any piece, the director may signal the next by extending the necessary number of fingers. Hat held high means to have the school song ready for a possible touchdown.

There is need for clear understanding about eating in the stands and also, leaving the stands. Some directors entrust control of this traffic to one boy and one girl who make sure that more than a specified number are never absent.

Preparation for difficult weather is necessary. If possible, metal clarinets should be available for issue to those having expensive wood instruments. White cotton gloves help take the edge off the cold wind (holes may be cut under the fingertips for the clarinet players), and brass players should have lip grease. Whether overcoats may or may not be worn should be clear in advance. Some directors make a definite rule: if the temperature is below x degrees when the player leaves home, he should wear an overcoat. There are also occasions when the appearance of the band is problematical because of intermittent drizzle, threatening clouds, or dropping temperatures, so, each fall arrangements should be made to take care of this contingency by telephone committees who will relay the director's decision.

TRIPS

Among the unusual facets of the instrumental director's job is that of tour guide. The possibilities range from an afternoon jaunt of fifty miles for an exchange concert or clinic, to a world's fair visit, or even a three month European tour. By and large, the importance of these excursions is probably overestimated. To some of the students they are merely a lark and many are definitely inconvenienced in their school work or other commitments. But some trips are educationally profitable if they are properly handled.

The purpose of a trip should be to participate in something that is musically worthwhile, in a setting which is not locally available. A huge festival or clinic, drawing many excellent performing groups and exhibits, is clearly such an occasion. Commercial and promotional events, during which the musicians are only massed together on a gridiron or marched past a reviewing stand, are open to question. After all, the mere excitement of a trip and an opportunity to see the world may not be the school's responsibility to provide.

When a trip is contemplated, administrative sanction is secured, the group is consulted, and the necessary transportation and financial support is found. Arrangements vary with the number of students, the distance, the time away from home, and the availability of financial support. The regular options are as follows.

(1) Volunteer transportation is found, and extra expense is borne by the individuals.

(2) The school provides entrance fees, use of school buses, or direct costs.

(3) Buses, train, or even airplanes are chartered, with all or part of the expenses being borne by a local industry or citizens' group.

(4) Prizes or mileage allowances from the promoting organization provide all or part of the expenses. Rooms and/or meals may also be provided (but high subsidization is likely to mean exploitation).

(5) Players' and/or parents' club conduct a fund raising campaign for the balance of expenses.

The musical preparation is made as for any concert, contest, or marching event.

It is difficult to move a large group and its luggage from point to point on schedule, and without damage to health, morals, or property. In this task, if the trip and personnel are extensive, the director should try to secure active assistance from other qualified individuals. Yet he is necessarily involved at all points, for only he knows the details pertaining to the players, their equipment, the times and places to be, etc. For major trips, the following measures should be noted:

(1) Complete information is secured from the sponsoring organization; times, places, and dates are confirmed; any necessary forms are completed and returned, together with any fees to be paid. When leaving the United States, customs regulations are checked and any required vaccinations and papers are secured.

(2) The dates, times, places, and mileages are checked and a time-table is drawn up.

(3) The personnel and needed equipment are listed, the number of carriers are determined, and these are engaged and informed of the itinerary and timetable. Insurance coverage on personnel is checked. Personnel and equipment are divided among the carriers and a list is made of who and what is in each carrier.

(4) If an overnight stay is involved, room reservations should be made, and confirmed, and meal reservations may also be desirable. Students choose roommates and lists are drawn up.

(5) Bus leaders or chaperones are secured, and their duties are assigned. For long tours a nurse should accompany the group.

(6) An equipment crew is selected and assigned specific responsibilities to load, unload, and set up the percussion equipment, racks, podium, etc. Sometimes bass drum, tympani, and racks are provided on location.

(7) Complete information is outlined and duplicated for each member of the party, including:

> detailed timetable
> what to bring (money, equipment, luggage) and packing
>   instructions
> bus or car assignments
> room assignments (if overnight)

listing of all assigned responsibilities (bus leaders,
    chaperones, stage and equipment crews, etc.)
procedures for embarking and disembarking
rules of conduct for the trip

If all is carefully planned, and if it is a responsible group, the director
need not be a nursemaid en route. His energies may then be conserved for
meeting officials and musical colleagues, and in handling the musical
presentation.

Smaller trips, such as a few players going by car to a clinic, are
handled much more informally. The players are simply reminded to be
ready, with their instruments, at a specific hour. Exactly the same
problems are to be faced, but on a more improvised basis.

EVALUATION

From the field of practical logistics, we move to the more abstract
realm of evaluation. Evaluation is the process of determining the extent
to which a student or an entire instrumental music program is accom-
plishing the established goals, with the understanding that revisions will
be instituted in instruction to improve the results. As such, evaluation
is a very definite aspect of program coordination in instrumental music.
Without it, directors can only operate by instinct and may go blindly
ahead for years inefficiently expending their energies.

Instrumental directors are especially concerned with devices for
measuring the musical potential of their volunteers, with the marking of
students in their classes, and with an estimation of the effectiveness of
the various phases of their program. Answers of this kind are needed for
any enlightened program of instruction. Good evaluation does not
necessarily mean a massive program of testing. Much time can be spent in
administering standardized tests that are unreliable in gathering the type
of information needed. Indeed, many talent tests are more promotional
than prognostic and the danger is not always avoided by constructing a
series of quizzes. The old terms validity and reliability are still important.
A test must consistently measure what it is supposed to measure.

It must be recognized that much pertaining to musicianship is not
revealed by tests alone. Listening to actual performance is obviously
the chief means to judge performing skills, while observation of choices of
music and recordings is one means of determining levels of musical taste.
Knowledge *about* music is discovered by test or interview.

Evaluation thus begins with the definition of what is to be determined, which suggests the kind of information to be sought and the
means of gathering it. Then the collected data must be interpreted in
the light of the original question.

Musical Potential

All school children possess some degree of musical capacity. Just how this is to be defined and measured is not readily clear. It is apparently more than simple ability to hear small differences in pitch, loudness, duration, and tone quality, and even the possession of absolute pitch is not a definite clue. The prevalent theory is that musicality is related to the perception and organization of tonal relationships as found in actual music. That is, a potential musician should be able to identify beat and phrase patterns, to anticipate tonal resolutions, and so on. To be sure, these abilities are learned, but so are the vocabulary and mathematical symbols usually employed in intelligence tests. This principle has been explored by several recently developed tests, but a completely satisfactory result is yet to be achieved. Even if the true musicality of an individual could be definitely measured, there are other important factors in his musical future. These factors certainly would include perseverance and motivation. This is why a few tests include questions on a student's interests, his parents' and siblings' musical backgrounds, and so on. We also like to know something about a student's intelligence, his school grades, and his physical conformation in respect to certain instruments. We may also interview him and his parents, and check his teachers' opinions.

It should be noted, however, that this kind of quest for information is rather time consuming and inconclusive, and it is often easier and safer to determine musical potential through actual trial. *This too is a method of evaluation.* The time spent on the dropouts is not wasted by any means, and indeed, almost everyone becomes a dropout at some point (even the music teacher).

Marking

The progressive educator dislikes marking students because a single grade of A, B, or C gives only a composite estimate of a student's progress toward the objectives of a course. In band or orchestra, for example, a student may make strides in musical knowledge and taste but develop quite slowly in playing proficiency.

A type of grade card often used in the elementary schools lists several qualities (growth in sight reading skill, knowledge of musical rudiments, development of musical tastes, and so on) which are judged separately in evaluating the students. However, nothing has been able to supplant the traditional marking system for convenience and clarity of interpretation.

The instrumental music teacher is placed in a difficult situation. The performing groups are elective and any loss of trained and selected personnel has a damaging effect upon the group. Hence, the director does not wish to discourage players by giving low marks. Often, deportment and attendance count more than musical progress (although these qualities of course are related). To academic colleagues, music courses seem to be snap courses in which an A or B may be easily earned.

The fact remains that the director needs some definite basis for his marks. The point system discussed in Chapter 5 is one answer, but too often it becomes a sort of merit badge plan rather than a true index of improving musicianship.

Marks must express individual progress toward the objectives of a course, and this relationship must be clear to the student. Any other system results in the pursuit of false objectives by the members of the class. For example, basing marks upon position within a section will cause students to work toward displacing their section leaders, while marks based upon auditions will result in extra practice on musical passages that are likely to be used in such auditions. Marks based in whole or in part upon a compliant attitude will cause efforts to please the teacher.

Any reasoned consideration of a music course should produce some definite goals related to the student's increasing facility, taste, and understanding of musical device (as discussed in the first chapter). This being the case, some means of discovering the student's development along these lines must be attempted. Ideally, this would mean a series of auditions (unless the player were already receiving individual instruction), assigned homework, quizzes, and conferences. However, with numerous students to mark every six weeks, the director cannot be so thorough since his time would be spent in evaluating rather than teaching.

What must happen is that while teaching, the director is constantly evaluating. For example, as he checks passages in the trumpet section he observes that the last chair player seems more certain than before. He also observes that one player warms up carefully for rehearsal while another does nothing constructive. He notes which students frequently take their music home and which ones mark their parts for more accurate execution. Such behavior is evidence of musical facility, taste, and understanding. This method of evaluation becomes not only a basis for marks (supplementing more formal procedures) but also each observed weakness calls for logical measures of correction through instruction.

Program Evaluation

An instrumental music program may be evaluated in terms of its *capacity* to produce results. This capacity is related to the facilities (plant and equipment), enrollments, the number and qualifications of the staff, the offerings, and the specific policies relating to instruction. All these factors can be rated in terms of favorability to produce good musical learning. Such a rating is sought when one is considering a position in a particular school, when ascertaining needs and preparing budget requests, and when seeking accreditation.

However, a more direct route to improved instruction is evaluation in terms of the program's *actual* effect upon the students. This approach is based on the same principle as individual marking, that is, the extent of progress of all the students toward the objectives. A good program has mostly *successful* graduates, i.e., graduates who exemplify the kind of musicians and players the teachers wish to produce. They will be acquainted with much good literature and will play with reasonable facility; they will understand the principles of music's construction and interpretation; they will like it enough to continue playing at least occasionally; and they will seek to hear good music whenever they can. A weak program will produce weak graduates. Many of these will not play very well and will have little knowledge of musical style and device. Few of these will ever play again, buy recordings, or become concertgoers.

Therefore, the director must be able to judge the kind of graduates actually being produced. When he observes that they generally sound well and perform adequately in any competition, he knows that he is doing the necessary job in the technical and expressive elements of music. If, on the other hand, he notes that few of the graduates *occupy* themselves with music, that there are few returnees to hear the high school groups, that few continue to play, and none select a musical vocation, then he may be sure that his instruction is not as interesting and meaningful as it should be. Measures to deepen the approach are clearly needed.

The forms of evaluation that have been discussed are a practical necessity. It should be apparent that the more time the director has, the more exact he may be in his collection of evaluative data. A class roll book and grade book is the first step, while files of prognostic test results is another. Regular dossiers may be kept of each student and follow-up questionnaires may be sent to graduates. Whatever is done, evaluation should be approached with sincerity and full understanding of its purpose. Only in this way can directors escape useless testing, expedience in marking, and false illusions about the results of their instruction.

Research

Evaluation is also a method of research when applied to a specific area of investigation. For example, if a director wishes to find better class instruction books, then he compares detailed progress records of one group of players who are using his regular materials, with another group who are using newly selected materials. He may similarly compare the results of class instruction with individual instruction. Such experiments should be handled carefully in order to achieve valid findings. The only sure way is to try it, regardless of prejudices or difficulties en route, and then judge in terms of recorded results.

SCHOOL AND COMMUNITY RELATIONSHIPS

We return, finally, to the consideration of instrumental music activities as part of the larger educational enterprise and the life of the community. Such relationships are implicit throughout the book, but require more detailed consideration, for instrumental music bears a unique relationship to other elements of the school and community.

One of the characteristics of instrumental music in the schools is its status as an elective and the consequent great variability in the extent and quality. It is thus partially dependent on promotional activity, that is, there is a direct relationship between the degree of success demonstrated and the support that accrues from the school administration, students, and community. Without this support the program never acquires enough staff, facilities, money, and students to make significant progress.

Another characteristic is that instrumental music is comparatively costly in instructional time as well as money. More teachers and dollars are required per student than in most educational subjects, which causes further stress on tangible results.

A third characteristic is that instrumental music has great possibilities as entertainment, which many people think is its only function. Consequently, there is a tendency to exploit the students to meet these demands.

But the basic factor about the instrumental music program is its irrepressibility. It is a noisy, active, cooperative endeavor that usually arouses considerable loyalty among the players and their parents, while some onlookers may be aroused to open or concealed resistance.

These characteristics give the instrumental program a special stance. Unique among the school subjects, its role must be played openly and vigorously, yet with the utmost patience and sincerity.

Students and Instrumental Music

To the instrumental director, students are either players or potential players. His inherent mission is to convert students to the pursuit of musicianship and to aid them in that endeavor.

As we have suggested, participation in band and orchestra is not the entire measure of this influence. The majority of students will be affected by the less specialized activities with rhythm, melody, and keyboard instruments, and in listening to good recordings and live performances by the school groups, and some of these are further exposed, for a time, to instruction on orchestral instruments but for various reasons do not achieve regular membership in the performing groups. Far from failing with these students (if the task was properly conceived and handled), a long step has been taken toward their useful musicianship in society. It is an inherent purpose of the instrumental music program to strengthen and extend these exploratory forms of experience.

Those students who become continuing members of the performing groups are especially sensitive to the atmosphere surrounding the activities. Under proper circumstances, a good number of students will center their interests around the supplemental activities in instrumental music. They practice after school, volunteer to form small ensembles, carry out assigned tasks, and make themselves generally useful around the department. Such activities sometimes reach the proportions of a club. This is entirely natural, for these students have acquired an absorbing interest and need to occupy themselves in it. Some are unconsciously weighing music as a vocation.

To some of these students, the director becomes a model, and they tend to reflect his attitudes and reactions. This becomes an important influence on the character and the future outlook of these people. It is a rare director whose advice has not been asked and, in giving it, he has established certain ideas and courses of action that seriously affect the lives and careers of students. This is an awesome responsibility. The director is not ordinarily qualified in psychology and counseling and should therefore avoid making judgments on problems which are better referred to more qualified personnel. The safest approach is undoubtedly along the lines of non-directive counseling, i.e., the counselor (director) avoids direct advice but he encourages the client (student) to discuss his problems and by adroit questioning and sympathetic listening, the student is helped to reason his way to his own decision.

Direct guidance within the field of music is more appropriate to the director. A promising young musician should be encouraged to make a career of music, and the necessary preparations for such a career should be explained to him. But meddling paternalism is never justified. By and large, the best form of guidance consists in opening the door of opportunity to the gifted musician—making sure that he can solo with the performing group, referring him to interesting professional books and articles, providing transportation to outstanding recitals, encouraging him to creative composition and providing opportunity for performance of his works, giving leadership opportunities and a chance to help and learn about the director's duties. This procedure is always more effective than talking.

Departmental Relationships

One of the most prevalent problems in instrumental music is a lack of teamwork among music teachers in a school. Often the vocalists and instrumentalists operate quite independently of each other. It can be seen how easily this causes a lack of effectiveness in the elementary music program and an improper sense of exclusiveness among the students in each field. Actually both fields should aim for about the same objectives, since the means are somewhat different, but complementary in effect.

But while vocalists and instrumentalists may possibly succeed in ignoring one another, the relationship of the band and orchestra programs is sometimes so close that active competition and antagonism is the result. If there are not enough players and equipment for both, and the school administration and public must choose, someone is going to get hurt. Such a result is tragic and should never be allowed to develop. Music supervisors and administrators should establish the tradition of joint planning between these two fields. Natural points of conflict (recruiting policy, budget requests, scheduling and calendar) should be approached on a cooperative basis. If the two fields threaten to become competitive, it is sometimes necessary to reassign the directors.

Intraschool Relationships

While musicians usually agree in principle, the relations with other departments often suffer because of conflicting philosophy. Since the academic fields are assumed to be the core of schooling, and instrumental music seems to swallow up a disproportionate share of time and money, music is often thought to be overemphasized. This may well be true in particular instances. The differences between legitimate schooling in music and misplaced emphasis are discussed in Chapter 1.

As one school discipline, instrumental music is charged to work with the others in the interests of the students. This principle needs to be considered in any decision regarding course requirements, scheduling, budget allocation, and the like. Instrumental music activity should be neither suppressed nor allowed to interfere unnecessarily with other subjects. However, certain special concessions to instrumental music are required to achieve equality. The cost of books and equipment for a field like English or mathematics would not support adequate musical instruction, and a policy of rigid scheduling will not allow students to elect ensembles and individual instruction.

An objective administrative approach is required if the special needs of the instrumental music program are to be recognized and fulfilled. Too often, administrative authority is not fully exercised in this area, leaving the instrumental program to fend for itself. In such a case, the program either languishes without the sinews of instruction or else it becomes increasingly self-sufficient and insensitive to the aims of the school. Administrators also should clarify the status of band and orchestra as credit subjects. In earlier days, of course, they were non-credit courses, but when the vocational implications were recognized, some schools allowed credit *after* a student completed music theory or some other preprofessional course. Today, band and orchestra are full credit offerings in many schools. However, each of these solutions is somewhat beside the mark. Band and orchestra are *laboratory* courses, and thus entitled to *partial* credit. Either a student should earn half a unit per year in such a group, or a full unit should be given during each of the junior and senior years and none before.

Administrative policy is usually influenced in a large measure by the climate of opinion among the faculty. If there is resistance to instrumental music, wise administrative measures are likely to founder anyway. In too many instances, the director is placed on the defensive by his colleagues, and unless he is unusually erudite and gifted in expression, his opinions on nonmusical subjects are quite likely to be ignored. He gradually subsides until even his pronouncements on music are dismissed as the views of a mere technician. Unfortunately, the specialized training and consuming interest of the instrumental director often justifies this reaction. The only means to combat this attitude is through a broader form of education for music teachers and special efforts by individual directors to concern themselves more forcefully with the total aspect of schooling.

The extent of such biased attitudes among academic personnel has a proportional effect upon students. A student will be hesitant about electing band or orchestra if he has been subtly given the opinion that it is an easy course and that he deserves better things.

It is even more disturbing when this negative approach is adopted by the school counselor; frankly we feel that the position of counselor requires more farsightedness and impartiality. We fear that some of these people are guided by certain vocational formulae on one hand and a liberal arts bias on the other (and neither position grants instrumental music much of a foothold). Fortunately, the power of music itself is intrinsic and difficult to overcome. As long as the director really feeds music to his students (and little else) his program can stand much assault.

Thus, it must be recognized that the instrumental music program is often set within a mildly hostile school environment. Although its value is admitted, every forward step is likely to be contested. The struggle often continues intermittently until the instrumental music program either accepts second class status within the school or breaks through to reign in uneasy splendor. This senseless conflict must be avoided whenever possible. The instrumental director should rise above these issues in dealing with his colleagues, seek strong leadership from the school administration, and devote his energies to developing the musicianship of his students.

Interschool Relationships

In a larger sense, of course, the welfare of a school's instrumental music program depends upon the status of similar programs in the vicinity and throughout the nation. As we have seen, instrumental music in the schools is a child of this century, and its strength seems to be increasing.

Although each local school system is unique, it tends to imitate successful practices in other schools, thus producing educational evolution. That instrumental music is part of this evolution is proved by the spread of marching bands, stage bands, new instrumentation plans, new techniques or methods of teaching, and new types of equipment. What seem to be gaps in the program, i.e., lack of instruction in strings and piano and sufficient playing experience in the elementary grades, will only be remedied when enough schools have demonstrated their value and practicability.

Thus, it is incumbent upon instrumental directors to observe one another's work and to cooperate with each other in refining and strengthening their mode of instruction. Fortunately, this tendency to look beyond the walls of their own schools has been one of the strengths of instrumental teachers and has probably been largely responsible for the rapid strides in school music. The director who travels alone is fairly rare.

However, the cooperation among instrumental directors can be improved, since much of this association is shallow. Many directors go to clinics, contests, and conventions to flaunt their performing groups, to advance in elective office, to find better jobs, or just for a holiday. This is good, if it can inspire real improvements at home and deliberate measures to upgrade the profession.

Instrumental directors should compare notes. They should not only hear the splendid bands and orchestras in performances that are thoroughly prepared, but should also visit one another's daily operations and see how these groups are achieved, and how the entire program is handled. But, of course, who has the time and opportunity? We would wish directors could occasionally exchange podiums. Meanwhile, a great deal is being done at the grass roots level through such mediums as exchange concerts, and cooperatively arranged clinics and festivals, whereby students and directors from several schools focus their efforts in a deliberately educational enterprise.

There should be more cooperation between the schools and institutions of higher learning. Collegiate music departments cannot develop their players from scratch and are usually placed in the position of competing for students through extensive programs of public relations and frank promotion. This should not be, and it seems to be largely the fault of the school instrumental teachers.

The college should be considered a natural extension of the high school just as the secondary school is an extension of the elementary school. A deliberate attempt should be made to interest students in attending concerts and clinics held at nearby colleges. Graduates should be *referred* to the colleges and encouraged to participate in the musical groups (which is no more than the high school director expects from the junior high and elementary staff). Colleges are also greatly dependent upon the school directors for scholarship recommendations; not every student who asks is qualified, but those who are highly talented and needy should be pointed out to the appropriate college official. By such cooperative measures, the energies of collegiate music departments will be more fully utilized for their true business of providing advanced and specialized musical training of the highest sort.

Such cooperation is also immediately helpful to the individual schools. The colleges can serve as natural sponsors of music clinics, festivals, and summer camps, while their teachers can serve as clinicians, private instructors, and resource people in the service of the schools (without promotional implications). In short, thriving school and college music programs usually exist together or not at all.

Instrumental Music in the Community

In American schools, the student is really not educated to take his place within a specific community. How many people live and die in one spot? Just because the local citizenry is largely employed in a steel mill does not mean that those children should be deliberately trained in that industry. Neither does the lack of a local symphony orchestra mean that a school's graduate cannot aspire to an orchestral post in another community. While the school is properly responsive to local needs and limitations, it is engaged in education for national and international, as well as local citizenship.

Similarly, the instrumental music program is *of* the local community, but not dedicated to the will of the community. Its business is to make the best possible musicians out of the children of the community, by the means at hand. However, the instrumental music activities need community support, which means mutual cooperation between the music department and the parents and community leaders.

Essentially, the community supplies the children, and the necessary moral and material support, while the school undertakes to provide an education for today's and tomorrow's world. To provide a check on the process, the community needs an opportunity to evaluate the educational results *en route*. This is the wonderful role of music in the schools, since it can be brought in to full view. How many school programs occur without some singing or playing by the children?

The needs of instrumental music are quite varied. Among these are:

(1) active backing of parents in the enlistment of pupils as beginners, and maintenance of their enrollment in musical groups;

(2) willingness of parents to purchase instruments and other supplies as needed by their children;

(3) parental tolerance, and encouragement of home practice by their children;

(4) parental consent for special projects involving their children, such as trips, fund raising campaigns, and extra assistance as needed for transportation, meals, etc.;

(5) adequate attendance at programs and concerts sponsored by the instrumental music department;

(6) favorable news media;

(7) understanding of the director's goals and problems, and reasonable tolerance of weaknesses and inadequacies in the program;

(8) avoidance of pressures for activities which the director sincerely considers impractical or miseducational.

A band parents club, music alumni, or a similar group may be of great help in securing this kind of backing. It can, however, become simply another special interest group which seeks to secure its own ends. This depends upon its leadership and organization. The helpful group is both militant and acquiescent, since all action is necessarily based upon the welfare of the members' children. Sometimes it is wrongfully used to pressure school administrative officials against their judgment, and whenever such tactics succeed, it is usually not long before the director himself is controlled by the group. In many cases it is better to work directly through the Parent Teachers Association, which has more broadly based membership.

Appearance by the director and his players in community functions is both a dividend of the support provided by the public, and a generator of new support, although the true purpose is to offer the program for public evaluation. It is important to present a *balanced* picture, since a citizen knows only what he sees and hears. The band will appear at parades and games, some will hear it in concert, and any contest results will be widely proclaimed. But will the public form an adequate notion of the kinds of activity going on day by day in the classroom and rehearsal room? Can they conceive the range of musical literature that is being studied and the methods employed? "Open house" at school is one answer, while another is music presented where people are. Most enlightened directors sustain a vigorous activity in presentation of various groups and soloists before all kinds of local gatherings. The danger is that music may become monotonous and its provision taken for granted, and also that flashier presentations are expected. Eventually the individual player sees that he is not playing for experience or so that his progress can be checked, but simply because a program is required.

Sometimes, too, the director's efforts to meet the community half way will boomerang. His musical selections may be termed too classical; his marches may be played too slowly for some at the games; or his concerts may be too long. Any attempts he makes to limit the appearances (even to avoid too much missed class attendance) may be considered uncooperative.

Such criticisms may or may not be justified. The director is really not the one to judge. If the criticism is continued and rather universal he must seek counsel from either his superintendent or most trusted colleagues. What is wrong and what is right? Perhaps he will find it necessary to use new methods and approaches. However, he must not bow to expedience in the name of public relations.

SUMMARY

Among the various factors supporting the task of instruction is that of finance. The needs of the instrumental program must be constantly surveyed and formulated. The resultant list forms the basis for appropriations from school funds, the collection of receipts and fees, and may suggest the need of special fund raising campaigns. Wise budgeting will serve to control purchasing.

Another vital factor is scheduling. Too often, the weekly schedule is based upon tradition. One must reconsider the various offerings and the time required to achieve the inherent objectives. This may result in a revision of the regular periods or some variation of the rotating schedule. The yearly calendar of events likewise needs to be well spaced and coordinated for the convenience of players and audience alike.

Critical to the development of good public appearances is effective programming, which requires judicious timing and contrast. Preparation of the music and publicity must also be carefully handled. Proper staging is a primary factor in a public presentation. Ensemble and solo performances, contests, and outdoor appearances are also public performances, each requiring certain special preparation.

Many public appearances demand the movement of personnel from one location to another. These excursions should not be undertaken without promise of educative results. Money and transportation must be secured and the disposition of personnel and equipment must be planned in detail.

A factor underlying all instruction is effective evaluation. This includes the estimation of musical potential, individual marking, and evaluation of the total program. In many cases, much effort is wasted in giving tests, gathering information, and making interpretations that are quite unrelated to the real goals of instruction. One must begin with a definition of desired results before he can determine the kinds of information he must seek.

The instrumental music program is part of the school curriculum and a definite factor in the community. It is an elective, and hence, is sensitive to reactions and influences from the students, academic staff, and local citizens. The music teachers should work together, and with their administrative and academic colleagues. This cooperation needs to be extended to other schools and colleges. Within the community, the task is to exhibit the results of instruction and to secure the necessary backing without sacrificing freedom of action.

QUESTIONS FOR DISCUSSION

1. Define and illustrate "minimum needs" and their relation to budgeting. How are budget priorities established?

2. What are the principal sources of funds for instrumental music? How are these secured?

3. How are various items ordered? What is the purpose of bidding?

4. What are some of the special difficulties in scheduling musical activities? How are offerings determined? What is adequate rehearsal time?

5. Describe typical scheduling patterns. How are these to be established?

6. Attempt an outline of a typical music calendar. What factors must be considered?

7. Describe factors to be considered in programming and program preparation. What types of publicity are suitable? What staging arrangements need to be made? What special arrangements are needed for outdoor appearances?

8. What seem to be the values and dangers in contests? What is the general process of preparation?

9. How are funds secured for trips? Describe the general process of planning movement of personnel and equipment.

10. What is the inherent purpose of evaluation? What kinds of answers are needed? How does one gather the information and what does he do with it?

11. In what way may the director serve as a counselor?

12. What are some of the inherent difficulties in relationships among music teachers, administrators, and academic colleagues? In what way may schools and colleges cooperate to greater advantage?

13. What is the essential relationship of school and community? What does the instrumental music program offer, and what may it expect from the community?

SELECTED REFERENCES

HINDSLEY, MARK H., *School Band and Orchestra Administration*. New York: Boosey and Hawkes, Inc., 1940.

HOVEY, NILO, *Administration of School Instrumental Music*. Rockville Centre, L. I., N. Y.: Belwin, Inc., 1952.

JONES, LLEWELLYN B., *Building the Instrumental Music Department*. New York: Carl Fischer, Inc., 1949.

MUSIC INDUSTRY COUNCIL, *Business Handbook In Music Education*. Washington, D. C.: Music Educators National Conference, 1959.

THE MUSIC TEACHER AND PUBLIC RELATIONS. Washington, D. C.: Music Educators National Conference, 1958.

THE NIMAC MANUAL. Washington, D. C.: Music Educators National Conference, 1963.

PRESCOTT, GERALD R. AND L. W. CHIDESTER, *Getting Results With School Bands*. Minneapolis: Paul A. Schmitt Music Co., and New York: Carl Fischer, Inc., 1938.

SNYDER, KEITH D., *School Music Administration and Supervision*. Boston: Allyn and Bacon, Inc., 1959.

WEYLAND, RUDOLPH H., *A Guide to Effective Music Supervision*. Dubuque, Iowa: William C. Brown Company, 1960.

WHYBREW, WILLIAM E., *Measurement and Evaluation in Music*. Dubuque, Iowa: William C. Brown Company, 1962.

TESTS OF MUSICAL CAPACITY

DRAKE, R. M., *Drake Musical Aptitude Test*. Chicago: Science Research Associates, 1954. Test of rhythm and musical memory on one LP recording.

GASTON, E. THAYER, *A Test of Musicality*, fourth edition. Lawrence, Kansas: Odell's Instrumental Service, 1956. A progressive test of rhythmic and melodic perception on one LP recording.

KWALWASSER, JACOB, *Kwalwasser Music Talent Test*. New York: Mills Music, Inc. Form A for secondary school and college students; form B for elementary school students. Similar to the Seashore *Measures of Musical Talent*.

SEASHORE, CARL E., *Measures of Musical Talent*. New York: The Psychological Corporation, 1956. The classic test for pitch, loudness, rhythm, timbre, time, and tonal memory on six 78 rpm recordings.

TILSON, LOWELL MASON, *Tilson-Gretsch Musical Aptitude Test*. Chicago: Fred Gretsch Manufacturing Company. A test of pitch, time, intensity and tonal memory on two LP recordings.

WHISTLER, HARVEY S. AND LOUIS P. THORPE, *Whistler-Thorpe Music Aptitude Test, Series A*. Hollywood, California: California Test Bureau, 1950. Test of rhythm and pitch recognition to be self-administered at the piano.

TESTS OF MUSICAL ACHIEVEMENT

ALIFERIS, JAMES, *Aliferis Music Achievement Test*. Minneapolis: University of Minnesota Press, 1954. Essentially a college entrance test in music theory to be played on tape.

FARNUM, STEPHEN E., *Farnum Music Notation Test*. New York: The Psychological Corporation, 1953.

KNUTH, WILLIAM E., *Knuth Achievement Tests in Music*. Philadelphia: Educational Test Bureau, Inc., 1956. Deals with recognition of musical form from written examples.

WATKINS, JOHN G. AND STEPHEN E. FARNUM, *Watkins-Farnum Performance Scale for All Band Instruments*. Winona, Minnesota: Hal Leonard Music, Inc., 1954. Sight reading exercises.

CHAPTER 9

The Instrumental Director

Besides the school children themselves, there are three basic groups of people concerned with the school program in instrumental music:

(1) school band and orchestra directors at any level, instructors assigned to piano and orchestral instruments, and instrumental music supervisors;

(2) classroom teachers and instructors of general music, who handle the broad and preliminary phases of instrumental music;

(3) all those who support the program, including parents and taxpayers, school administrators and officials, private music teachers, instrument manufacturers and retail dealers, and collegiate music departments which prepare the teachers.

While cooperation of all these people is vital, those in the first named group are the ones who hold the initiative and without whom, instrumental music in the schools would retrogress to its Nineteenth century status. For these people we have used the term instrumental director in a generic sense. This book has surveyed the problems of the instrumental music program largely from the viewpoint of the instrumental director. It is time to look more directly at that individual upon whom such wide responsibility rests.

It should be understood that no one person is entirely effective in all the areas of an instrumental director's job. There are good directors and poor directors, and if the qualities that make a good director could be ascertained and more widely attained, the school instrumental music program would increasingly flourish.

This chapter covers the qualifications and preparation necessary for a music teaching career, certain factors in securing a teaching position, and on-the-job relationships. It also deals with further study and various types of professional activity.

VOCATIONAL DECISION

It would be comforting to have a more exact, or scientific, method for discovering the musical vocation. As it stands, the process is still haphazard. Many who choose music are not particularly qualified, and many others who show early promise fade disappointingly. Statistics are not of much value here. It is known that there is a need for instrumental music teachers, that there is frequent turnover, and that there is a chronic lack of really good talent. This could be said of most professions today. Unfortunately, many likely prospects who are at least equally qualified in other fields turn away from music teaching.

The problem has three aspects: (1) how the individual himself may arrive at a sensible estimate of his qualifications, (2) how teachers and the college admissions staff may best check and review this decision, and (3) how students are to be selectively encouraged or discouraged in their choice.

Whatever the answer may be, a certain percentage of the population may not be coldly and scientifically selected to fill a specific number of vacancies in the field. The number and quality of candidates from any locality depends upon the relative richness of the musical environment and, in turn, upon the success and magnetism of certain instructors who have helped produce this environment. That is, a good band with a popular director will tend to produce more than its share of future band directors.

The point at which anyone first entertains the idea of teaching instrumental music can scarcely be determined. It probably begins when an individual looks forward to rehearsals and practice sessions, and when others credit the player with a certain precociousness or superiority of musicianship. Those who learned to play easily and well, who have risen to the top of their sections, and who are locally acclaimed as soloists are likely to become conscious of music as a possible profession.

This thought then develops by stages. At first, there is only a generalized feeling that music would be a good thing with which to work. Then, an idealized image may grow of one's self as a famous concert artist or conductor, or a teacher somewhat like one's own teacher. Finally, if the individual is lucky, he realizes that his natural aptitudes are especially suitable to instrumental music teaching as a field of endeavor.

Competing with this line of thought, of course, are considerations of other vocations. The individual cannot escape comparisons of the roles *as he sees them* in terms of his own values. If he *must* be rich and believes teachers are poor, then he will regard music only as a good avocation.

Among the chief characteristics of this profession are: (1) great love of music and the desire to promote it in all students, and (2) constant ingenuity and perseverance in the task. Instrumental music teachers might be regarded as missionaries. He who considers this profession must therefore ask if he really possesses superior musicianship, love of the art, and the energy necessary for the task. The future instrumental director should feel a strong urge to bring children and music together.

Parents, high school counselors, and collegiate music departments observe and guide this search for a vocation to the best of their ability. There are aptitude tests and talent tests for music and teaching. However, the best test is demonstrated achievement, which is comparatively easy to perceive in this field. When a student plays with ease and freedom, he shows promise, and when he also shows initiative in actively assisting with the school and community musical enterprises, his possibilities are even more striking. If he also shows dependability and integrity and is the kind of person one naturally likes and respects, then he has certainly passed the test.

Too many school instrumental directors are disappointed symphony conductors, while many others wished to become professional performers, but realized they could not meet the competition. Many regard a teaching certificate as a form of insurance and accept a job only as a temporary expedient. Those who possess such confirmed distaste for the vocation should obviously be spotted before they go too far along the road to certification. It is difficult, however, to make definite judgments on this, since some very successful instrumental teachers have acquired their real love for the profession after beginning to teach. Thus, the creative and performing ambitions of the potential music major should not be suppressed, but neither should he be allowed to turn his back on experiences that would develop his teaching competence.

Chapter 8 lists some methods used by directors to encourage promising music students—by giving them opportunities to solo, to conduct and coach small groups, and to compose and arrange. In addition, the director may bring certain books and pamphlets[1] to their attention, and discuss questions which may arise about colleges, courses, and fees. Such students should also be brought to the attention of nearby collegiate music departments. In essence, music majors are made by channeling their thoughts and energies into musical activity.

There are also those who elect to major in music education in spite of rather unpromising records. But it is dangerous to reject these people summarily, for strong motivation has often altered the picture. The actual potential can only be determined by a period of college work. However, there are others who do well enough scholastically and in performance, but who have serious weaknesses in personality and/or attitudes that make them unfit for a teaching vocation. These traits must be brought to

[1] Such as *Careers In Music* (Washington, D. C.: Music Educators National Conference, 1961).

the attention of such candidates and, if no improvement is noticed, they should be led to abandon their major in music education in favor of some other endeavor.

We should mention, parenthetically, that there is a prevalent and false notion that women are not fitted to be instrumental music directors. Nothing could be further from the truth, although it is true that their vocational career is sometimes shortened by marriage and that they face severe competition for high school positions. The best way for them to meet the competition is to develop the breadth of background in piano, strings, and band instruments that will make them indispensable in any school situation.

PREPARATION FOR TEACHING INSTRUMENTAL MUSIC

Those who have chosen to become instrumental directors face a serious job of preparation. This begins, consciously or unconsciously, in elementary and secondary schools, is intensified in college, and continues on the job.

Once the thought is seriously entertained, the individual should seek and accept every opportunity to extend his musicianship. Too often, the choice of a vocation narrows one's vision, so that the wind player scorns string or vocal music, and *vice versa*. On the contrary, a future instrumental teacher *should* join a church choir and take over a Sunday school orchestra, if the opportunity arises, or he should join a dance band, if he is qualified. He should also begin to build a good record library and to study and collect musical scores and books on music. He should learn to play one or two other instruments and become familiar with the fundamentals of their construction and adjustment, and he should dabble in arranging and composition. The more he does along these lines *before* entering college, the better. No fact or skill related to music should ever be considered unimportant to a musician.

Upon graduation from high school, the student may still not be completely certain of his vocational choice. However, if it is likely to be music, he should consider the musical environment offered by several colleges. Nearby institutions naturally have the advantage because of distance and costs, and because the student may have become somewhat acquainted with their programs. But many young people are unduly influenced by attractive literature, flashy touring groups, and aggressive recruiting through scholarship offers. These are some of the factors to be considered.

(1) The primary strength of a collegiate music department lies in the breadth and quality of its teaching staff. This can be evaluated by the general morale of the music students and the relative success of the graduates.

(2) The apparent prestige of a school should be carefully examined,

since it sometimes rests more on tradition than fact. Most schools are better in some fields than in others. Thus, they may be known for their choir, their operas, their theory department, or their applied music staff. Naturally, a future instrumental director wants to attend a school where there is a reasonable emphasis on instrumental music education.

(3) Size of a school and the quality of facilities are important factors, but not necessarily indicative of the quality of training.

(4) Relative costs can be determined from the total of living expenses and tuition, less any financial aid. On this basis, a sizeable scholarship may be quite deceptive. However, small differences in cost should not be figured too closely, for the best possible education is the wisest investment anyone can make.

(5) The school may or may not make the approach to the student, but once a student indicates an interest in attendance he may expect a warm and personal interest in his future. Coldness at this point may also mean impersonality after enrollment.

We have not mentioned the courses offered in colleges as a factor in the choice of school, because these are remarkably similar in outline. There are slight differences in course titles and credit, and some basic differences in emphasis, but the essentials have been stabilized for some time. The real differences lie in the actual organization and conduct of instruction.

To give a better idea of the methods and goals of teacher education we quote (intact) the "Music Education Curriculum," drafted by C. B. Hunt, Jr., Lee Shackson, and Robert House, and adopted in November, 1962, by the National Association of Schools of Music:[2]

MUSIC EDUCATION CURRICULUM

The Bachelor of Music Education, Bachelor of Music in School Music, Bachelor of Science in Music Education, and the Bachelor of Arts in Music Education, are some of the terms applied to degree programs designed for teacher education in music. These typically comprise 120-132 semester credits (180-192 quarter credits).

Whatever degree is offered, preparation for music teaching must include certain specialized forms of learning designed to develop the basic musicianship of the student, extensive skills in performance applicable in teaching, and ability in the teaching process. It is deemed impractical to try to specify here the course titles, content, and credit allotment, for there is much variation in the needs of students, the types of institutions, types of classification within the institutions and state certification laws. It is important, however, to outline the type of background needed by students who are to teach music and the broad means by which this may be achieved; this outline can be used as a standard in the construction and evaluation of programs of music education.

[2] *Bulletin*, February, 1963, Office of Secretary, Thomas Williams, Knox College, Galesburg, Illinois, pp. 74-78.

1. GENERAL EDUCATION

The future music teacher needs a comprehension of the more important elements of our cultural heritage. These include:

a. Habitually effective use of written and spoken English.
b. Broad acquaintance with and appreciation of great literature.
c. Acquaintance with the development of man, his social and economic institutions, and of his rights and responsibilities as a citizen.
d. A sense of historical perspective.
e. A sense of moral, ethical, and aesthetic values.
f. An understanding of scientific thought and method.
g. Ability to use and interpret basic mathematical concepts.
h. A continuing attitude of intellectual curiosity.

Depending upon the individual's pre-college background, these qualities may be developed by judicious selection of courses from:
English composition and literature
Speech
History and Social Studies
Fine Arts
Natural Science and Mathematics
Such a process implies recognition of effective pre-college studies through testing, counseling, and much flexibility in the curriculum. It should occupy 30-35% of the total curriculum. Where institutional patterns include music courses as part of General Education, this proportion may be revised accordingly.

2. MUSICIANSHIP

A. *Basic Music.* The future music teacher must possess broad musicianship worthy of serving as a basis for his task in the schools. Such a background would include:

a. Functional knowledge of the language and grammar of music.
b. Ability to hear and grasp the basic elements of musical compositions—rhythmic, melodic, and harmonic.
c. An understanding of the methods by which music is conceived, constructed and scored.
d. Knowledge of the development of the art of music.
e. Intimate acquaintance with a wide selection of good musical literature from the principal eras, forms and idioms.
f. Maturing standards of musical taste and discrimination.

Objectives of this type are ordinarily emphasized in courses in:
Harmony and Ear Training (or Music Theory)
History and Literature of Music
Form and Analysis
Orchestration and Arranging
Composition
Counterpoint
There is no particular division of courses and credits which will satisfy every situation. Indeed, these same goals are also promoted in the area of performance. In any case, it is strongly suggested that these important concepts and generalizations be developed through a process of practical and intimate contact with living music. This task should occupy 20-25% of the curriculum. Where institutional patterns

include music courses as part of General Education, this proportion may be revised accordingly.

B. *Musical Performance.* The prospective music teacher must be a thoroughly competent performer in order to understand and deal with the problems of his students. Practical and thorough development in this field implies:

a. Fluency in sight reading.
b. Ability to perform from memory and "by ear."
c. Technical facility and depth of repertoire in the principal applied field sufficient to meet the needs of artistic self-expression and demonstration.
d. Functional ability in those applied fields (piano, voice, orchestral instruments) appropriate to the student's future teaching needs.
e. Thorough understanding of musical interpretation combined with adequate conducting and rehearsal skills.
f. Appreciation of the values and problems of musical groups through effective participation.

Music students generally enter vocational preparation with some performing ability in one, two or possibly three fields. Skill in at least one of these should be developed to the utmost level through private instruction, solo performance, ensemble participation, and intensive practice. Such competence is essential for artistic music teaching and contributes greatly to the teaching of those fields related to the needs of the prospective band, orchestra, or choral teacher. The foundations of technique in these latter fields may be acquired through private or class instruction.

Similarly, the future music teacher needs to participate throughout this period in the ensemble of his choice, but should have opportunity also to acquaint himself with the special literature and techniques of other types of musical organizations. The mature student deserves the opportunity to observe and participate in the operation and conducting of such organizations.

The work in this area thus comprises:
Private instruction in one's principal performing field
Class or private instruction in appropriate secondary fields
Appropriate large and small ensembles
Conducting

Because of the great variety in the performing experience of entering students and their different needs for specialization, specific requirements in the area of performance need to be interpreted quite broadly. It is necessary to reserve 25-30% of the curriculum for the work in this field.

3. PROFESSIONAL EDUCATION

The task in professional education is to develop competence in applying one's musicianship in school situations. It involves:

a. An understanding of human growth and the learning problems of students.
b. Working knowledge of effective methods, materials and facilities for musical instruction.
c. An enlightened philosophy of education and of music education.

   d. Acquaintance with school patterns, procedures, and professional relationships.

   e. Understanding and skill in the teaching process.

   f. Ability to plan, lead, and cooperate in the work of the school.

   g. Desire for professional growth and stature.

The professional phase of teacher education is usually undertaken in courses in:

     Educational Psychology
     Historical and Social Foundations of Education
     Curriculum
     Music Methods and Materials
     Observation and Student Teaching

In the judgment of this association, most of these matters are best dealt with in a musical rather than a theoretical context, with much opportunity for the student to examine, test, and report his findings. Professional education should occupy 15-20% of the curriculum.

4. ELECTIVES

By applying the minimum percentages recommended above, as much as 10% of the curriculum may be reserved for electives.

The above outline shows something of the broad coverage and relationship of subjects in the preparation of music teachers and should help clarify the requirements listed in catalogs of individual colleges.

The outline should also give an indication of the actual goals which underlie the professional curriculum, and any college music student might profit by comparing his current background with these objectives.

In order to achieve these goals, the student has many choices. Usually, in the area of General Education, he may elect various courses in the humanities, social sciences, and natural sciences. In music, he has some choice among the instruments he will study and the ensembles in which he will participate. Some schools offer much more latitude than others. Whenever the student has a choice, however, he should take the option which would most enrich his background and stimulate him to action. Instead of electing the easy courses, he should choose those which excite his curiosity and those in which the teacher has refreshing ideas. Too often, professorial advisement on courses to be taken is highly superficial and mechanical.

The college student can also choose how he will spend his time outside of class. Many, who are released from the classroom to classroom routine of the public schools, imagine that time outside of classes is leisure time. On the other hand, the prudent music major realizes that twice as much time is needed in the practice room, listening room, and library as is spent in class. Only the remaining waking hours are available for work and recreation.

Such application (of time and mind) is related to actual learning and hence, improved liberal and vocational qualifications. It is also related to opportunities for good teaching positions and graduate study, since adequate marks and teachers' recommendations are absolute requisites. Grade averages, if they do not truly measure learning, at least reflect mental application, which is also important, while a teacher's good opinion is a priceless commodity.

PLACEMENT

It is curious that so many thoroughly prepared instrumental directors are lacking in the ability to secure positions that are commensurate with their desire and qualifications. It is probably due to lack of professional foresight, weakness in appraisal and judgment, and some element of bad luck.

All collegiate institutions have some form of placement service. One of the values of attending a large, established institution is the geographical coverage and influence of this agency. There are also several commercial agencies, with regional or national coverage, which usually charge a fee of five percent of the first year's salary for their services. Although one would like to avoid this charge, these commercial agencies perform a service, which will be needed until job notices become more widely disseminated to school placement bureaus, or some central clearing house. In any event, the director is wise to keep up-to-date credentials in two or three locations, if he is seriously considering a move.

The first step is to complete the placement forms and secure the necessary recommendations. In self interest, one should be careful to avoid any possibility of a damaging reference, since it would exert a tremendous drag on any career. Real friends and supporters are always better than "names" as references.

The next step is to develop and duplicate a personal summary of qualifications, which should be revised and updated every few years. This is a crucial adjunct to any application, and it frees the writer to discuss the particular position. A condensed sample is shown on page 265. Such an outline should be expanded to include all pertinent facts and later job experience, new references, graduate work, any publications, compositions, professional memberships and offices.

A good placement bureau compares each job notice with the qualifications of its members (as determined by forms and interviews). The job description is then given or sent to the most likely candidates, who must decide whether they are interested in the particular position. Each individual must determine whether he is qualified for the position (as described), and whether it is likely to be an improvement over his present position (or the best he can do at this time). These are the preliminary considerations.

(1) Are the duties suited to the director's interests and qualifications?

John Doe
Present address: 111 College Street, Jackson, Md.   Phone 622-4211
Permanent address: 222 Park Place, Blackville, N. Y.   Phone 721-1422
Born: 4/8/46 Blackville, N. Y.   Marital status: single
Military service: National Guard since January, 1966 (including 6 months of active duty)

Education:
  Blackville High School: diploma, 1964
    member of band, orchestra, and woodwind quintet
    superior rating in bassoon, state contest, 1964
    debating team
    National Honor Society
  State University: B. Mus. Ed., 1969

English	6	Music theory	14
Speech	3	Music history	6
American government	6	Form and analysis	4
Sociology	4	Counterpoint	2
Humanities	4	Arranging	2
Biology	5	Bassoon	16
Physical science	5	Piano	4
Physical education	3	String class	2
French	6	Brass class	2
Educational psychology	3	Band	4
Hist and phil of education	3	Orchestra	4
School curriculum	3	Conducting	4
Student teaching	8	Music methods	4
		semester credits	127

    Freshman scholarship
    Music fraternity, president senior year
    Dean's honor list, 3 terms
    Soloist with orchestra, Mozart Bassoon concerto, 1969

Work Experience—
  YMCA camp counselor, summer, 1967
  Student teaching Longfellow High School
    (conducting and tuning band, coaching small ensembles, private instruction of beginning woodwinds)
  Private studio experience, 3 summers at Blackville, N. Y.
    (15 to 20 woodwind students, and ensembles)

References:
  Dr. James Jones, Head, Dept. of Music, State University
  Prof. John Brown, woodwind instructor, State University
  William Wood, instrumental director, Blackville, N. Y., schools
  Robert Ward, YMCA Director, Collegeville

(2) Does the size of the school and the reputation of the instrumental music program hold promise of potential development?

(3) Is the salary adequate?

If the answers are negative, the director so notifies the placement bureau. If they are affirmative, he notifies the bureau to forward his credentials, and makes immediate application by letter, telephone, or personal visit. The application has two purposes: (1) to discover any additional factors that may be needed for a decision (if the job is offered), and (2) to effect the most favorable, but honest, impression. That is, he can ask what he should know about the extent of the present program, the quality of musical groups, financial support and school policy, administrative expectations, salary and tenure provisions. By his questions and responses, he reveals something of his philosophy, personality, and experience. Simultaneously, the hiring official is doing his best to explain the situation while investigating every pertinent factor about the applicant. This process may involve several indirect inquiries, calls, letters, and visits from either or both parties.

The knowledge of the opening may not come through a placement bureau, but through someone who knows both the director and the changing situation at that particular school, (in which case the application is made and the credentials are forwarded later), or the director may be well known to the school officials (who believe he is the person they want), and they contact him directly, to explain and offer the job.

Eventually, the applicant will be either informed that another candidate has been chosen or that he is being offered the position under stated terms. At this point the applicant may still withdraw because (1) he now is either considering a more promising position or has become suspicious of this situation or (2) he has certain amendments or stipulations to propose (such as a higher salary or a larger music budget). However, if the school has negotiated in good faith, any inordinate delay or drastic stipulations are entirely unethical at this point.

The factors which finally influence the decision to accept or reject a position depend upon an individual's definition of a good (or better) job.

(1) The director usually wants a position which gives him the widest latitude to accomplish his mission. That is, he must feel assured that the current program has real potential for growth and improvement, that he can make reasonable revisions to improve instruction, and that the administration will support his efforts and carefully consider his future recommendations.

(2) The director must feel assured that the city will be a pleasant and stimulating place to live, and that the school and community will understand his philosophy and methods.

(3) The director wants to feel that his effort (if successful) will be rewarded by appropriate improvements in salary, status, and working conditions.

If the picture is generally favorable, the contract or appointment should be accepted and its conditions faithfully observed.

However, the definition of a promising position depends partially on the current circumstance in which the director is placed. A director may change positions in order to escape chronic problems, only to find other and even more serious disadvantages. For example, the administration is disappointing, the community seems uncooperative, or the school staff is antagonistic. However, these and similar difficulties may be related to the director's own approach. One director's difficulties are not always inherited by his successor.

It is difficult to generalize about the proper length of a director's stay. Some directors move frequently, with little or no improvement, while others' moves are keyed to rapid advancement, and some directors stay in one place practically for life. In any case, an instrumental director should always proceed as if his job tenure were to be for life, while at the same time he is always open to a bigger and better challenge elsewhere.

THE ROLE OF THE DIRECTOR

This book treats of the various aspects of the director's task in some detail. Still, any experienced teacher will recognize that each job has its special emphasis and limitations. The teacher must survey the local situation and design his approach to meet it.

In teaching instrumental music there is always a discrepancy between what *should* be and what *can* be done. The director should be aware of this fact and having established his general philosophy and conception of proper procedure, he must often accept the limitations imposed by local circumstances. Meanwhile, he must take steps to alter conditions so that his ideals may be more logically pursued. The important thing is not to forget the ideals. For example, a band director may hold a strong belief that marching is only a subsidiary function of a school band. Yet he finds that the school and community, in which he works, judges the band almost entirely as a marching unit. He has three choices:

(1) to accept the prevailing opinion and strive to build the best possible marching band,

(2) to ignore the prevailing opinion and take steps to de-emphasize marching in favor of concert work,

(3) to build an adequate marching band, while gradually developing the ability and taste of the players for fine concert literature, until the climate of opinion changes in favor of concert music and its emphasis.

It is clear which is the practical and enlightened approach.

Similarly, the director may be faced with a serious lack of funds, a poorly designed teaching schedule, inadequate facilities, and an apathetic community. Although he must learn to work under those circumstances, he must never accept them as permanent.

The instrumental program will never advance beyond the director's vision nor his effectiveness as a person. He must be able to secure the respect and cooperation of people. The extent of his acceptance is usually determined during the first months of the director's tenure in a position. During this period he fixes his goals and establishes the kinds of relationships which will almost certainly prevail in the future.

People develop fixed opinions about those who are in the public eye as much as an instrumental music teacher. He will be considered gregarious, aggressive, visionary, pompous, meek, incompetent, shy, inspiring, dashing, hard-working, weak, or some combination of such traits. Of course, each of his acquaintances will develop a somewhat different estimate, depending upon the complex psychological patterns of human relationship. The fact remains that *whatever the director attempts to do will be discounted in terms of these individual conceptions of him.* Once people have decided that the director is weak, they will tend to ignore him; if they think he is overly-aggressive, they will suspect and resist him; and when they view him as a sensible and effective individual, they will be disposed to support him. The director's job is to establish the right kind of image. This is not done simply by being pleasant and agreeable with everyone, but by assuming a natural, straightforward approach with those who are contacted in the ordinary course of activity.

The most important relationships of the director are with the students whom he must teach and if he is successful in these, the other relationships will follow. But, it is hard to say just what can be done to gain the confidence of students. Some directors treat students with an easy familiarity, while others are more serious and reserved—with equal success. Apparently, the secret lies in the instinctive *concern* of the director for his students, coupled with essential competence as a person, musician, and teacher. This is in line with the child psychologists' theory, that children who know they are loved by their parents can absorb much abuse, but parental indifference is fatal. Similarly, students (in rehearsal) will accept some harshness or ineffectiveness from their director, if they are convinced of his true concern for their welfare. This feeling of concern is usually expressed in having the time to listen to students, in anticipating their needs, and in giving them the benefit of the doubt. This quality is the root of the entire teaching-learning process, and cannot be successfully faked.

A similar approach becomes the basis of good relationships with local citizens and teaching colleagues. However, one is not bound by duty (as with his students) to like or cultivate everyone. The director *gives* to students, but *cooperates* with his fellowmen, whenever their interests and problems coincide.

A particularly vital relationship is with school administrative officials. These people (superintendents, principals, and their staffs) are charged

with the organization and direction of the school. They provide the facilities for instruction—including buildings, teachers, equipment, and cur-
ricular arrangements, and thus, they are both masters and servants of the
teachers. In one sense their wishes are law, while in another, their role is
to minister to the needs of the teachers and students.

The school administrator does not *own* the school but is charged with
its operation by society. The director's proper role is not to execute
directives, but rather to take the initiative in recommending the policies
and actions that he deems necessary. To put it another way, the director
is supposed to be the expert in his field, so he must outline his needs and
tactics while conceding the administrator's duty to adjust and regulate all
factors in the school in order to produce a balanced, well-coordinated
operation. The exact relationship between administrator and director,
however, depends upon the personality and competence of the individuals.
There are both weak and strong superintendents, but in either case, the
director's approach should be positive and constructive.

The teaching staff in a school (the director's professional colleagues)
have naturally complementary interests in their task of educating the students. They form a team, but, at the same time, they are in competition
with one another for the students' time and efforts, and also for support
of the school administration and community. The primary job of the
director is to secure the respect and cooperation of his colleagues without
sacrificing the interests of his program, which can be best accomplished
by taking a sincere and useful part in appropriate non-musical activities.
The director who can take an interest in the team, sponsor clubs, participate effectively in deciding academic issues, and who generally takes
an all-school approach, is doing the best possible service for his own
program.

To the director, the local citizenry includes his students' parents, his
golfing and bridge partners, his grocer and haberdasher, his concert audience, and an anonymous group which exerts general control over taxes,
elections, manners, and morals. The mass of people establish the particular
tone and outlook of a community.

The director may wish to join various community organizations
(church, country club, service club, or fraternal group) but social climbing,
for professional reasons, is usually ineffective. This is because the effort is
insincere and no benefit is gained, unless the individual participates
wholeheartedly in any organization he may join. Indeed, there are no
"right people," except those that happen to strike a responsive chord with
the director.

It is more important to be known as an upright, honorable citizen, of
good moral repute, financially solvent, and a supporter of those forces
which advance the community. This does not mean that the director may
not drink, smoke, or borrow money, but as a schoolman he *is* a responsible

professional man and should not be subject to aberrations which would seriously compromise his professional task.

Therefore, as the director moves around the school and community, he needs to "make friends and influence people" in a naturally constructive way. He tries to be as enlightened, progressive, sensible, and democratic as possible. He does not curry favor but enlists support wherever available. His essential role should be that of an educator who is interested in the musical welfare of the children and youth.

FURTHER STUDY

The instrumental music director, who remains for a length of time in the profession, is almost certain to undertake additional study beyond his undergraduate preparation. A career can hardly be sustained without some attempt to remedy shortcomings in preparation and to develop familiarity with new philosophies and techniques as they are developed.

Informal Study

It is often forgotten that a great deal of this effort is undertaken rather casually and informally, and without college credit. Careful reading of professional journals and books, participation in locally organized workshops and clinics, attendance at summer music camps and conferences, foreign travel and language study, and private study of instruments or voice are some of the forms of education undertaken by instrumental directors. Teaching activity, itself, is highly educational.

Non-Degree Study

Formal supplemental study at collegiate institutions has been a feature of the profession, since the normal schools first developed from the short courses and Chautauquas, during the Nineteenth century. At first, a minimum course of study was designed for temporary certification which was to be followed by the supplemental work that was required for certificate renewal. In this way, certification requirements have been gradually raised to the baccalaureate degree, and the trend now seems to be evolving toward a five-year requirement.

The patterns are still not universal. Some localities and states require a specific number of additional credits every few years to maintain certification, while others are now requiring a fifth year to be taken after teaching begins, but before a certain number of years have elapsed. This work may be on the undergraduate or graduate level, or both. The idea is to provide the teacher with an opportunity to remedy inadequacies in his preparation or to pursue new specializations that he has developed. Thus, the band director who has started a string program can now concentrate in this field, while another will need special work in arranging, conducting, or instrument repair.

A large amount of study of this nature is accomplished not because it is required, but because the director has some free time and he becomes aware of a course or two that especially interests him. His work may not only accomplish the learning he desires, but it also may eventually amount to the equivalent of the fifth or sixth year that raises him on the salary scale. Often, the impetus is also acquired for study toward a graduate degree.

Graduate Degrees

THE VALUES. The inherent purpose of graduate study is the development of professional leadership. Degree candidates are assumed to be bright, ambitious people who will advance to greater heights of professional service. The degrees themselves, when finally granted, are only incidental to this result.

However, graduate schools are closely tuned to the needs of the teaching profession, where degrees are valued quite highly. To an educational institution, an advanced degree represents specialized knowledge and professional purpose. Another school has so certified, and students and colleagues respect it. Thus, possession of the master's degree means several hundred dollars annually to the director, while it is a prerequisite to college teaching. In turn, the doctorate becomes a factor in competing for positions, and attaining higher rank and salary in most collegiate institutions.

Degree candidates also have an advantage in obtaining new positions. The individual in residence develops new professional associations, acquires additional and current references from his professors, and secures the services of a new placement bureau.

But the values of degree study are not automatically conferred. Too many candidates are only average musicians and scholars who are motivated by extrinsic rewards. These may obtain their goal, but only those who are moved by the urge to learn and achieve will secure the ultimate values: wider horizons, greater professional freedom, and confidence.

DEGREES AND REQUIREMENTS. It should be realized that the titles of graduate degrees are often grossly misleading. In many instances, the degree was first authorized under a particular title, and then the content was changed to meet the practical needs of the situation. Fortunately, employers are usually cognizant of this fact and are much more concerned about the quality of the institution granting the degree, the general emphasis of the student's program, and his record, than with the specific degree title.

However, one generally expects that the Master of Music degree will be designed for specialization in performance and/or music theory and composition, while the Master of Music Education degree will emphasize the needs of school music teachers. To be sure, many courses will apply equally to either degree, since the music teacher needs practical work in music, in addition to the study of instructional device.

Many schools offer degrees in Arts (M.A.) or Science (M.S.) which, with a major in music or music education, are practically indistinguishable in content from the standard music degrees mentioned above. If anything, the M.A. and M.S. degrees may imply broader coverage, with possibly some work in related fields.

Requirements for a master's degree are usually equivalent to one school year of full-time study (thirty semester or forty-five quarter credits). But the vocational, marital, or financial situation of many candidates requires them to pursue their study on a part-time basis. Transcripts and examinations may also reveal deficiencies that must be remedied, so that minimum time in residence becomes the exception, rather than the rule. A popular and effective plan is to enroll for three, four, or five summer terms; this enables one to hold his job, spreads out the financial burden and results in increased placement opportunities.

The doctorate is based upon two further years of study (sixty semester or ninety quarter credits) but a longer period of time is often necessary. At least two consecutive terms in residence are ordinarily required. The Ph.D. (in music) has academic overtones, and is primarily associated with specialization in musicology, or music theory. The Ed.D. (in music education) is a professional degree for the teacher of music teachers. In recent years another degree has evolved, the Doctor of Musical Arts, which is designed primarily for the studio teacher or composer.

All of the advanced degrees mentioned above involve certain requirements beyond taking courses and passing them. The candidate must first submit his transcripts and he may need recommendations from his former instructors. If he appears to have the necessary prerequisites and evidence of scholastic aptitude, he will be considered a likely risk. Further screening, in the form of an audition and examinations in subject matter appropriate to the field of study, will occur before or soon after he enrolls. Often more generalized tests pertaining to scholastic and/or musical aptitude are also administered.

Once admitted to candidacy, the student must plan his course of study with his adviser, maintain high marks, fulfill any language requirements, select and complete a special project, and pass final written and/or oral examinations.

Although a foreign language requirement is not universal, for the Ph.D., a reading knowledge of two languages (French and German preferred) is commonly required. A language is sometimes expected of M.A., M.Mus., and D.M.A. candidates, but few institutions demand any foreign language for a degree in music education.

The special project takes many forms—scientific research, field study or survey, musical composition, orchestration, or recital. The type of study and its extent is largely determined by the level of degree and the major area of study. Results at the masters level are expected to be modest, but well-organized, while the doctoral effort is expected to be larger, more original, and more significant.

MAKING THE DECISION. The production of leadership in all the professions is highly critical to the maintenance and improvement of our social institutions. As a primary means to that end, the major share of the costs of graduate study are borne by society. This fact points up the moral obligation to reserve such study for those who can profit by it. The instrumental music teacher should not consider an advanced degree if he is an average scholar or musician, or if he has failed to develop a strong sense of calling for his profession. It should be realized that only a fraction of the population possesses the necessary intelligence and motivation to complete a rigorous masters program, while a much smaller group is eligible for the doctorate.

However, even the most promising student must carefully choose the time and place, since he would be unwise to begin before his personal and financial affairs are in order. It is equally frustrating to find one's self in an unexpectedly difficult, or dull situation, or one that is unsuited to his special interests.

Of first importance in choosing a school is the quality of its faculty and program. One should never take graduate work at a school that he considers inferior, or where he seems to be unappreciated. It is wise, particularly on the doctoral level, to take a summer term before arranging for the year's residence, because if conditions are unfavorable, it is possible to transfer to another school.

Another factor in choosing a school is its prestige, even though this may not reflect the actual condition of the program. A school may have developed such a reputation in some phase of music, that employers return for replacements in that field, although the reputation may no longer be deserved, and lesser known schools (or even "diploma mills") can offer equally good instruction. However, these latter usually accept weaker students, so that any work done there is discounted.

The cost of graduate study is often a controlling factor. One should carefully compare all costs—tuition (less any fellowship or assistantship), living and traveling expense, and residence requirements (which may affect one's regular income). However, financial assistance often tends to lengthen the period of residence. An assistantship will involve teaching undergraduate courses several hours a week. This means a reduced program of graduate study, additional time needed to complete the degree, and actual loss of income on a long-term basis.

PURSUIT OF THE DEGREE. Those who have taken no graduate work seldom understand the critical importance of the adviser. Student and adviser are so closely associated in the task that mutual respect is essential.

The entrance examinations should be taken as soon as possible. Very little preparation can be made for these examinations except to brush up on a solo or two, practice some part writing, and perhaps review two or three basic texts. Since the principal tests will measure general musical and scholarly background, the results will depend upon the individual's industriousness during the past ten or fifteen years. If one fails these tests, he should go home with no regrets, while if he does well, he may push on with renewed confidence.

As soon as the degree work is well launched, it is wise to make up a tentative outline of courses to be taken, and plans for the required project should begin almost immediately. It is unfortunate that *most incomplete degrees simply mean incompleted projects.* The usual candidate puts too much emphasis on courses and tends to defer the project, and once he is away from the adviser and the library or practice room, the task becomes more remote. If possible, the course work and project should be completed simultaneously, since this helps coordinate study, and tends to produce a better final examination.

In choosing the topic for a written project, it is well to evaluate one's special interests and skills. The director may find that his principal preoccupation is with the literature he uses, his methods of presentation, the counseling of students, course organization, evaluative procedures, housing and equipment, or a parallel phase of the task. When such an interest is identified, it becomes a likely *area* for his topic. Then, he should re-examine his basic approach to problems. Is he a reader-philosopher, a good fact-gatherer, or a natural statistician? The answer will determine the *kind* of topic to pursue. Finally, a topic should be as specific as possible and the necessary data should be readily accessible.

When the project is completed and the final examination has been passed, the real test of the value of graduate study is the *difference* it makes. The music teacher must *apply* what he has learned. He teaches with increased vigor and quality and finds his professional influence is vastly multiplied.

PROFESSIONALLY-RELATED ACTIVITY

Beyond the director's specific school tasks lie areas of activity that grow naturally from his educational and vocational background. He may direct a church choir, play in a civic orchestra or a dance band, work actively in music educators groups, and so on. Any such activity has definite promotional, financial, educational, or avocational overtones.

Basically, however, all such activity is essentially *creative*. While the director is a teacher of his pupils, he also wants to perform, compose, or cooperate toward general improvement within the profession. The results of such work directly or indirectly affect his daily tasks in the school. If nothing else, the director sees his ordinary successes and failures in proper perspective and acquires motivation to meet his problems. No director should confine his efforts entirely to the school.

Conducting

Most instrumental music teachers become rather accomplished conductors by virtue of daily application. However, great delicacy and finesse in interpretation are difficult to exercise with school children. For this reason, the conductorship of a church choir, civic orchestra, or municipal band becomes quite attractive. The loyalty and support of such a group is also helpful and the additional salary is welcome.

Among the problems of these groups (which were discussed in Chapter 6), is the possibility that the conductor may come to regard his non-school group as his principal responsibility, in which case, he should resign from one post or the other.

Private Teaching

A director who is a fine performer and teacher on a certain instrument may be prevailed upon to take a few pupils who are not enrolled in his school. To an extent, this is a professional obligation (regardless of the fees), but such altruism should never occupy any major proportion of a director's time.

Business Operations

A somewhat similar situation exists when a teacher has become an expert in instrument adjustment, reed making, or piano tuning, and he can sell these services to those who need them. Other directors accept commissions on the sale of instruments through certain dealers. Obviously, great care is needed to remain within ethical bounds, even though the customer may be greatly assisted, and this kind of activity needs special clearance with the school authorities.

Performing

Probably the most common form of extra-curricular activity among directors is performing in church choirs, dance bands, civic bands and orchestras, chamber music groups, and appearing as soloist or accompanist. This activity is natural because their interest in music ordinarily began with performing, and the skill must be used in order to maintain it. In fact, many directors have let their performing skill rust and have come to regret it.

Most young directors have good intentions of continuing their practice and repertoire development while they engage in teaching, but, because of the pressures of time, few succeed. The only answer is to join some group with regularly scheduled rehearsals. This act alone tends to maintain proficiency, and any added individual practice or study will enable one to forge ahead. This also leads to the discovery of new repertoire, new friendships, immense satisfaction, and possibly a bit of extra income, and it is an excellent example to one's students as well.

Composition and Arranging

The arts of composition and arranging are not only fascinating but also quite useful in developing settings for one's groups. Those directors who have the knack and experience usually do some arranging for the football band, variety shows, and similar occasions. Others are able to compose or transcribe works for their groups in concert. For example, a fine soloist may have prepared a solo which is not scored for the orchestra or band, and it is not difficult to make a transcription from the piano part (observing copyright rules). Such activity has a stimulating effect upon the students.

Particularly successful works can be taped and sent (with score) to likely publishers, and if they fill a need at the particular time, their chance for publication is enhanced. However, one should not count heavily on this possibility. The proportion of works published is very small, since each new number must compete with all the established works for a place in the repertoire.

Writing and Research

Graduate study often develops skills in writing and research, and if the director has such talents, they should be used. Neither field is often lucrative but can be a source of great satisfaction, since the scientific and philosophical talents have full sway. Creative endeavor of this kind has an incalculable effect upon the profession.

Many researchers have received grants from various corporations and foundations. To be considered for such a grant a detailed prospectus must be submitted in advance, and a similar type of outline is also the usual approach to publishers.

Participation in Professional Organizations

Today, individual effort is rather ineffective in changing or maintaining anything, except through special interest groups. The local instrumental music program, in fact, would be easy prey for its critics without the strength of various state and national bodies, such as the

Music Educators National Conference, the Music Teachers National Association, the American String Teachers Association, and the American Bandmaster's Association. It is a duty to be a member and support such bodies. Much can be learned by reading the journals and attending the conventions, where one becomes acquainted with new compositions, absorbs new ideas, renews acquaintances, and meets new people.

Many directors take a more active part in these groups as officers or members of committees and commissions. Much of this activity is quite frustrating and useless, since communication is difficult, and some members do not discharge their responsibilities. However, it is remarkable what the right people can do with a good idea. The director who has strong convictions, as well as patience, should be present at the meetings pertaining to his special interests. If he is reasonably gregarious and has any professional stature, he will eventually find himself named to some group considering a particular problem.

In the group process, each plays a different role. Some are idea-men, some are editors, and others play the roles of chairman, critic, and promoter. Whatever role the director may fill, his inherent purpose is to help create the policies, documents, and activities that will advance the profession.

Since all organizational activity is aimed at bringing about improvements at the grass roots, there is no need for professional jealousy and even less need for routine and trivia. When these conditions exist, the director should not waste his time.

Indeed, it is apparent throughout this volume that the instrumental music director has a great mission, with a variety of means, and must possess competence, vision, energy, and the time to do the job. The rewards are many, but they exist mainly in the minds and hearts of his students and the future students throughout the nation.

SUMMARY

Candidates for the profession of instrumental music teaching are essentially the successful products of a rich musical environment and the call to this profession should be analyzed and confirmed. These people need opportunity to acquire preliminary leadership qualities. Many failures seem to be traceable to personality deficiencies and lack of motivation.

Preparation needs to have great breadth. Specific competence must be sought rather than credits and grades.

Definite procedures should be followed in seeking a teaching position. A personally developed summary of training and experience is a great help. One must also acquire the knack of securing information about the job, while underlining his own qualifications.

The director must establish a good working relationship on the job, and always strive to overcome the basic obstacles to his task. Each position requires different procedures.

The director needs further study to remedy his shortcomings and to pursue special interests as they develop. This may take the form of graduate degree work, and in such a case, care must be exercised in the choice of school and the selection of a project.

Several other avenues are open to the director who is interested in professional development. He may participate in various kinds of nonschool performing groups (as player or conductor), he may teach privately, compose or write, and he should participate in professional groups of music educators. The extent of all such activity is to be measured by this test: will the time spent finally hamper or enhance the director's program of instruction?

QUESTIONS FOR DISCUSSION

1. What influences seem to lead to the decision to become an instrumental music teacher? What are some of the needed traits?

2. How should one select the college for his training? What kind of program should he expect?

3. Describe the general process and ethics of job placement. What constitutes a "good job?"

4. In teaching, how does one reconcile the practical situation with his ideals? How does the factor of personality relate to the teaching task? What is the essential approach to students, colleagues, and acquaintances?

5. What types of post-baccalaureate study are open to the instrumental director? Who is qualified for graduate work? Review the general requirements and the procedure for graduate degrees.

6. What kinds of professionally-related activity are open to the instrumental music director? What are some of the basic advantages and problems in such activity?

SELECTED REFERENCES

BOWLES, MICHAEL, *The Art of Conducting.* Garden City, N. Y.: Doubleday and Company, Inc., 1959.

A Career in Music Education. Washington, D. C.: Music Educators National Conference, 1962.

DAVIS, ENNIS M., *More Than a Pitch Pipe.* Boston: C. C. Birchard and Co., 1941.

JONES, ARCHIE N., ed., *Music Education In Action.* Boston: Allyn and Bacon, Inc., 1960.

MORGAN, HAZEL N., *Music Research Handbook.* Evanston, Illinois: The Instrumentalist Co., 1962.

Post-Baccalaureate Grants and Awards in Music. Washington, D. C.: Music Educators National Conference, 1963.

REIMER, BENNETT, "The Market for Music Teachers," *Music Educators Journal.* February-March, 1963, pp. 42-44; 50-54.

SUR, WILLIAM R., *Your Future As a Teacher of Music in the Schools.* Washington, D. C.: Music Educators National Conference, 1959.

WAGNER, JOSEPH, *Band Scoring.* New York: McGraw-Hill Book Company, 1960.

Index